TO SERVE THE COMMUNITY

THE STORY OF TORONTO'S BOARD OF TRADE

G.H. STANFORD

# To Serve the Community
# The Story of Toronto's
# Board of Trade

PUBLISHED FOR THE BOARD OF TRADE
OF METROPOLITAN TORONTO
BY UNIVERSITY OF TORONTO PRESS

© The Board of Trade of Metropolitan Toronto 1974
Printed in Canada
ISBN 0-8020-3325-3
LC 74-75829

The Board of Trade has played a notable part in the development of this city and, I suppose, the history of the one is inseparable from the history of the other, as of two friends who have grown up together. It is by the vigour and by the enterprise of her sons that Toronto holds so proud a place among the cities of our Commonwealth, and surely no single organization represents and expresses those qualities more faithfully than does the Board of Trade.

*The Viscount Halifax, on the occasion of the celebration of the Board of Trade's One Hundredth Anniversary*

# Contents

# I
# Beginnings

The streets of Toronto in 1834, the year it officially became a city by an Act of Parliament passed 6 March, had already begun to show signs of the mercantile vigour that was to contribute so much to the formation of its permanent character. King Street, the main thoroughfare, was lined with little shops offering food and drink and dressgoods and ironmongery. Although many local needs were being met by adjacent farms, flour mills and sawmills, blacksmiths and cartwrights, and by makers of candles, clocks, hats and shoes, a high proportion of the goods on the shelves was imported, largely from Britain. A class of merchant traders was developing who eventually became pure wholesalers and were destined to dominate the commercial life of the community for a hundred years.

In its earliest days Toronto had been known as 'The Carrying Place', the Lake Ontario starting point of a route that led up the Humber River and ultimately by land and water to Georgian Bay and Lake Huron. The French, engaged in a strenuous competition with the British for the lucrative fur trade, realized the value of this 'Toronto Passage' and in 1751 built Fort Rouille, a strategically located and defended trading post better known as Fort Toronto. In the course of the Seven Years War, they burned it and withdrew before an invading British force and it was not until 1788 that the Governor-in-Chief of Canada, Sir Guy Carlton (Lord Dorchester), who had been assigned the task of consolidating the lands north of the Great Lakes under the British Crown, negotiated the purchase from the Mississauga Indians of the site on which the present city stands in order to secure control, so important to the fur trade, of the passage from Lake Ontario to Lake Huron.

After the separation of the territory into the two provinces of Upper and Lower Canada in 1791, John Graves Simcoe was appointed as the first Lieutenant-Governor of Upper Canada. After some deliberation he chose Toronto as the provisional centre for his new administration, promptly renaming it York in honour of the Duke of York, son of George III, whose European victories were being celebrated at the time. An important factor in Simcoe's choice of Toronto for his provincial capital, officially confirmed in 1794, was its unparalleled harbour, almost completely encircled by a narrow spit of land. It provided a safe anchorage for the ships that were the only means of access and facilitated defence against possible incursions from the south – the times were still uneasy.

While wholly practical considerations of trade, defence and communication were thus at the root of Toronto's origins, there may have been other attractions. Joseph Bouchette, one of Simcoe's surveyors, later wrote:

In 1793 the spot on which York now stands presented only one solitary Indian wigwam .... I distinctly recollect the untamed aspect which the country exhibited when I first entered this beautiful basin. Dense and trackless forests lined the margin of the lake and reflected their inverted images in its glassy surface. The wandering savage had constructed his ephemeral habitation beneath their luxuriant foliage, and the bay and neighbouring marshes were the hitherto uninvaded haunts of immense coveys of wild fowl.

By the time Toronto attained city status it had an adequate street system and roadways had been built linking it with the developing lands to the north, east and west, but the city still depended heavily on the harbour for the import of essential goods. Trade with Europe had been facilitated by the opening of the Erie Canal in 1825 and the Oswego extension three years later, which provided a water route between the Great Lakes and the port of New York that by-passed Montreal. Since merchandise trade was the backbone of its business structure Toronto had to compete vigorously with Montreal in the early years to overcome the severe handicap of its location. Upper Canada was, moreover, developing a reputation as a producer of high-quality wheat and the grain trade was becoming increasingly important in Toronto's economy. If, as its businessmen foresaw, the city was to become the principal distributing point for goods imported from overseas and for the agricultural products of the region, it was essential to provide cheap and effective means of transport over which it could exercise full control. Pressures were applied for needed harbour improvements and in 1833 Parliament granted a sum of £2,000 and appointed a commission to design and superintend the required works. A further sum was allotted several years later for additional expansion of the port facilities. Above and beyond these improvements, the idea of re-establishing Toronto as 'The Carrying Place', the main terminus of a portage from the Upper to the Lower Lakes and hence to seaboard, continued to simmer and was for many years the subject of ambitious thinking.

Banking services were available to assist business transactions: the Bank of Montreal had established an agency in the precursor town of York in 1818, and the Bank of Upper Canada had received its charter three years later. While the development of financial enterprise was not always considered to be commensurate with the needs of an increasingly active commerce, sufficient resources were generally available and they were gradually improving as the potential became more evident.

Since the availability of most raw materials was restricted and uncertain and the market area was scarcely larger than the immediate environs, manufacturing operations remained on a very limited scale. The first industry of any account was a tannery established in 1812 by Jesse Ketchum at the corner of Yonge and Newgate (now Adelaide) Streets, but industrial production was not materially stimulated until assured supplies of cheap bituminous coal for the generation of steam power became available and the efficient movement of goods was made possible by the advent of the railways.

The population of the city at the time of its incorporation was under ten thousand, and since a large proportion of its citizens were immigrants from Britain, it still retained many characteristics of a colonial outpost. The municipal boundaries were Peter Street on the west, Parliament Street on the east and a line not far north of Lot (now Queen) Street, although the so-called 'liberties', those territories available for future expansion which came under the city's jurisdiction, extended some distance beyond these limits. The base for the street system was the grid of ten rectangular blocks laid out by Alexander Aitken in his original design for the town of York, which was situated at the eastern and best protected part of the harbour near the mouth of the Don River. Development had been quite haphazard and years passed before it was considered necessary to give it direction.

Under the Act incorporating the city a council responsible for the administration of civic affairs was elected for the first time. The new council immediately chose from among themselves the notorious William Lyon Mackenzie to serve as mayor. Not surprisingly, the administration got off to a bad start: its members were inexperienced, there were sharp political differences and money was short. The city's credit was virtually non-existent and any suggestion of increased taxes on real and personal property was strongly resisted by the merchants, who saw in all such imposts a threat to their still somewhat hazardous enterprises.

Through these formative times, however, the city was undoubtedly sustained by its merchants and commercial opportunists, who foresaw that Toronto would become the economic centre of Upper Canada and devoted their considerable skills and energies to making this happen – not, perhaps, in an excess of public zeal, but as a means to an end by which they themselves would be enriched. As staunch believers in free enterprise they were ready to prove that the public good was best served by individual initiative taking calculated risks in the hope of future profit. Their attitude toward government was no doubt shaped by the fact that so many were small proprietors who had employed common sense, thrift and hard work to build up their own businesses and who were not disposed to see authority at any level undermine their hard-won prosperity or dissipate their earnings by levies for purposes they considered ill-advised or unnecessary. The financial fumblings of the early administrations enraged them and were no doubt a primary reason for the decision made by some of the prominent businessmen to organize themselves in a way that would permit a forceful expression of their views.

Furthermore, with Toronto clearly launched on a course of commercial growth, measures were needed to bring greater stability into commercial operations by creating means whereby market information could be made more readily available and common agreement reached on forms and procedures. Transportation, too, was a continuing problem and a united effort might improve the city's primitive facilities. Nevertheless, the prime motivation toward organization was undoubtedly the average businessman's distrust of the provincial legislature and the municipal council, neither of which had given him confidence that his future well-being and prosperity would be ensured. A united business front was therefore expected to influence legislative decisions.

Organizations of merchants and craftsmen into bodies designed to provide safeguards and benefits for their members appear to have been in existence almost as long as the occupations themselves. The guilds that had their origin in the Middle Ages are a notable example of how men with like interests could group together, gain substantial power and make genuine contributions to the development of skills and the improvement of working and trading conditions. Early organizations were principally composed of those with specific skills or well-defined interests – goldsmiths, tanners, fishmongers and so on – and their concern was really to create elites in their various categories. They became monopolistic and their activities not infrequently brought them into conflict with the state; curtailment of their powers, suppression of their privileges and, in some cases, the outright cancellation of their charters resulted. The guilds were in some respects the precursors of both trade associations and trade unions.

An organized affiliation of various business interests first took effect in France with the formation of the Marseilles Chambre de Commerce in 1599. It seems to have functioned mainly as a court of arbitration in mercantile affairs. Similar bodies later appeared in other French cities, but by then they had acquired a quasi-official character, collaborating with the government to promote trade and giving advice on public works likely to affect its progress. In 1750 thirteen merchants of Halifax banded together to form an 'Association for the Benefit of Trade', thus establishing the foundation for the first such organization in North America and indeed in the British Empire. Eighteen years later similar associations were founded in Great Britain and New York. A meeting to launch a Committee of Trade, forerunner of a Board of Trade, was held in Montreal in 1822. Throughout the early nineteenth century Boards of Trade and Chambers of Commerce (the names are interchangeable) proliferated and became recognized bodies with fairly well-defined structures and aims. They were independent groupings of businessmen, chiefly traders, working together to develop their communities and create conditions which would advance their own commercial interests, and they recognized no conflict between these objectives.

By the 1830s the time was ripe for the formation of such an association in Toronto.

On 15 January 1836, a Friday, the following notice appeared in *The Patriot*, a Toronto newspaper:

BOARD OF TRADE
The General Annual Meeting will be held at the News Room,
on Monday Evening next the 18th inst. at 7 o'clock p.m.

By order
J. W. Brent
Secretary

In *The City of Toronto and the Home District Commercial Directory and Register* for 1837 there is the following listing:

CITY OF TORONTO BOARD OF TRADE
Hon. Wm Allan – President
J. W. Brent –Secretary

There was thus a Toronto Board of Trade at least as early as 1835 and it is possible that it may have been formed in the year the city itself was incorporated. There seems to be no record of how it was constituted or what its functions were. The *Patriot* gives no account of the proceedings at the Annual Meeting held on 18 January, nor are there notices of subsequent meetings. The President, the Hon. Wm Allan, was a wealthy merchant and landowner, and the fact that he was also a member of the executive council in the government of Upper Canada suggests that the Board of Trade of that day may have enjoyed some official recognition. In any event the first Board was apparently no longer functional when George Percival Ridout and others got together in 1844 and decided to set up an incorporated body to serve as an independent medium representing the interests of the general business community.

George Percival Ridout (1807–73) was born in Bristol, England, a grandnephew of Thomas Ridout. He and his brother Joseph emigrated to the United States in 1820, where they worked in or organized branches in Philadelphia and New York for Messrs Taratt, hardware merchants of Wolverhampton, England. George came to York in 1832, where he took an active part in commercial life and was a Toronto member in the provincial legislature from 1852 to 1854. His brother had preceded him and they established themselves as Ridout Brothers & Co., Hardware Merchants, with a shop near the corner of King and Yonge Streets; the stock was advertised as 'the heaviest and most extensive in this country.' George died in 1873, and when Joseph retired in 1876 the firm was taken over by James Aikenhead and his partner Alexander Crombie. It was restyled the Aikenhead Hardware Co. in 1893, and the business has continued to flourish.

George Ridout's immediate collaborator in the formation of a local Board of Trade was Thomas Clarkson, an Englishman who had come to the town of York in 1832 and later became a prominent merchant and financier. The new Board of Trade was brought into effective existence in 1844, and an Act incorporating the Board of Trade of the City of Toronto was passed by the legislature of Canada on 10 February 1845. The charter members, in addition to Ridout and Clarkson, were Peter Paterson, John Mulholland, William Leadley Perrin, Duncan McDonnell, J. McGlashen, Timothy J. Farr, Henry Rowsell, Thomas Rigney, Thomas D. Harris, John Thomson, William Wakefield, Joseph Workman, R. C. McMullen, Joseph D. Ridout, K. M. Sutherland, J. B. Sutherland, John Harrington, William Rowsell, Robert Wightman, A. Badenach, John Shaw, Walter Macfarlane, William Henderson, James Beaty, M. J. O'Beirne, George Michie, John Robertson, Peter Freeland, Alexander Murray, L. Moffatt, George Denholm, J. R. Armstrong, Alexander Ogilvie, Frederick Perkins, Robert MacKay, Angus McIntosh, Charles Robertson, George H. Cheney, Thomas Brunskill, John Sproule, Samuel Phillips, J. McMurrich, E. F. Whittemore and Samuel Workman.

George Percival Ridout was the first President, an office he was to hold until 1852 when he was elected to the legislature. The Vice-President was Joseph Workman, M.D. Henry Rowsell was Treasurer and the Council members were John Mulholland, William Leadley Perrin, Peter Paterson, Duncan McDonnell, John Thomson, Peter Freeland, Thomas D. Harris, James Beaty, William Henderson, J. Shaw, R. H. Brett and E. F. Whittemore. The Council, elected by the membership at large, was to concern itself with policy considerations, exercise administrative control, and implement the decisions of the Board made in general session. In its Act of Incorporation, which was subsequently amended on a number of occasions, the Board's principal objectives were:

To promote and/or support such measures as, upon due consideration, are deemed calculated to advance and render prosperous the lawful trade and commerce and to foster the economic and social welfare of the City of Toronto ...

To advance in all lawful ways the commercial interests of the members of the Corporation generally and to secure the advantages to be obtained by mutual co-operation.

It was provided that

... each and every person carrying on trade and commerce of any kind, or being a Cashier, Manager or Director of any Financial Institution, Railway or Insurance Company, shall be eligible to become a member of the said Corporation.

That there was some continuity from the Board of Trade of the 1830s is evident from the fact that J. W. Brent, the Secretary of the earlier group, acted in the same capacity in the newly-incorporated organization. Operations began in a small office over banking premises and, starting in the mid-1850s, meetings were held in the Mechanics' Institute at Church and Adelaide Streets. These did not at first fall into a regular pattern but rather the Council met as often as necessary to deal with routine affairs, and the full membership met quarterly or when issues of substance required a consensus on which a formal statement of the Board's policy could be based. At the Annual Meeting in January or February a report was made on the state of trade and on the activities of the organization. Occasional public meetings were convoked when wider support was sought for the Board's position in matters of special significance. Records of proceedings in the earliest days are few and the new body did not at first appear to make much headway or public impression. Mercantile and financial men did not show as much interest in its deliberations and proceedings as might have been expected; many business leaders questioned in a deprecating way the value of a Board of Trade and remained aloof. By 1856 it had acquired only sixty members and for a number of years attendance at meetings was poor; often business could not be transacted through lack of a bare quorum. As in so many voluntary organizations the bulk of the work was left to a few energetic members but those few proved dedicated and capable.

It may well have been the deliberate intention of the officers to tread softly until some experience had been gained and methods devised to deal with problems in such a way as to produce positive results. In the 1850s, however, the Board began to reach its stride and entered into a career of growth and activity which has continued unabated. Procedures were developed to deal with issues of consequence and the Board gradually became recognized as a substantial force in the life of the growing city. When it was strongly convinced of inequities or vigorously advocated a course of action in the community's interests, the Board worked over the years with remarkable tenacity and considerable success to achieve its goals.

Canada experienced its first period of sustained prosperity in the first half of the 1850s, but the country was still in a state of transition. Its parts were loosely joined, with the seat of government alternating between Ontario and Quebec, and French Canada remained in a state of simmering rebellion against British rule. Lines of communication were poor and there was little evidence of any real community of interest among the main population centres. Business was good, but it was not built on solid foundations, and businessmen were eager to dispel this insecurity by whatever means they could employ. The issues were for the most part not local ones, and although the Toronto Board was ostensibly a body of strictly limited jurisdiction, it had to be concerned with much more than local affairs. If there was to be a business system permitting the desired and expected growth, there had to be recognition and adoption of sound policies which could be relied upon to provide a reasonable degree of permanence and gain a wide acceptance. The Board came to regard itself as the spokesman in Upper Canada not only for those engaged in trade, but also for citizens in general; for the most part its views did seem to represent those of this larger community.

Until well into the 1860s most members of the Board were traders, predominantly wholesalers. Few were native-born Canadians, the majority having come to the new land to make their fortunes, and trade was the way to wealth. Manufacturing was still in its infancy, and the other main interests represented had to do in one way or another with the movement rather than the production of goods – commission merchandising, warehouse operation and retailing. Not unnaturally they were concerned with maintaining the greatest possible freedom of trade: the Reciprocity Treaty with the United States was supported, much effort was expended in attempts to lower tariff barriers and a recurrent theme was the establishment of better means of transport and the elimination of restraints on the use of navigable waters. This preoccupation with trade and merchandising however, began to lessen as the more able and farsighted business leaders came to realize that if the community's total economy was to be stabilized and developed it had to be attended by strong institutions providing supplementary services such as banking and insurance. Members took a direct interest in the establishment and functioning of financial institutions as members of their boards of directors, and the Board increasingly came to represent a cross-section of the total business community and hence to speak with fuller appreciation of its varied concerns.

It was all business. The professions and the arts had as yet no part in the Board's deliberations, and not until much later was any attention paid to another of its ostensible purposes, 'to stimulate ... social intercourse among the members of the Corporation.' The Board at first limited itself to immediate business objectives and left the expression of its members' social or cultural interests to individual initiative. Many were wealthy men, concerned in their private lives with humanitarian issues, and certainly many of them contributed in a genuine way to ensuring a certain charm for the growing city by employing the best architects and craftsmen available for building projects over which they had responsibility. It is indeed rather remarkable under the circumstances that utilitarianism was not the only rule, and that so many of Toronto's buildings of this period managed to combine elegance with their solidity.

While party politics were an important element in the life of the community, the Board maintained a position of strict neutrality. Its members might hold what views and party affiliations they liked and might – as in fact many did – participate wholeheartedly in political activities, but the organization itself remained aloof since it did not wish to jeopardize its persuasive powers with changing governments. Although reluctant to admit to the title, the Board was in fact a pressure group and its usefulness at first consisted almost entirely in its ability to influence governing bodies.

Money was the important thing: it made the wheels turn and its proper management seemed the key to all the glorious things that assuredly lay in the future of this rich new land. Most businessmen felt instinctively that governments were incompetent to handle financial affairs in a way best calculated to serve the total needs of the community and actualize its growth potential. In 1850, for example, the Council was indignant over some provisions of the new Assessment Act and petitioned the Legislative Assembly accordingly. Its main objection, which was sustained over many years, was to the 'personalty tax' whereby municipal taxes levied on land and buildings were increased by a six per cent impost on the assessed total value of the average stocks on hand. That an organization such as the Toronto Board should be so upset by this tax is understandable in view of its high proportion of merchant members with warehouses full of goods, all taxable, whose taxes rose when trade was poor and inventories did not move. What particularly irritated them was the inequity of the tax: it fell heavily on the commercial and trading sector while financial institutions and the professions for the most part escaped.

Among the reasons given by the Board for its objection to the Assessment Bill in its petition were the following:

Because a tax upon personal property cannot be imposed without being extremely unequal in its operations, and in many instances causing double taxation, especially in the case of securities on landed property, mortgaged lands being taxed as real property in the township and as personal property in the town;

Because income is taxed and also the rent paid out of that income;

Because bank issues are already taxed as such and should not be also taxed as personal property;

Because it would be highly injurious to tax personal property such as stock in trade and furniture of the net value of £1000 and which will probably produce the tradesman no more than from £200 to £250 per annum, to an equal amount with a fixed income of £1000 a year;

Because it will drive English capital from the Province, if income derivable from England and already taxed there should be taxed in this Province;

The clause enabling City Corporations to suspend a personal property tax is considered highly objectionable, as giving too great a power, and because it might create an invidious competition between rival cities.

The Council therefore recommended that incorporated towns and cities should be altogether exempt from assessment on personal property. They did not get very far. Governments needed money and this was a relatively easy way of getting it. Although the Board repeatedly attacked tax methods, and some minor adjustment of assessment procedures was secured, it was not until 1905, fifty-five years later, that the retiring President, J.F. Ellis, could say: 'The abolition of the personalty tax as embodied in the new Assessment Act is a subject for congratulation.'

Very early in its existence the Board began to take a direct interest in the question of railways, an interest it sustained until the railway-building enthusiasm began to wane in the 1880s. Until mid-century, Toronto had to maintain a high degree of self-sufficiency; inland lines of communication were tenuous, its excellent port gave only limited access to other market areas and was closed tight during the long winter months, and for essential goods imported from overseas it was heavily dependent on the port of Montreal. In 1852 the Board recorded its objection to English mail being channelled through Montreal to Toronto, a 360-mile overland haul which in winter took eight days. Better means of transport and communication were urgently needed and Toronto businessmen were clearly frustrated by their inability to function as effectively as they thought they could.

Toronto's opportunity to establish itself as a major distributing point and resume its role as the 'Toronto Passage' occurred when Britain repealed the Corn Laws and the Navigation Act in the late 1840s. Duties on wheat imported into Britain were lowered, and Canada's primary products no longer had to be transported to Britain on British ships. The way was open for the development in Toronto of a cheaper route for western grains on their way to Britain through the Erie Canal and New York. In 1850 the freight charge on a barrel of flour shipped from New York to Liverpool was 1s. 3$^1$/2d., while from Montreal it was 3s. 0$^1$/2d. There was thus a real incentive to establish a Toronto-centred railway system which would permit overseas forwarding arrangements to be made locally and establish the city as a principal clearing centre. The race was on.

Nevertheless, in 1850 the Board's Council took strong objection to a proposal by the city council to assist the Ontario, Simcoe and Huron Railway by issuing debentures to the value of £100,000 on the grounds that the information available on the proposed line was inadequate and outlays from the city's coffers would inevitably result in a heavy tax impost upon ordinary taxpayers. This position was later modified when the Board passed a resolution approving the construction of the railroad and recommended civic assistance in the form of a £25,000 contribution in twenty-year debentures, to be issued when satisfactory progress had been made in construction and there was adequate evidence that the line would be completed. The city later decided on a sum of £50,000 and the building of Upper Canada's first steam railway line was assured. This line had been originally chartered in 1849 as the Toronto, Simcoe and Lake Huron, then took the name Ontario, Simcoe and Huron, and in 1855 became the Northern Railway. Its chief instigator was Frederick Chase Capreol, who conceived the line as a portage between Lakes Ontario and Huron, proposing a lottery to finance its construction and the purchase of 100,000 acres along the route; the increasing value of the land would soon repay any remaining indebtedness. The lottery idea, strenuously opposed by the Board of Trade, fell flat and Capreol then sought direct subvention.

At the Board's Annual Meeting on 24 January 1852 President Ridout reported that twenty miles of the railway had been graded and he had every reason to believe that the road to Barrie, sixty-four miles distant, would be completed and in working order by 1 December. It was in fact operative by 1853, and by 1855 had been extended to Collingwood, a distance of ninety-five miles, thus providing a railway link between Toronto and a port on Georgian Bay. By 1872 it reached a second port at Meaford and in 1875 was further extended through the Muskoka territory as far as Huntsville. The first locomotive for the new line to the north was imported from Portland, Maine, and arrived in Toronto by boat on 3 October 1852. The second engine, the *Toronto*, was built by James Good in his shops at the northeast corner of Queen and Yonge Streets and was delivered on 26 April 1853 to the railway company at the foot of York Street where a temporary railway station had been erected adjacent to the Queen's Wharf.

Toronto's next railway link was the Great Western line to Hamilton, open in December 1855, which provided a connection with Buffalo and the United States system. The Grand Trunk opened a line to Guelph in June 1856 and one to Oshawa in August of that year. The first passenger service between Toronto and Montreal began on 27 October 1856, giving Toronto rail access to a Canadian seaport and avoiding the hazards of the St Lawrence canal system. By 1859 this line had been extended westward to Sarnia. Feeder lines throughout southern Ontario proliferated and by 1876 there were over 5,000 miles of track under the control of thirty-seven companies. Toronto had become the main supplier for the entire region as well as the channel through which flowed a major part of the agricultural produce bound for overseas destinations. Of special importance was Toronto's linkage with American lines, which assured a steady flow of imports through the port of New York without reliance upon Montreal. However, the attitude of the Board of Trade toward this dominant American connection later became somewhat less than enthusiastic. There is no doubt that Toronto's harbour and the rapid creation of an efficient railway network with Toronto as its hub were the factors which contributed most significantly to the city's consolidation as a commercial centre of first importance. Referring to the splurge of railway construction, Charles Mulvaney in his *Toronto: Past and Present* remarks that 'no other one thing has contributed so materially in building up the city. It has made it really the metropolis ... the mart of Ontario.'

But railway building is an expensive business. In the absence of an organized money market the provincial government in 1852 had created a Municipal Loan Fund on which municipalities could draw for essential public work. Many used the available funds to make grants to or subscribe for the stock of railway companies in order to ensure the construction of lines considered important to their development. Quite a few municipalities soon found themselves in deep financial trouble as a result of their railway speculation. The Loan Fund was radically revised in 1859 to deter misuse, and by 1873 the provincial government was forced to step in and relieve the embarrassed municipalities of their burden. In *The Railway Builders* Oscar Skelton observes that 'the eight or ten years following 1849 are notable not only for a sudden outburst of railway construction and speculative activity throughout the provinces, but for the beginning of that close connection between politics and railways which is distinctively Canadian.'

Toronto's complementary asset, its harbour, had been in use since the French regime. The first Canadian mail steamers began operations from the port in 1826, carrying mail to Niagara for distribution in the United States and for onward forwarding to Europe via the port of New York. The Board of Trade demonstrated its interest in the harbour by inaugurating a campaign in 1844 to bring about the formation of a Harbour Trust and the transfer of complete authority for the administration of the facility to that body as a means of improving the accommodation for vessels, goods and passengers. It was six years before the campaign bore fruit with the passage of an Act to provide for the Future Management of Toronto Harbour whereby administrative authority was transferred to appointed Commissioners. The first Chairman of the Harbour Commissioners was J.G. Chervett and the Board of Trade appointed its President and Vice-President, Messrs George P. Ridout and P. Paterson, as Commissioners in conformity with specific provisions incorporated in the new Act.

The city council retained control of the waterlots and waterfront lands which it had acquired by Crown Patent in 1840. This control imposed upon the city the responsibility of constructing a boulevard paralleling the waterfront, and by 1852 a plan was worked out providing for a proportionate contribution by the waterlot occupants, with the city acting as co-ordinator. But by this time a problem had been created by the entry into the waterfront area of the railways, and the feasibility of the 'Esplanade Project' as it was first conceived was in some doubt. A tentative plan was worked out nonetheless and a contract was awarded to Gzowski & Co. for its implementation. A right of way along the Esplanade for the Grand Trunk Railway was proposed, and a sum of £10,000 was included in the estimates for the construction of bridges at George, Church, Yonge, Bay and either York or Simcoe Streets to give access to the wharves. There were important afterthoughts and the contract was later cancelled. The whole question of the development and use of the waterfront remained a major issue for the Board of Trade, and efforts to ensure access to the harbour area through the railway lines, which eventually created an effective barrier between the city proper and the shoreline, later constituted one of the Board's most vigorous and sustained campaigns.

In 1855 the Board became enthusiastic (and slightly hypnotized) by a plan to build a ship canal connecting Georgian Bay and Lake Huron with Lake Ontario and the St Lawrence route at the port of Toronto. Apparently the scheme was well thought of by mercantile men in Chicago, Milwaukee and Oswego, and the Board appointed a sub-committee authorized to employ an engineer to undertake a feasibility study. A sum of £110 was subscribed for the purpose. The sub-committee under the chairmanship of M.P. Hayes reported the following year that it had met with delegates from Chicago, Oswego and other places to receive a report of Kivus Tully, C.E., on the practicability of the project. Tully had made an initial survey in 1846 and another in 1851 and seems to have concluded that it could be done. At any rate the Council decided to proceed with a thorough survey immediately and Tully was authorized to undertake it in collaboration with Col. R.B. Mason, chief engineer of the Illinois Central Railroad. Tully later reported by letter:

... with regard to the practicability of a work for the construction of a Ship Canal between Lakes Ontario and Huron, I have to state that from recent examination, and from actual survey, I have no hesitation in saying that there are no insuperable obstacles to the construction of the above work.

On the contrary, the explorations have tended to dispel what appeared at first to be impracticable difficulties. In this opinion I have been fully sustained by Col. R.B. Mason.

The Board's interest in this project was to make Toronto the clearing point for western grains by providing a portage for ships from the Upper Lakes, thus avoiding the longer haul around the southern Ontario peninsula. Ships could then proceed either via Lake Ontario and the St Lawrence to Montreal or Quebec for trans-shipment overseas, or via Lake Ontario and the Oswego canal system to New York, Boston or Portland. The haul from Chicago to Quebec would be reduced from 1,450 to 1,150 miles, and from Chicago to New York from 1,415 to 1,015 miles. Toronto would be a focal point of the system, a consideration which undoubtedly contributed substantially to the Board of Trade's enthusiasm for the scheme. Trade would be opened up with the fertile regions around the Great Lakes, delays caused by overcrowding in the Welland Canal would be avoided, the trend of western grain shipments through Buffalo and the Erie Canal to American ports would be checked and impetus would be given to better utilization of the St Lawrence route instead of shipping through the Oswego Canal, again to American ports. It was even suggested that the portage would have military value by giving Great Britain better access to Lake Huron.

The proposed alignment followed the Humber and Holland Rivers to Lake Simcoe, and from there down the Nottawasaga River to Georgian Bay. Lake Simcoe is 469 feet above Lake Ontario and 109 feet above Lake Huron so that 44 locks were needed, each with a rise of more than 13 feet. The 28 miles from Toronto to the head of navigation in the Holland River alone required 34 locks. The canal would be built to accommodate only lake vessels of not more than 11 feet draft, or approximately 1,000 tons burden, not ocean-going vessels, so that cargoes would have to be trans-shipped for their overseas voyage. The cost was put at something under £5 million, and the Board of Trade worked hard with the other interests directly concerned to promote the idea and secure government grants which would permit first a full survey and later the chartering of a company to undertake construction. But interest outside of Toronto was lukewarm and the government in any event had far too much on its hands with the railway and canal-building program to which it was already committed to countenance this immense added expenditure. The prosperity of the early 1850s had bred a heady optimism among Toronto businessmen; if undertaken with good intentions and sufficient energy, nothing seemed impossible. However, implementation of the grandiose plan for a Toronto-Georgian Bay Canal needed more than enthusiasm: it needed a financial input which was enormous for those days, and one which the government was not only unwilling but probably incapable of supplying.

The project simply faded away, although the idea continued to have great attraction for Toronto business interests and it was later revived in different terms.

The Board was ever alert to the advantages of opening up new territories and hence new opportunities for trade. By 1856 it was casting eyes on the vast new field of enterprise lying in the Hudson's Bay Territory which stretched from the Gulf of St Lawrence right across to the west coast. Here was surely a huge new field for development with a potential that could hardly be visualized, and the Board was convinced that the inhabitants would welcome commercial relations with the more developed regions of the southeast 'so soon as the stern rule of the Hudson's Bay Company will permit of free action.' A petition against the Hudson's Bay Company's monopoly was prepared in January 1857 urging the annexation of its territory to Canada. 'With the advantage of the Canadian constitution extended to its most distant settlement,' it said, 'and the civilizing influence commerce spreads over it, who shall limit the future greatness of this noble country, with its Eastern boundary resting on the Gulf of St Lawrence or the Atlantic Ocean, and extending West to the Pacific?' Twelve years later all lands owned by the Hudson's Bay Company were transferred to Canada for a consideration of £300,000. The Saugeen territory, newly settled and improving rapidly, also held great promise. Sandford Fleming had been appointed by the directors of the Canada North-Western Railway Company to examine the features and prospects of this region and to recommend a proposed route for a railway to connect Saugeen and Owen Sound on Lake Huron with Toronto. The outcome was clearly important to the Toronto mercantile community.

Nor were the Board's eyes turned only westward. It joined the Montreal Board of Trade in seeking a government subsidy for a weekly steamship service between Montreal and Liverpool. It supported the Northwest Transportation Company, which was incorporated in 1858 to open up new territories and whose first activity was the operation of the steamship *Rescue* to transport freight, passengers and mail from Collingwood to the head of Lake Superior. It advocated lower tolls on the St Lawrence canals and generally took the position that any extension or improvement of facilities contributing to the economical movement of goods should be supported in order to assist the country's growth and mercantile health.

The Board's outward-looking attitude was partially the result of a growing realization in the business community that, in spite of Toronto's favourable economic position and many assets, there was still some risk of its being bypassed in the development of the country's trading pattern. It was therefore essential to acquire the widest possible marketing area and ensure a dominant position for Toronto in that area.

Conditions affecting the actual processes of trade concerned the Board's Council a great deal in the early years. Essentially an organization of traders, the Board worked consistently for the removal of all barriers to the free movement of goods. A proposed Reciprocity Treaty with the United States providing for free trade in a wide variety of natural products was supported since it would stimulate business and contribute to an increase in the value of most leading articles of export. However, at the Board's 1851 Annual Meeting, held in the St Lawrence Hall, President Ridout had this to say about the suggested agreement, which was still under consideration by the United States Congress:

The agitation seems in a great measure to have died away with the cause which gave it birth, namely, the high price of wheat and other grain which obtained in the markets of the neighboring States when compared with those of this Province, – the high price existing in those markets was evidently temporary, caused by the partial failure of the harvest in the Western and Middle States and by speculators who have since paid the penalty of their folly, and the low price in this Province caused by the abundant harvest with which we have been favored. That which should have been a source of thankfulness to all classes of the community was tortured by some into a cause of dissatisfaction with our own condition, and of complaint against the Government of the country. As the markets have since settled down to an equality, a better spirit seems to possess even those who carried their dissatisfaction so far as to agitate for the annexation of this colony to the United States – a movement which cannot but be deplored and condemned, when viewed in connection with the capabilities of this Province, – its unbounded resources rich in all the material which constitutes wealth, its forests of timber, its mines of metals and minerals, its noble rivers and still more noble lakes teeming with wealth, superadded to which may be the Anglo-Saxon spirit which is extant and which is surely and rapidly turning to account advantages which our adopted country possesses in no ordinary degree.

The reluctance of the United States government to agree to reciprocity was nevertheless regretted, and alternative recourse to differential duties was deprecated. Ridout's 1851 report continued:

In the opinion of your Council, it would be unwise and impolitic to call for differential duties on articles coming from the United States ... it is obviously the interest of this Province to have its wants supplied wherever it can do so the cheapest – our own resolution would not be the less prejudicial to our own capital and industry because the American Government persisted in maintaining impolitic regulations.

Contending that 'the best and only effectual method of combatting hostile tariffs is by free imports,' the Board viewed with satisfaction a reduction in the duty on a few articles and advocated that this be followed forthwith by a general lowering of 'the present very high schedule of duties.' Although Toronto businessmen attributed their free-trade stance to the highest motives of national good, it was easy to see a substantial vein of self-interest and the government, always in need of revenues, was not much influenced by their persistence. The Board's actions, however, may have applied a brake on tariff increment tendencies.

From the time of the Act of Union in 1840 until Confederation in 1867 the Province of Canada derived four-fifths of its total revenues from customs duties. Until 1846 it had no fiscal freedom since the duties levied by the colonies of British North America were fixed by the Imperial Parliament in London. In that year Britain abandoned its system of colonial preferences, and as a consequence the colonies were given some control over their own tariff structures. However, it was not until the British North America Act was passed that the Dominion was accorded the sole power to levy customs and excise duties. Indignation was expressed in 1851 over the conduct of the local collector of customs, who 'has been in many cases harsh, over-bearing and insolent to parties, Merchants of this City, and others having business with the office, and ... has also in some instances hastened the sale of goods seized in a manner unprecedented and not contemplated by law.' An investigation was recommended with a view to removing these causes of complaint, but the government declined to act.

In spite of the traders' resentment of tariffs, the country's external trade steadily improved and exports increased from £47.4 million in 1842 to £71.2 million in 1850 as a result of a natural increase in productivity, the opening up of wider markets in the United States and Britain, and the gradual introduction of commercial policies affording considerable freedom in trading operations.

In June 1854, after long debate, a treaty was finally effected 'between Great Britain and the North American Provinces on the one part and the United States of North America on the other,' bringing about a reciprocity of trade in such items as grain, flour, meats, fruit and vegetables, fish, butter, eggs, cheese, ores, timber, lumber and other products generally in the category of natural or unmanufactured commodities. The Board noted that this treaty brought about a speedy increase in the export of agricultural products and a correspondingly large increase in the import of free goods. The production of many staple export products was stimulated by the assurance of a steady, quick and active cash demand for them. The Board lost no time in recording its opinion that the benefits derived from these partial measures indicated that vastly greater advantages would accrue to both countries by 'a full, complete and well-considered measure of reciprocity.'

A deficiency of the new agreement was considered to be its failure to provide for complete freedom of navigation for the vessels of both countries, a condition which the Board felt would not only help implement the idea of reciprocity but would also give impetus to the development of Canadian lands, particularly on the south and east shores of Lake Huron. The Toronto Board noted with satisfaction that its advocacy in this respect was supported by the New York Chamber of Commerce in a statement directed to the United States Congress. It is interesting that at this early date the Board was sufficiently impressed by the idea of reciprocity to propose a reciprocal trade agreement between Canada and the British West Indies as a means of bringing about a mutually beneficial exchange of staples.

In 1851 the Board was advocating the reform of postal arrangements, recommending that effective steps be taken to encourage immigration and to improve the system of land grants to new immigrants under favourable terms, and was recording its views on the inadequacies of existing currency laws. Money matters figured prominently in the Board's deliberations during its early years, and in 1852 the usury laws – 'these obnoxious laws which continue to deface the statute books of the land' – came under heavy fire. A modification of these laws was secured by Stat. 16, Vic. c. 80 so that all parties except chartered banks and insurance companies could lend money at such rates as they might agree upon, subject only to the forfeiture of surplus interest over 6 per cent if the borrower should think fit to repudiate the payment. The Board's Council considered this a step in the right direction, but urged total repeal of all legislative trammels on the trade in money. It was felt that '... all partial enactments giving limited freedom of action in the transactions between borrowers and lenders can only tend to perpetuate and increase the evils which they are intended to remedy, without bringing about the influx of capital into Canada which would undoubtedly follow the total repeal of all restrictive enactments on the trade.' It was recognized that the government probably feared an unrestricted trade in money by the banks, and suggested that, if so, a seven per cent limit be imposed in such transactions (as was currently in effect in New York State) with no restriction on trade between private parties. This theme was pursued for some years, with little success. While it might appear that the members of the Council, as substantial businessmen, were interested only in getting their maximum return on money loaned, it must be charitably conceded that their objection to a limitation on interest rates, at least ostensibly, was that it inhibited the flow into the country of new money so badly needed for resource development.

Of related concern was the need for bankruptcy legislation, another issue which occupied the Board's attention over a long period. In 1855 the Council expressed its opinion that 'a well-considered bankruptcy law should be enacted to protect both creditor and debtor – the former against undue preferences when no legislative control exists, the latter against possible debarment from recuperation if any creditor refuse discharge. The law, however, should be very carefully enacted, and every precaution taken to prevent its fraudulent and tyrannical application.' In 1856 the Parliament passed an Act for the Relief of Insolvent Debtors which the Board promptly condemned as inadequate for the prevention of unscrupulous practices.

The mere existence of adequate supplies of money became a matter of some consequence to businessmen with the increase of trade and general prosperity in the mid-1850s. In 1855 President Clarkson noted that banking capital had nearly doubled in the previous two years, but that in his opinion there was an immediate need for almost as much again. Banking facilities were not keeping pace with the acceleration of commercial activity and money was not being made available in supplies commensurate with the development of new sources of wealth. At this period the Board seems to have been somewhat critical and wary of prevailing banking practices.

Canadian currency had had a rather strange history and its remarkable variety had done nothing to facilitate commercial operations. For a time in the earliest days beaver skins had been the ordinary medium of exchange and until 1664 there were very few coins in circulation, most of them French. Soon after, there was a flood of foreign coins of all kinds, and these became over-valued to the point where laws had to be enacted to reduce and standardize their values. By 1681 the Spanish piastre (or dollar), was circulating widely, brought into the country through trade with the English colonies to the south, and an ordinance was passed requiring these and all other foreign coins to be valued according to how their weight compared to a set standard. As a convenience, all full-weight coins were over-stamped with a fleur-de-lis. In 1685 there was a temporary money shortage, and

Intendant De Meulles tried to solve the problem by issuing the first paper money – playing cards cut into four, each part stamped with the amount it was supposed to represent. After the English conquest the Spanish dollar became the standard coin. In Quebec the 'Halifax standard' was adopted which, reckoned in pounds, shillings and pence, rated the Spanish dollar at six shillings. Montreal employed the 'New York standard' based on the York shilling at eight to the Spanish dollar. This confusion was resolved in 1777 by making the Halifax standard the legal money of account for the whole country, with a reduction in the value of the Spanish dollar to five shillings. About 1792 an attempt was made by a business group in the colony to obtain a charter authorizing a banking operation. It was not granted, but the group appears to have conducted some kind of banking business for a while as a private company, issuing its own notes. During the War of 1812 and for some time after, the colonists used Army Bills, issued by the Army Bill Office, as an expedient for raising war funds. They were redeemable either in cash or bills of exchange and appear to have served their purpose satisfactorily.

The Bank of Montreal was founded in 1817 and appointed an agent at York, but the town's own banking operations began with the chartering of the Bank of Upper Canada in 1821. It was under substantial government control and was concerned almost wholly with commercial transactions, but by issuing bank notes it relieved the shortage of currency and greatly facilitated the transaction of business. Coinage of great variety was still in circulation, however, much of it in worn and mutilated condition and becoming debased in spite of repeated attempts to establish legal valuations. Copper coins in particular were in such bad condition that many private firms were importing coinage until, in 1837, the banks began to issue their own copper coins. In 1853 a decimal system was devised with a dollar unit equivalent in value to that of the United States and on an equal footing with the Halifax currency as money of account. By the Currency Act of 1858 the decimal system was made the official system for the whole of Canada and came into general use. The first Canadian coins corresponding to the new system – five-, ten- and twenty-cent coins in silver and one-cent coins in bronze – were issued in this same year, although the banks continued to issue their own notes. The first Canadian government paper money was issued in 1866 by the Province of Canada.

For some time merchants were plagued by the large-scale circulation of United States coinage throughout the province, trading at par. The market value of silver in New York made it six to eight per cent cheaper than gold which led to large quantities of American silver entering Canada for the purchase of goods and for exchange into Canadian currency. In addition, gold was being withdrawn from Canadian banks for sale in New York at a profit. The amount of American silver circulating at last became so large that the Board recommended a 4 per cent discount be imposed on it, and over a period of time this was done and proved effective. The dislocations later brought about in the United States by the Civil War became so severe that by 1863 the discount on American silver was increased to 8 per cent.

An important advance in the transaction of business was indicated in this press item of 26 July 1852:

It has for some time past been in contemplation to establish a Stock Exchange in Toronto, for the purpose of affording to all parties interested in the transfer of stocks and other public securities, greater facilities in effecting their respective operations than are at present possessed, and also to extend the circulation of Canadian credit and establish a uniform charge for the transaction of all business coming within the range of stock or share brokers. With this object in view a meeting of gentlemen engaged in this business was held today for the purpose of taking this subject into consideration.

The gentlemen present at this meeting constituted themselves into an association which they named the Toronto Stock Exchange. For some years its activities were minimal. In October 1861 a meeting was held at the Masonic Hall on Toronto Street to draw up rules and regulations for the conduct of the Exchange's business and thereafter daily sessions were held from 11 to 11.30 a.m. The value of a seat on the Exchange was $5 and the average attendance at the sessions was five. Members were elected annually by ballot. In 1863 the first official list of members was published and the daily listing of quotations was begun the same year. Transactions were mainly in municipal and government bonds and mortgages, and an attempt in 1864 to develop interest in manufacturing and other joint stock enterprises proved unsuccessful.

Better conditions for the conduct of trade were gradually being established during the 1850s. Transport and communications media were available and statutory regulations governing the conduct of commercial affairs were being formulated and applied. A recently-created Toronto Exchange, dealing in commodities, was proving a marked success and Board of Trade members were urged to make fullest use of it in negotiating purchases and sales, in exchanging market information and for general personal intercourse. Gratifying evidence of Toronto's escape from its former isolation was provided when two large first-class ocean vessels – the *City of Toronto*, built locally, and the *Reindeer*, built on the shores of Lake Huron – cleared its port in 1855 for Liverpool and London respectively. In this year, too, the Board was pressing for the appointment of a Canadian representative in Washington, taking care to add that if Canada's naming of an ambassador was considered to be 'an infringement of the Royal Prerogative,' the Canadian government should pursue the matter in consultation with Great Britain. Failing such action it was proposed that Boards of Trade in Canada should consider the appointment of their own commercial delegate.

General prosperity continued through 1856, largely due to abundant harvests and good prices. The Board continued its vigorous opposition to high tariffs on imports, some of which had been increased to as much as 50 per cent. It saw no justification for a high-tariff policy and considered it prejudicial to trade. Frequent rate changes were especially resented on the grounds that they destroyed confidence and added to the uncertainty of long-range planning. The value of imports at the port of Toronto grew from £634,722 in 1850 to £1,738,657 in 1856, while over the same period exports increased from £67,557 to £551,333. Up-to-date statistical information was scarce, however, and the Board repeatedly applied to the Inspector General to release export/import figures from the books of the Customs Office on a weekly or monthly basis. A need was also felt for a better method of adjudicating commercial disputes. Although the Board itself each year appointed a Board of Arbitration, it was little used and the suggestion was made that a Court of Merchants be legally constituted as arbitrators and that their decisions be final. The existing jury processes were proving costly and unsatisfactory and it was considered essential that differences between business concerns be dealt with expeditiously by those accustomed to trade usages.

Some uneasiness was already felt in 1856 about what had been hoped would be continuing economic progress. A sudden downturn came late in 1857; few were prepared for it and casualties were high. By the beginning of 1858 twenty-five firms had failed with liabilities totalling nearly $3 million. Although Toronto was hard hit, the trade depression was by no means a local phenomenon; in both the United States and Europe rapid economic deterioration caused near panic in the money markets. The value of produce plummeted 'so that one dollar would now purchase more than double the quantity of flour or grain it would have done last year.' Canadian banks were battered but they survived. The banks were not held blameless in the disaster, however, since it was alleged that

... the directors of these institutions, participating in the general spirit of speculation which has obtained during the last few years, have for the sake of more
immediate large profits been in the habit of granting individuals accommodation to
an extent not justified by any principle of sound policy; and as a natural consequence much of our banking capital that should be available at all times in assisting
to develop the agricultural and productive resources of the country is now locked
up.

While the depression was largely imported, there were local causes.
Farmers could in no way be held responsible for the drastic decline in the
prices obtainable for their produce, nor for a poor harvest, but they had,
during the prosperous days, been speculating heavily and unwisely in
marginal land, until 'in their desire for speedy wealth they overstepped the
bounds of prudence and made large investments in wild lands and other
unproductive property.' Merchants, as well, carried along by the general
optimism, had imported heavily and found themselves with massive inventories they could not liquidate. The effect of the personalty tax in these
circumstances became well-nigh unbearable. They had, moreover, been
entrusting large quantities of merchandise for country distribution 'to
inexperienced people not alert to the evils of excessive credit.' Even the
railway builders came in for criticism. The huge costs involved in building
and maintaining the railroads had 'soon made themselves felt in the increased value of every article of consumption for domestic use, doubling
expenditure without in most cases increasing their income.'
Probably because of the desperate straits in which many businesses
found themselves, the Board's membership increased and more attention
was given to its attempts to solve problems which in good times had seemed
insignificant. Moreover, it appeared that if trade were to be revitalized it
would probably require an effort which only a body like the Board of Trade
could organize. Most of the problems were old ones, made more acute by
economic stringency; bankruptcy laws were wholly unsatisfactory to both
creditor and debtor; the currency situation was confused: the decimal
system and the circulation of Canadian coins of standardized values had
not yet passed into law and the Board pressed for such legislation. Although statutory limits on the interest chargeable on borrowed money
reduced the availability of emergency funds, the government seemed ob-
livious to Toronto's concerns and reluctant to adopt measures which
would restore commercial confidence and stimulate trade.
Ridout, the Board's first President, had resigned in 1852 and was succeeded by Thomas Clarkson, who had taken an active part in the

community's civic and cultural affairs and was involved in the establishment of the Bank of Toronto in 1856. He later spent some time in the United States, returning to Toronto in 1864 to found the trustee and accounting business which still bears his name. Clarkson resigned in 1859, saying that 'he looked forward hopefully to the day when a greater number of intelligent commercial men would fill the places in the halls of the legislature of those wily lawyers and political demagogues, whose sole desire and ambition was to raise themselves to wealth, rank and power, and when those long harangues of weeks and months would cease.' He was followed in the presidency by E.F. Whittemore, who died during the year, William P. Howland being chosen to succeed him. In March 1856 J.W. Brent, who had acted as the Board's Secretary from the beginning, resigned, and M.P. Hayes was appointed in his stead.

The city had grown in population from 25,166 in 1850, to 41,760 in 1856. Property in the former year was valued at £132,360, producing £9,788 in taxes at a rate of 1s. 6d. By 1856 the value was £427,981 and taxes £55,362 at a 2s. 6d. rate. The highest price paid at property auctions was £40 per foot frontage for a lot 180 feet deep on Front Street near York. A three-storey brick house on King Street west of York brought £1,900, while on Garrison Reserve, two miles from the city's centre, lots were selling for £5 to £8 a frontage foot.

Toronto citizens were expressing alarm over the number of fires of undetermined origins occurring in the city, and the Board in 1856 recommended that an 'inquest' be held into their cause. Since the seriousness of fire loss was enhanced by the paucity of insurance coverage usually available, the Board opposed a government plan to impose restrictions on the operation of foreign insurance companies by requiring them to hold government bonds on the grounds that this would discourage the entry of new companies. However, a few years later, the Board indicated its concurrence that some regulation was probably desirable.

Poverty and disease were still rife in the community and were, as everywhere else, considered to be an inevitable concomitant of urban living. That the leaders, both political and business, worked hard to correct the conditions which gave rise to these evils is indisputable, but it does appear that their concern was sometimes motivated more by a desire to rid themselves of a costly nuisance than by a true social conscience. *The Annual Review of Commerce of Toronto* for 1860 noted more salutary conditions: '... within the last few years or since the clearing of the country and the completion of our railroads and public works, the consumption of quinine has fallen off fully 90 per cent owing to the almost entire absence of ague and bilious fevers. Druggists and medical men assert that from this change in the climate of Canada West it is now one of the most healthy known.'

The year 1860 saw the end of an important decade in Toronto's affairs and the beginning of a return to more prosperous times. Trade and financial conditions in the United States and Great Britain were steadying, the harvests were better and prices for agricultural products moved up. The shock of two bad years had resulted in a more cautious attitude on the part of Toronto merchants and the removal by attrition of some of the weaker and more flamboyant elements from earlier boom times. The clear signs of recovery greeted with such relief in the early part of 1860 were shadowed before the end of the year by the political crisis brewing in the United States. Over the next several years Canadian affairs were to be profoundly influenced by the chaos of the American Civil War; for example, export trade in a number of important commodities was seriously affected. The United States had been taking two-thirds of Canada's entire grain crop and all of its lumber exports. While the trade in grain continued, and indeed for a while increased, lumber shipments dropped to nil. For a long time the uncertain outcome of the civil strife had a generally repressive effect on Canadian enterprise, but there were some compensations. Several American companies notably tobacco processors, established operations in Toronto and in other parts of the province.

Throughout the early 1860s the Board continued its campaigns for ameliorization of the tariff, amendment of the assessment laws, abolition of usury laws and the introduction of effective bankruptcy and insolvency legislation. It kept, besides, 'a general watchfulness over the formation of doubtful institutions which, although established with the sanction of law, were placed under the control of irresponsible parties; several of these dangerous concerns have been checked in their operations, and ultimately put down through the instrumentality of the Board.' It would be interesting to know more about these 'dangerous concerns', but we are not told.

Toronto was steadily consolidating its position as a centre for the distribution of goods throughout Upper Canada and its commission and wholesale houses flourished. They were heavily dependent upon Great Britain as a source of supply and it was the constant concern of the mercantile community to keep the trade channel to Britain in good repair, to maintain at Toronto all facilities necessary for the efficient handling of goods shipments both into and out of the city and to cultivate new markets wherever and whenever the opportunity arose. In pursuit of these objectives it pressed for better warehouse accommodation at the waterfront and, seeing itself also as a potential main centre for the trade in both western and local grains, advocated the erection of large-capacity grain elevators. Since successful grain marketing depended upon conformity to standards, the Board supported a proposal to establish a system of official grading stations throughout the province and worked to ensure that one such station was opened in Toronto.

Although primarily concerned with trade and its problems, and with ensuring Toronto's role as broker in the grain trade, by 1860 the Board was beginning to pay attention to the need for developing local manufacturing industries. Progress was already being made in this direction: among the established plants were Childs & Hamilton for boots and shoes, the Phoenix Foundry for stoves, Wm Matthews Soap and Candle Manufactory, Crawford's Spice Factory, Mason's Sperm Oil Manufactory for the refining of whale oil, Peter R. Lamb for blacking and glue, and a number of others, all relatively small with twenty employees or less. One of the first and largest organized as a full-scale factory operation was the Toronto Locomotive Works, founded in 1852. The bulk of the citizens' needs were still being met by imports and the made-to-order services of local craftsmen, although the latter's skills slowly fell into disuse as the factory system took over. The Board's aim was to increase the scale and diversity of industrial production and by so doing improve the availability and price of commodities in constant demand by a growing population. A further aim was to reduce unemployment and so relieve 'our numerous poor during the long winter who for want of work become idle and vicious, entailing a moral disgrace and a heavy pecuniary burden on the community.'

The vicissitudes of the grain trade were a major factor in the general condition of Toronto's business, and indifferent crops in the early 1860s were cited as one substantial cause of economic sluggishness. In 1864 there was a good harvest accompanied by high prices and brisk demand, which was reflected in a general heightening of prosperity. The termination of the Civil War renewed a demand from the United States for farm stock, cereal products and other staples, even manufactured items and goods imported from England. Economic stability was being re-established, one of the first observable indices being an improvement in land values. Customs returns were up almost a million dollars over the previous year, and between August and October currency in circulation rose from $8.5 million to more than $14 million.

A dark cloud in 1864 was the proposed abrogation of the Reciprocity Treaty with the United States. It had come to be regarded as a prime element in Canada's overall trading picture and the prospect of its annulment was alarming. An invitation received by the Board of Trade at this time to attend a convention in Detroit of delegates from Boards of Trade and Chambers of Commerce in the United States and the British Provinces for the discussion of matters of mutual concern was accepted with alacrity. The Toronto Board took the initiative in organizing the Canadian delegation and convoked a preliminary two-day conference in Toronto attended by fifty representatives from ten Canadian Boards of Trade to attempt a consensus on the issues to be discussed with the Americans and the positions to be taken. High on the list was the reciprocity question, and it was agreed that every effort should be made to secure its renewal. Another decision reached at the conference, which was probably the first attempt at a national business forum, was to urge the Canadian government to act promptly to enlarge the Welland Canal and deepen the St Lawrence.

The Detroit conference itself appears to have been moderately satisfactory, at least insofar as there was a unanimous expression in favour of the negotiation of a new treaty of reciprocity between the United States and the British North American Provinces. However, the American government later confirmed its resolve to terminate the treaty, and the best the Toronto Board could then do was to press the Canadian government to take measures for the extension of Canadian trade in other foreign countries. It also urged Canadian businesses to promote the production of articles suitable for export to these new markets. When reciprocity with the United States was finally abrogated in 1866, the Board found to its surprise that the general level of trade was not much affected. Markets were being opened up or extended in Britain, and it was noted with some satisfaction that sales there were in many cases supplanting those formerly made by the United States. The question of Canada's trading relationship with the United States was to continue to occupy the Board's attention, and in 1887 it again became a matter of extensive debate.

By 1864 the Board had 111 members, although responsibility for the conduct of its affairs still fell upon its officers and the twelve members of its Council. Meetings continued to be held in the old Mechanics Institute, and it was felt that the time had come to establish better quarters. There was talk, too, of amalgamating with the Corn Exchange, an association of produce dealers, which would necessitate improved accommodation. Accordingly, rooms were taken in the Merchants' Exchange Building at the corner of Leader Lane (then called 'Change Alley) and Wellington Street, where the Board's offices remained until it erected and occupied its own building in 1890. To support the added costs of operation the membership fee was advanced from $4 to $8 annually.

Toronto was steadily growing, with an annual population increase of 1,200 between 1861 and 1871. Its immigrant inflow was greater than that of any other Canadian city. A high proportion of Irish were fleeing the famine in their country and, indeed, in 1860 the city contained more people of Irish than of English birth. The city by this time comprised over four square miles extending about three miles along the waterfront from the Don River to Dufferin Street and roughly a mile and a half from what was then the shoreline north to Bloor Street. It was 1870 before development began on the east side of the Don, and no substantial construction took place north of Bloor or west of Dufferin until the 1880s. There was still no attempt made to regulate land use, and the pattern of development was governed by historical circumstances or mere convenience.

Commercial and industrial activities were expanding. Messrs J. & J. Taylor, established in 1855, were producing between three and four hundred safes a year; the Gooderham & Worts distillery, erected in 1861, was annually consuming half a million bushels of grain in the production of 2.5 million gallons of spirits; the Wm Davies Company, pork packers, occupied new and enlarged premises in 1865. The harbour in 1865 received 905 steamers and 1,453 sailing vessels from Britain and 95 steamers and 96 sailing vessels from the United States. By the same year the Esplanade, forty feet wide and accommodating the Grand Trunk Railway's right of way, had finally been built and paved along the waterfront at a cost of more than $1 million.

The harbour had previously been almost wholly enclosed by a spit of land extending in an arc from the east with access only through a narrow westerly gap, but on 13 April 1858 a violent lake storm breached the peninsula and created an eastern passage, cautiously used by shipping in May of that year. By 1859 the eastern gap had been buoyed by the Harbour Commissioners and it came into general use as a second entrance to the harbour. New wharfs had been built to take care of increased ship movements and by 1862 grain storage facilities, advocated by the Board of Trade, had been installed at the waterfront.

The development of the port of Toronto and effective harbour management were traditionally areas of great concern to the Board, and two of its members continued to serve as Harbour Commissioners. In 1858-9 the Board had acted vigorously to oppose action by the city of Toronto to assume effective control of the harbour at the expense of the Commissioners, and the city's bill with this objective was defeated in the legislature. In 1865 an Act respecting the Weighing, Measuring and Gauging of Certain Articles of General Consumption was passed, which assigned responsibility to the Board of Trade for developing rules and appointing referees to act in any matter of dispute respecting quantities of goods received at the port of Toronto. To this day the Board appoints an Official Weigher, Measurer and Gauger and establishes the general conditions under which his functions are discharged.

By the mid-1860s Toronto had become a thriving financial centre served by no less than eight substantial banks: the Bank of Montreal, the Bank of Toronto, the Ontario Bank, the Bank of Upper Canada, the City Bank, the Quebec Bank, the Commercial Bank of Canada, and the Bank of British North America. Two of these, the Commercial Bank and the Bank of Upper Canada, later failed. Referring to their collapse, the Board's President, James G. Worts, remarked in 1867 that it had occurred 'when money was abundant and without any undue pressure on our banking system, which has withstood the test of many years. Various causes have been assigned ... it is evident that in both cases mismanagement characterized their business operations for a number of years past; this is shown in their unusually large advances to corporations and irresponsible parties.' A number of merchants and others at this time were nevertheless experiencing difficulty in obtaining funds to conduct their businesses owing to the very conservative policy of the Bank of Montreal in granting loans to businessmen, especially to those in western Canada. Since the bank could not be shaken in its policy, the Hon. Wm McMaster, then a director, severed his connection with the Bank of Montreal and in 1866 applied for a charter for a new bank. This was granted, and when his Bank of Commerce commenced operations in the following year its stock to the value of $1 million was eagerly taken up. McMaster continued as president for the next twenty years. New banking legislation was adopted in 1871 which led ultimately to Canada's enviable position as possessor of one of the world's strongest banking systems.

Toronto had been well served almost from the beginning by retail establishments but a notable event in this field, though not much remarked on at the time, was the opening of Timothy Eaton's dry-goods shop on Yonge Street in 1869 with four clerks and a policy of plainly marked prices and cash-only sales. Robert Simpson opened a similar establishment in 1872. These two rival shops were to grow over the years to mammoth department store proportions.

In 1849 H.B. Williams, a cabinet-maker, had built four omnibuses to provide a public transportation service between the Red Lion Hotel in Yorkville and the St Lawrence Market. Toronto became one of the first cities in North America with a street railway system when Alexander Easton received a charter in 1861 giving him the sole right for a thirty-year period to operate public vehicles on tracks following rights-of-way on the principal streets. By the end of that year Easton's Toronto Street Railway Company was operating with horse-drawn cars over six miles of track and was soon carrying 2,000 passengers daily. There were three lines, one running up Yonge Street from King to Bloor (the city's northerly limit), one along Queen Street from Yonge almost to Dufferin, and the third from the Don River to Bathurst Street. The company ran into financial problems in 1869 and was sold to new owners without any interruption in service. It was several years, however, before there was any material extension of track- age.

Although Southern Ontario was by this time criss-crossed by railroads, the Board of Trade was still pressing for lines to open up new territories into which Toronto's trade could expand. It favoured the construction of the Toronto, Grey and Bruce and the Toronto and Nipissing Railways, the Board's Council in 1866 'deeming it their duty to aid and assist the provi- sional companies who are promoting these enterprises, it being expected that the construction of these railways will give a decided impulse to the industry of the city, largely increasing its population and bringing to a common centre the trade of an extensive and imperfectly developed field, hitherto placed at a great disadvantage for want of the means of transit.' At about this time, too, the Board gave a good deal of attention to the feasibility of light narrow-gauge railways. It was believed that these had the ability to perform any service required, and construction costs were con- siderably less than for the standard-gauge lines. The Toronto, Grey and Bruce line to Owen Sound and the Toronto and Nipissing line to Coboconk and Sutton were both originally designed to narrow-gauge standards, but the proposed technique was discarded since it prevented effective integra- tion with other railways in the network.

In his report to the members in 1865 President Worts observed that

Canadian credit abroad has been in an unsatisfactory state ... our securities have undergone violent fluctuations and have ruled considerably below the rates of last year. And we cannot expect any decided improvement in this respect till our political future is more definitely settled. The presence of a powerful neighbour, with large standing armies on our southern and western borders with all the disturbing elements engendered by a terrible civil strife of four years' duration, must render our securities anything but a first-class investment so long as we are divided as at present. We would like to indulge the hope for the good of the country that these Provinces may within the present year be erected into a strong united government ensuring the blessings of freedom and guaranteeing the perpetuation of British institutions.

The proposal to divide the Province of Canada into the provinces of Ontario and Quebec and unite them with Nova Scotia and New Brunswick to form the Dominion of Canada, thereby establishing a more cohesive political and economic entity, was looked upon with great favour by Toronto businessmen. By doing away with frustrating trade barriers it would provide greater business opportunities, at the same time creating a strengthened nation of greater attractiveness to foreign investors. Hitherto Toronto had been only one of several cities in a British territory, almost unknown to the world beyond the American border towns and the wholesale interests of Montreal and New York. It was confidently expected that Toronto would achieve its true position as the leading city of a major provincial unit in the more powerful confederation. The birth of the new Dominion was appropriately celebrated in Toronto on 1 July 1867, and the first parliament of the new province of Ontario met in Toronto on 27 December, with the Hon. John Sandfield Macdonald, Q.C., as Premier and Attorney General.

The Montreal Board of Trade reacted promptly to Confederation by issuing an invitation to delegates from all parts of the newly-integrated provinces to meet in Ottawa for the purpose of promoting unity of action in commercial matters. The Toronto Board heartily endorsed the move in the belief that such a meeting would contribute to the formulation of recommendations to the central government promoting commercial interests, encourage the adoption of uniform standards of money, weights and measures, and lead to agreement on appropriate customs and usages of trade. However, the Maritimes declined to take part and the project for the time being was put aside.

The Board saw a major objective achieved in 1869 when the Dominion of Canada purchased the vast territories of the Hudson's Bay Company and provided for their admission to and government by the Dominion. Here was another immense field for new commercial enterprise, although to be sure very little was known about it.

# 2
# Consolidation

The years from 1871 to 1874 were ones of great prosperity, as indicated by Toronto's growth of assessment from $29.3 million to almost $43.5 million. Then followed another period of depression in general business from 1875 to 1879, and so the cycle continued. Each year's harvest was a matter of first importance to the business health of the community, and the economic structure was also very sensitive to a number of outside influences over which it could exercise little control. Good commercial relations with Great Britain and the United States were vital, and businessmen were apt to worry about maintaining the stability of these relationships. A proposed new treaty of reciprocity with the United States came under the Board of Trade's scrutiny in 1874. At a general meeting to discuss the question a resolution was adopted to the effect that 'while approving generally of the principle of Reciprocity, it is the opinion of this meeting that the present draft of the Reciprocity Treaty is unfavourable to the country and that the equivalents offered are too great.'

By 1876 there was further evidence of a change in the Board's attitude toward tariffs. Free trade was all very well when the primary need was a simple exchange of natural products for manufactured ones, but with the advent of local industries the need for protection was manifest. The Board put itself on record as favouring 'an increase of duty on imports in the interest of native manufacturers' and requested their parliamentary representatives 'to urge upon the Government the necessity of rescinding the free list (except upon such raw materials as are not produced in Canada) so far as the United States are concerned, so long as they continue to impose

heavy duties on articles now included in the list.' Thus was foreshadowed
the attitude which led to Sir John A. Macdonald's 'National Policy' of
protective tariffs on which he appealed to the electors in 1878.

In 1872 the Board advocated the repeal of the Bill and Note Stamp Act
'considering that the comparatively small revenue derived therefrom
hardly compensates for the onerous and troublesome duties entailed upon
all classes of the community in its observance.' The following year it
pressed for uniformity in the forms and conditions of the policies of fire
insurance companies doing business in Canada. These differed widely, and
in the Board's view there were not only too many conditions but a number
of them were overly protective of the insurer's interests.

In spite of some reservations on the expansion of railway services based
on the high cost and the fact that these costs, partially subsidized by the
government, were reflected in taxes, the Board in 1873 placed on record its
recognition of the contribution made to the stimulation of the country's
trade development by the rapid extension of railways throughout Ontario,
and advocated railway communication with Manitoba. 'The early construction of the Canadian Pacific Railway,' it said, 'in its broad sense is an
undertaking demanding the most serious consideration at the hands of our
legislators.'

Contrasting opinions about the possible future of the Dominion of
Canada were evident at this time. There were many sober businessmen
with long experience in the country who confidently foresaw an extended
period of healthy development of its vast resources, given reasonable
stability of government and freedom from undue restraints on commercial
operations. There were some opportunists who came to the country with
the sole aim of making a quick fortune by resource exploitation and who
were little concerned with the tedious process of building the foundations
for a future nation. Financial strength for the building process was not
great, and the accomplishment of major development projects depended
substantially on a capital inflow from outside sources, mainly Great
Britain, and often on imported advisory assistance. That some took a jaun-
diced view of the Dominion's future is clear from the comments of an un-
named editorial writer in an 1871 English newspaper:

The Canadian Pacific Railways has begun to launch its bonds. A group of
Montreal and New York bankers have undertaken to float ten million dollars' worth
of Company's Land Grant Bonds. The New Yorkers are keen gamblers, and yet it is
impossible to believe that they are such fools as to put their money into this mad

project. I would as soon credit them with a willingness to subscribe hard cash in support of a scheme for the utilization of icebergs.

The Canadian Pacific will run, if it is ever finished, through a country frostbound for eight months of the year, and will connect with the Western part of the Dominion, a province which embraces about as forbidding a country as any on the face of the earth. British Columbia is a barren, cold mountain country not worth keeping. Fifty railroads could not galvanize it into prosperity.

The Canadians must know that the railroad is never likely to pay a single red cent of interest on the money sunk in it. A friend of mine told me, and he knew what he was talking about, that he believed the much-touted Manitoba Settlement would not hold out many years. The people who have gone there cannot stand the coldness of the winters. Men and cattle are frozen to death. Those that are not killed outright are often maimed for life by frostbite.

A word or two on Canadian finances in general would be in season. Canada is one of the most overrated colonies we have. The country is poor and is crushed with debt. The Province and City of Quebec are notoriously bankrupt.

In the end the Dominion will have to go into liquidation. One day, when the load gets too heavy, Ontario is pretty certain to go over to the States, into which it dovetails, and where its best trade outlet is.

The Dominion is in short a 'Fraud'.

Throughout the 1870s and 1880s the Toronto Board of Trade persisted in a program of activities which it believed would foster growth in the community, recognizing, however, that any local prosperity was utterly dependent upon the creation and maintenance of a climate throughout Ontario and the Dominion that would encourage initiative and maintain a field in which business would be free to operate under rules it felt were fair and equitable. The nature of the relationship that should exist between business and government was not always easy to determine. Quite obviously the entrepreneur wanted the least possible interference in his affairs; as a rule he suspected politicians of being either unskilled in matters of trade and finance, or of motivations that did not accord with his own. On the other hand, the conduct of commercial affairs clearly needed ground rules and an umpire, and these could be provided effectively only by representatives of an assumedly unbiased government. It was necessary, therefore, to strike and attempt to preserve some kind of mutually acceptable balance.

In 1879, for instance, traders found themselves frequently in dispute with railway interests over the matter of freight rates. They considered many of the rates they were required to pay to be discriminatory and formulated by a railway combine determined to derive the utmost return from the services they supplied, regardless of the possible effect upon the users' interests. The response of the Board of Trade to this situation was to enter a plea for the creation of a railway commission which, as a function of government, would have power to arbitrate rate disputes and, if necessary, produce and enforce rate schedules. More than twenty years passed before this advice was translated into legislation.

The Board spent much time debating Prime Minister John A. Macdonald's new National Policy and offered a number of recommendations arising from special meetings called in 1879. Macdonald had taken advantage of the depression in the 1870s to oppose the Mackenzie government's free-trade or low-tariff policy and offer an alternative of tariffs designed to give protection to Canada's developing secondary industries. The policy appealed to the growing nationalist sentiment in central Canada and when Macdonald swept into power he established the basis for a lasting tariff structure. The Board of Trade's early free-trade stance had changed, and, while still insisting on moderation in trade barriers, it was prepared to accept government policies that appeared likely to bolster the fragile state of local manufacturing. Its position was a somewhat delicate one, considering that a high proportion of its membership strength still lay in the wholesale field and wholesalers are not fond of tariffs. At this time the dry-goods trade in Toronto, almost wholly based on imports, was bigger than any single industrial operation.

Throughout the 1870s, although the Board's work was carried on in all the areas that concerned its members, it still did not attract the wide support of businessmen necessary to make its approaches to governments forceful and persuasive. Its affairs were guided by able Presidents (see list in Appendix) who for the most part succeeded one another annually, and by an elected Council reasonably representative of the city's broad business interests. The Board had not yet succeeded, however, in building an administrative structure upon which broader operations likely to appeal to the ordinary businessman could be based. The decisions of the Council were implemented by the officers themselves or by a hard-working secretary upon whom fell all the responsibilities of management. J.W. Brent and M.P. Hayes, the first men to hold the position, had been followed in 1861 by Charles Robertson, in 1869 by Edward T. Bromfield, shortly afterwards by John Stevenson and in 1880 by J. Rollo.

There were few meetings in 1881, a quiet year according to the reports. The Board continued to take a deep interest in agriculture, an area which employed three-quarters of the entire population and the products of which represented by far the largest and most important part of the country's exports. That agriculture in Ontario was not flourishing had been attested in reports produced by a British delegation two years before and by an Agricultural Commission appointed by the Ontario government. For want of sufficient skill in the cultivation of crops and their proper rotation, a high proportion of the farms in the parts of the province first settled had been so seriously impoverished as to be incapable of producing grain of high enough quality to command the market. The quantity also had been diminishing to the point where wheat farming was becoming unprofitable. In 1880 the President of the Corn Exchange Association pointed out that Ontario grains were unable to compete in American markets, and that the Montreal standards for grain and flour were so much above the average of Ontario production as to be well-nigh useless. A revision of the standards was requested.

The Board of Trade in turn advocated a drastic revision of agricultural policies. Some signs of redirection and improvement were evident: cheese and butter factories were being established in some parts of the province, and an increased British demand for cattle encouraged conservation of the soil by turning the land to pasture. But the effort to steer the farmer away from his familiar grain-growing preoccupation was not easy.

The timber trade was reviving, but here again there was cause for concern. Quality was deteriorating because the easy first-quality cut was fast disappearing – indeed, in 1880 it was estimated that twenty-five to thirty years would exhaust the supply of pine in Canada east of British Columbia. The forests were being depleted by severe fires: in 1881 a fire in Muskoka had particularly devastating effects. The Board of Trade strongly urged the provincial government to put into effect measures to protect against fire losses. Mining was in its infancy, although there appears to have been a growing awareness of the underground wealth the province probably possessed. Phosphate was being mined in the Ottawa region for shipment to England as fertilizer.

In 1881 it was noted that progress was being made in the construction of the Canadian Pacific Railway and that immigrants were pouring into the west and northwest. There would apparently be three independent railway lines connecting Ontario with the west – the Grand Trunk, the Great Western and the Canadian Pacific–Midland combination. If these proved to be competing lines the Board was satisfied it could expect favourable rates, whereas if, as appeared possible, they were to amalgamate, shippers would be at the mercy of the only service available and high tariffs seemed inevitable. The Council considered which of two rival companies should be favoured for the construction of a railway connecting the Ontario system with Sault Ste Marie and decided to throw in its lot with the Northern Railway as a local line more likely to promote Toronto interests than the Grand Trunk. With the completion in 1882 of a new independent line between Port Huron and Chicago, thus establishing an unbroken connection between the latter city and Portland, the Grand Trunk Railway invited the Toronto, Montreal and Quebec Boards of Trade and the Toronto Corn Exchange on a free ride over the new route. In spite of any feelings the Toronto members might have had about the Grand Trunk, the invitation was accepted with alacrity and on 25 March a party of four hundred departed at noon in fifteen Pullman coaches, arriving in Chicago the following morning where they were royally entertained for the next four days by the Chicago Board of Trade.

An earlier expression of the need for some official body to arbitrate railway disputes was reaffirmed in 1882 when the Council appointed a special committee to prepare a report addressed to the Dominion government. The committee advocated the appointment of a commission to adjudicate on all matters in dispute between railway companies and forwarding companies, and between railway companies and individuals, with power to settle cases of unjust discrimination between certain points on the various lines running into Toronto. The Board complained that the railways quoted better rates to preferred customers and paid no attention to the remonstrances of those who considered themselves ill-used. It felt that the railways were quasi-public bodies responsible for the maintenance of equitable rate schedules, but, in spite of the Board's strong appeal, the government showed no inclination to act in the matter.

The merchants of Toronto in 1881 inaugurated what they called 'Trade Sales' as a means of stimulating business. This was an arrangement with the railways whereby special rates were granted to buyers in all parts of the province to come to Toronto to make their purchases for the coming year. The first effort proved successful and it was felt that the event should be repeated annually. The following year, however, the railways balked, perhaps on the grounds that they were merely discounting a normal revenue. Only after considerable pressure from members of the Toronto dry-goods trade was a restricted program put into effect from 25 August to 30 September 1882, applicable only to buyers in this specified trade. The Board of Trade interested itself in this project and entered into negotiations for its continuance in succeeding years. 1,700 buyers were brought to the city in 1883 under the reduced fare plan and 2,300 the following year; the plan was maintained for many years, largely at the instigation of the dry-goods trade.

Further proposals were made to the government with respect to water traffic. Toronto citizens had been shocked by a shipping disaster in the port of London on 24 May 1881, and the Board of Trade urged the Minister of Marine to institute without delay a system which would ensure the adequate inspection of steamboats for seaworthiness. The Stamp Act continued to irk businessmen, and in the same year the Toronto Board joined other Boards of Trade in presenting a petition for repeal of the Act. The action was successful and gratification was expressed over the removal of this source of annoyance and expense.

An event of considerable importance to Toronto was the establishment in 1879 of the Toronto Industrial Exhibition as a permanent annual exhibition. As early as 1846 a Provincial Agricultural Association and Board of Agriculture for Canada West had been organized to hold fairs which would stimulate advances in every branch of the economy. The first fair was held in Toronto in October 1846 on the grounds of Government House at the corner of King and Graves (now Simcoe) Streets, with the cattle show in a meadow behind Upper Canada College, then on the north side of King Street facing Government House. It was successful, and fairs thereafter were held annually in various places – Hamilton, London, Cobourg, Kingston and Brantford. For its return to Toronto in 1858 the city had secured ownership of some twenty acres of land south of the Insane Asylum on Queen Street and erected there a permanent exhibition building, the Palace of Industry, more popularly known as the Crystal Palace and modelled after the famous Crystal Palace of London's 1851 Exhibition. The fair continued on its rounds, however, returning to Toronto only about every fourth year. By 1878 Toronto had negotiated a new fairground comprising nearly fifty-two acres on the old Garrison Common, and was working to secure the fair as a permanent Toronto feature. Substantial civic funds had been committed to making it an outstanding presentation, and there was great disappointment when the provincial delegates chose Ottawa as that year's site. At the urging of Alderman John J. Withrow, civic leaders established a new organization, the Industrial Exhibition Association of Ontario, with the express purpose of conducting a permanent annual exhibition in Toronto for the encouragement of agriculture, horticulture, arts and manufacturing, the first such exhibition to be held during the first three weeks of September 1879. The Association was incorporated on 11

March, Withrow was elected president at the first meeting of the directors on 29 March, and preparations for the great event proceeded at an almost frenzied pace.

The first exhibition was duly and officially opened by the Governor General, the Marquis of Lorne, accompanied by H.R.H. the Princess Louise, on 5 September 1879. It was a splendid success. There were 8,234 exhibits, nearly $20,000 was awarded in prize money and 100,000 people paid to enter. As the years went by it became an eminent event in Toronto's calendar and amply fulfilled the expectations and hopes of its founders.

The Board of Trade was associated with the fair, later to become the Canadian National Exhibition, from its beginning. Representatives of the Board participated in the formative discussions, and the Exhibition Association's original structure provided for two representatives from the Board; this number was later increased to five. The Board undoubtedly regarded the Exhibition as a powerful stimulant of civic development, and for many years it exercised its not inconsiderable influence to publicize the Exhibition and foster its growth. A number of its representatives served as officers and directors of the Exhibition Association, and over the years the relationship between the two organizations remained close and cordial.

Although by the 1880s the Board was operating effectively, it still had not attracted the breadth or extent of support from the general business community that was desired by those who were active in its affairs. This was due in part to the fact that it had not yet created a strong public image and was not appealing to the small merchant and the professional man who tended to regard it as an instrument of the larger commercial interests. This situation changed materially when Henry W. Darling assumed the presidency in 1883 and the Board amalgamated with the Toronto Corn Exchange in the following year. Darling headed the very successful dry-goods firm of Messrs McMaster, Darling & Company, founded in 1844 by the Hon. Wm McMaster. He possessed a vigorous personality and brought to the Board not only enthusiasm and energy but new ideas for organization and programs he felt would stimulate the interest and participation of businessmen.

The question of union with the Corn Exchange had been in the air for some time, and it was at last accomplished largely on Darling's initiative. The Exchange had been formed in 1866 and for several years was known as the Produce Merchants' Exchange. Its purpose was to bring together every business day the dealers in all kinds of grain and produce, both local and out of town, to receive telegraph reports and other information about the state of the market. Statistics were collected on the receipts and shipments of produce, and means were provided to facilitate commodity marketing. Previously this business had been conducted informally in street markets or private offices without access to reliable data on market conditions, and the Exchange was designed to provide an effective medium wherein buyers and sellers would be brought face to face. The original President was Robert Spratt, and it was incorporated in 1872.

Telegraph communication was used sparingly in the early days of the Exchange, but in 1867 it introduced telegraph report services from Chicago and Milwaukee which were made available to members on payment of a $100 fee. By 1888 a complete service was established with daily cables from Britain, continuous market reports from Chicago, frequent despatches from the New York Stock Exchange and from Montreal, and twice-daily reports from Milwaukee, Duluth, St Louis, Toledo, Detroit and Oswego. In 1867 the Exchange had actively collaborated with the Boards of Trade of Toronto and other cities in Ontario and Quebec to press upon the government the need to establish proper grain classifications and a uniform grain inspection system throughout the Dominion. This effort was successful and the appointment of flour and grain inspectors in Toronto, a statutory function of the Board of Trade, was customarily made on the recommendation of the Corn Exchange.

The interests of the two bodies thus corresponded closely in many respects, and after a series of negotiations application was made for amalgamation and it was granted by a special Act of Parliament in April 1884. It provided that 'the amalgamated corporation shall have, possess and enjoy all the rights, powers, privileges and franchises of both of the said corporations.' A joint committee worked out a consolidation of by-laws, and the unified organization commenced operation under the presidency of Henry Darling, with William Galbraith, President of the Corn Exchange at the time of amalgamation, as Vice-President. With the union the Corn Exchange as such lost its identity and the Board of Trade assumed a new character. All the grain- and produce-trading functions of the Corn Exchange were added to the traditional operations of the Board and for a long time they remained a dominant feature. The membership of the Board shot up from 250 in 1884 to 822 the following year and by 1888 had reached 915; this in spite of a $100 entrance fee introduced on 1 January 1887.

The development of the Board in its new form was described as 'almost marvellous'. A whole new sense of interest in public questions of a commercial character was evidenced by a considerable increase in the number of meetings. During the full year 1887 there was a total of no less than 515 meetings, nineteen of which were general Board meetings, twenty-six were meetings of the Council and the rest sittings of the Board of Arbitration and meetings of groups with special interests, such as bankers and contractors, who were beginning to establish themselves. These groups worked within the framework of the Board of Trade and comprised members of a particular occupation with their own problems and concerns. Their operation was provided for in the by-laws of the Board, and they possessed a substantial degree of autonomy within their own spheres of interest. It was specifically provided, however, that any action they contemplated on their own behalf which might have implications for the general business community should be subject to the control of the Council of the Board, an obvious necessity to avoid the possibility of conflict between policies of the Board as such and one of its constituent parts. In practice, a Trade Section, having discussed and come to a conclusion regarding an issue of consequence in its own field, usually recommended a course of action to the Board's Council. The Council would base its decision on the facts of the case, taking into account that anything done in the Board's name must represent a consensus of all its members, not merely a group with an axe to grind. By the mid-1880s seven Sections had been set up: Bankers, Contractors, Lumber and Grain, Wholesale Hardware, Malt and Hops, Coal Dealers and Dry-goods. These sections continued to play an important part in the Board's overall operations over the years. New ones were formed from time to time as the need arose, and some broke away from affiliation with the Board as their stature increased to form their own independent trade associations. Others became inoperative through decline of interest or for a variety of other reasons.

In 1886 the attention of members was directed to the recent formation of the Institute of Chartered Accountants, which was holding its meetings in the Board's rooms. Support for the new Institute was solicited, and business owners were urged to employ the services of registered accountants in the administration of their affairs.

In his capacity as president, Darling also encouraged the use of the arbitration facilities provided by the Board. Each year a Board of Arbitration was appointed to deal with commercial disputes, but its services had been used infrequently, most members apparently preferring 'the glorious uncertainty of the law.' In 1884 only three cases had come before the Board and all were settled satisfactorily. There continued to be much complaining about the inadequacies of the courts in such cases, and it seemed clear that the Board could provide a useful service. Over the next few years successful arbitration procedures dealt with through the Board increased materially, and unexpected demands were made on the Board of Arbitration to adjudicate disputes between employers and their employees.

The Board was still complaining bitterly about the government's reluc-tance to enact adequate bankruptcy legislation. Prior to Confederation the only statutory conditions governing insolvency were those enacted by the provinces. A federal Bankruptcy Act introduced after Confederation was repealed in 1880 so that the only legislation remaining dealt solely with winding-up operations. Darling visited England in 1884 to ascertain the conditions there and found deficiencies similar to those in his own country. The Board had joined with sister organizations in principal cities to apply almost continuous pressure on the government to act in the matter, and by 1885 it appeared that some progress was being made. A Bill had been introduced in Parliament which would have implemented many of the Board's proposals and which, if enacted, would have provided uniform measures throughout the Dominion to govern the collection of debts and control insolvent debtors and their estates. The Board heartily supported the legislation but it was not enacted and there were many more years of frustration before this question was satisfactorily resolved. In the mean-time amendments of provincial legislation in this field had been secured which regularized the conditions of assignments for the benefit of creditors. This was fine as far as it went but it did not go far enough. There were still grave omissions, notably provisions regarding the fraudulent concealment of assets, disposal of goods and the destruction of records. The Board was convinced this was a federal matter, and that only legislation applicable uniformly in all provinces would remedy the existing deficiencies.

Supplies of money for capital purposes were chronically short due to high interest rates being forced on the chartered banks by the government, which was offering four per cent on deposits placed in its own and Post Office savings banks. These deposits increased from $26.2 million in 1883 to $30.3 million in 1884, while bank deposits declined in the same period from $96.6 million to $92.4 million. The Board regarded this as improper competition and a harmful withdrawal from normal circulation of money which could be made available for commercial purposes, but the govern-ment proved indifferent to the Board's complaints. Business conditions generally were not satisfactory in this period. The fact that 'our tariff-stimulated industries have not yet found their way out of the ''slough'' of over-production' resulted in extreme competition, falling prices and smal-ler profits. The grain and milling trades, still a vital element in the commer-cial scene, had not recovered from a serious setback they had received in 1882–3.

The prospect of a new reciprocity treaty with the United States was welcomed in 1885 as a potential trade stimulant in both countries, but the Board recorded its hope that before entering into any agreement the government would give commercial organizations the opportunity to comment on the proposed provisions and their probable effect. Reciprocity was not renewed, and a few years later the whole question of commercial relations with the United States again became a subject of much soul-searching among members of the board.

A number of general meetings were held during 1887 to determine the Board's position on the vexed question of a possible commercial union with the United States. There were divergent views, but at length a resolution was formulated and received unanimous endorsement from the members:

That this Board desires to place on record the conviction that the largest possible freedom of commercial intercourse between our own country and the United States, compatible with our relation to Great Britain, is desirable.

That this Board will do everything in its power to bring about the consummation of such a result.

That in its estimation any treaty which ignored any of the interests of our own country, or which gave undue prominence to any one to the neglect or to the injury of any other is one that could not be entertained.

That in our agricultural, mineral, manufacturing, and our diversified mercantile interests, in our fisheries, forests and other products, we possess in a rare and in an extraordinary degree all the elements which go to make a people great, prosperous and self-reliant.

That these are fitting inducements to any nation to render reciprocity with Canada a thing to be desired, and such as should secure for us a reciprocal agreement with the United States of the broadest and most generous character which, while fully recognizing these conditions, would contain guarantees which would prove of mutual and abiding advantage to both nations; but that this Board cannot entertain any proposal which would place Great Britain at any disadvantage as compared with the United States, or which would tend in any measure, however small, to weaken the bonds which bind us to the Empire.

The McKinley Tariff Act of 1890 erected highly protective tariff walls and reduced the American market for Canadian agricultural products. This grievance was accentuated by the generally unfriendly attitude of McKinley and others in the United States Congress. By 1893 the Board of Trade was still hopeful that a mutually acceptable base for a reciprocal trade agreement would be found, although there was a strong feeling that such a base could only result in political union. There was no doubt about the Board's attitude toward such an eventuality. 'Canada,' said former President D.R. Wilkie at the 1894 Annual Meeting, 'will never consent to barter her national and political individuality for any commercial consideration.' A significant result of these debates was renewed realization of Canada's need to develop other export markets for her products and particularly to strengthen her trading relations with Great Britain. In 1886 the Board recommended to the Dominion government the addition to the cabinet of a Minister whose undivided attention should be given to questions of trade and commerce. Matters of this kind had 'hitherto been administered by the heads of several Departments in a very imperfect manner and treated as of only secondary importance.'

Canada's foreign trade had been subject to many vicissitudes; in the Board of Trade's view, the fault lay partially in the absence of a sustained policy on the part of the government. Although total trade had steadily increased between 1869 and 1873, it had gone into a slow decline as a result of the world-wide industrial and commercial depression following the crisis of 1873. The introduction of a protective tariff policy in 1879, which raised the general level of duties from 17½ to 20 per cent, nevertheless stimulated the manufacture of goods for export and led to a trade revival which increased Canada's total trade between 1879 and 1883 from $153.5 million to $230.3 million. Then a new decline set in, reaching bottom at $189.7 million in 1886, in spite of a further increase in some customs duties. The cycle went on, upward to $247.6 million in 1893, then down again to $224.4 million in 1895. Businessmen came to regard the ups and downs with a resigned air, and certainly they were often due to circumstances quite beyond their control, but the feeling persisted nevertheless that greater stability could be achieved if the government could be induced to apply common-sense business principles and continuous effort toward trade stimulation.

An event overshadowing all others in the year 1885 was the completion of the Canadian Pacific Railway from sea to sea. The construction of 3,327 miles of line, not including 600 miles of leased line, at a cost in the neighbourhood of $140 million was considered, as indeed it was, a feat of immense significance to the future of the Dominion, in which Canadians could feel themselves participants and take great pride. Toronto impatiently awaited its own connection with the CPR at North Bay by means of the Northern and Pacific Junction Railway so that it could have access to the important markets of northern Ontario and western Canada.

The Board continued to voice its objection to the powers arbitrarily exercised by the railways in the matter of freight rates. Its representatives appeared before the Railway Commission in 1886, taking the position that an authority was needed with greater power than that of the Railway Committee of the Privy Council to compel the railways to recognize the rights of the public and give uniform treatment to all classes of customers. What still infuriated the Board was the railways' practice of playing favourites in the matter of rates and their high-handed attitude when objections were raised. The Board urged the government not to be deterred by the apparent difficulty of finding an adequate solution but to act promptly in establishing a competent authority.

It was in 1884 the Board first became directly involved in the Esplanade Project and the whole question of waterfront development. It was to remain involved for the next forty years, leading the campaign for a railway viaduct from which it eventually emerged victorious. The creation of the waterfront Esplanade, along which ran the railway right-of-way at grade, had formed a serious barrier between the city proper and its docks and harbour facilities. The situation worsened as the trackage needs of the railways increased. The blockage was inconvenient and dangerous, but for a long time there was little evidence of any forthcoming solution to the problem. A proposal to erect bridges over the tracks at several of the main crossings had been prepared in 1852 and some steps had been taken toward its implementation, but the project was hurriedly abandoned, probably because of its high cost. In 1889 a competent engineer, A.M. Wellington, c.e., was asked to examine the existing and proposed railway facilities along the waterfront and to submit his own proposals, but again it became evident that the city would be financially incapable of participating in any major remedial undertaking. The railways themselves had tentatively proposed that bridges be built to give access to the area south of the Esplanade, but the Board by this time was convinced that a viaduct completely separating the railway and street grades was the only proper solution and stuck to this conviction throughout its long and arduous campaign.

The waterfront problem had been brought into prominence by the pressures of the city's development. By 1884 population had increased to 105,200, and among many civic improvements was the laying of 8.42 miles of block pavements and 11.5 miles of sewers. New buildings had been erected in that year to the value of over a million dollars, and by 1885 the total assessed value of real estate had risen to $57,546,816. Land transactions were proceeding at a great pace, and the Board of Trade noted with gratification the ambition of Toronto citizens to own their own homes. It warned, however, against the dangers of land speculation.

At the Board's Annual Meeting in January 1887 President Darling somewhat grandly remarked: 'The extent to which our country has been favoured with a healthful climate, freedom during the year from plague and pestilence, and a bountiful harvest, vouchsafed peace in our borders and employment for willing hands with reasonable remuneration, should call forth the deepest gratitude of our industrious, law-abiding, freedom-loving, self-governing people.' Just a year earlier the Board had had occasion to refer to the city's many poor, including 'idle, vicious, depraved and improvident classes,' who constituted a problem for which it was felt the Board of Trade might establish a committee to seek a solution. An English visitor in 1890, Sir Charles Dilke, observed that 'Toronto has no great beauty, and its site upon a flat lake shore gives it no natural advantage to the eye; but there is about the city an air of business animation which yields an agreeable impression of vigorous growth. The educational and religious activity of "The Queen City" is as striking as its commercial enterprise.'

In 1885 the Board congratulated the Postmaster on his successful and satisfactory establishment of postal delivery by carriers, considered a great improvement over the old box system. Now the Board said, a city ordinance was needed to compel residents to provide 'a sufficient letter-box on the outer door.' The first telephone was installed in Toronto on 13 February 1879. The explosive incursion of the telephone is illustrated by the fact that the basic patent for the transmission of speech over wire had been issued to Alexander Graham Bell on 7 March 1876, and the first line was in use a year later. In 1878 Hamilton, Ontario, missed by a few months being the first city in the world to establish a telephone exchange, and Toronto was not far behind. The Toronto telephone directory of August 1879 listed 121 names; by July 1884 there were a thousand users and instruments were being installed at the rate of one a day. Telephone use was greater in Toronto than in any other city in Canada, and lines extended throughout the province. Nor was there any diminution in the use of the electric telegraph. Toronto was the centre of the Dominion's telegraph network and sixty-seven wires connected it to all of the continent's important cities.

An 1887 municipal by-law to improve the city's water system was defeated, much to the Board's chagrin. There was concern about the adequacy of the city's water supply, particularly for fire-fighting purposes; as an alternative to the aborted by-law, the Board suggested that the city authorize funds for a survey of the practicability of a new gravity-feed system from Lake Simcoe and offered its assistance in such an undertaking. The idea of using Lake Simcoe as a source of the city's water was bandied about for a long time but gradually faded away as existing facilities were improved and worries about adequate supplies abated.

There was one civic development project about which the Board of

Trade had reservations: a proposed new City Hall and Court House. A new Court House had been contemplated for some time and design competitions were held in 1885 and 1886. Cost estimates exceeded the limits the city had imposed, and it was decided a more practical approach would be to erect one structure combining the functions of a City Hall and Court House. At this point the Board of Trade became alarmed, taking the position that, while both facilities were needed, to take on the combined project at an estimated cost of $600,000 to $750,000 was unjustifiable and, in addition to other commitments, would lead to an unduly high tax rate. The Board felt, moreover, that the project had not been adequately considered and that the city had been deficient in not securing firm estimates of costs. President Darling commented in 1885: 'Pure water and a more suitable place of deposit for the sewage than the bay in front of the city are of infinitely more importance to our progress and prosperity than the proposed erection of a new and costly City Hall or even a new Court House.' The Board's opinion that the citizens should not be committed to an indefinite expenditure on such an ill-considered project was not heeded. E.J. Lennox was appointed as architect for the new civic building and built it was, at a cost of some $2.5 million. Open on 18 September 1899, it remains a notable Toronto landmark.

The Board of Trade was not happy about the state of the civic administration in this period, and was critical of the business community for taking insufficient interest in the city's affairs and avoiding responsibility for what it called 'the present critical state.' Again, it was a matter of businessmen distrusting the management capabilities of politicians and feeling that strong citizen participation was needed to control heedless expenditures and a constantly rising tax rate. The Board itself was pre-eminently exercising this function and the growing membership was strengthening its voice. Continued objections were made to the personalty basis of taxation in the Assessment Act, which the Board called inequitable, unjust and inquisitorial and as such a hindrance to commercial operation and growth. Instead, it proposed an adult poll tax to cover the cost of what all enjoyed in common which, with a classified business tax and a tax on real estate, would provide all the revenue the city needed.

In its new and enlarged form the Board was functioning well, and both by its example and direct encouragement stimulated the establishment of corresponding bodies in other Ontario cities. 'Hereafter,' said President Darling in 1887, 'the measure of unity and the spirit of enterprise animating the business men of any community in Canada will be gauged by the activity and success of its local Board of Trade.' Darling retired from the presidency at the end of 1886 after four active and fruitful years, and on 16 February 1887 an appreciative membership tendered him a banquet at the Rossin House, attended by five hundred of the city's leading businessmen. On 30 December 1887 the Board inaugurated its annual dinners at the Rossin House. The Rt Hon. Joseph Chamberlain, British Plenipotentiary to the United States on the fisheries question, was the distinguished speaker on the first occasion, responding to the toast 'The Commercial Interests of the Empire'. So great was the demand for places that the next event, on 4 January 1889, was held in the Pavilion of the Horticultural Gardens with 582 present and 450 ladies in the galleries. The dinners were carried on regularly for a number of years and became prominent events in the city's calendar.

The by-laws of the corporation were amended in 1887, establishing an entrance fee of $100 for the first one thousand members; the fee thereafter was $200. Each member then paid an annual fee of $10. Beginning in March 1886 certificates of membership were issued and in most cases were prominently displayed in members' places of business. In 1887, for the first time in the Board's history, two members were suspended for conduct unbecoming to members of the corporation, and one member was expelled for breach of the Act of Incorporation and its by-laws. Edgar A. Wills was appointed Secretary of the Board in 1884, and held that post for the next twenty years.

The Board was still occupying its old premises in the renamed Imperial Bank Building at the corner of Wellington Street and Leader Lane. They had been altered to meet expanding needs and the building was a commanding one in an excellent central location, but it had become apparent that new and larger accommodation would soon be needed, and ambitious plans were afoot. Negotiations were completed in November 1887 to purchase for $55,000 the site occupied by the old American Hotel at the corner of Front and Yonge Streets, part of the estate of the late Alexander Rennie, on which a Board of Trade Building was to be erected. This necessitated an amendment of the Board's Act of Incorporation extending the Board's powers to hold property and issue debentures. A special committee was appointed with responsibility for all arrangements entailed in the building process.

Since the American Hotel site was insufficient for the building contemplated, an additional twenty feet on Front Street was purchased from the Wilkes estate in June 1889 for $14,500, providing a total area of 9,323 square feet – 101 feet on Yonge Street and 109 feet on Front Street. The American Hotel was demolished in May 1889, and the winner from seventeen entrants in an international competition to obtain an outstanding design for the new building was Messrs James & James of New York. The initial estimate of the total cost was $400,000, somewhat higher than expected owing to the additional land purchase. The undertaking was financed by debentures: $250,000 as first mortgage at 4³/₄ per cent, $125,000 as second mortgage at 5 per cent, and $48,000 as third mortgage at 5 per cent. Building operations began in May 1889. Reporting on progress at the Annual Meeting in January 1890, President Wilmot D. Matthews said that 'the success of the financial scheme is in a great measure due to the public spirit displayed by our members and monetary institutions in so heartily subscribing for the second debentures, thus making the first a gilt-edged investment. The revenue is already assured, as enough of the space has already been let to return the entire amount of interest on the debentures issued.'

In the latter part of December 1890 the Board commenced operations in its spanking new building. The design of the building, described as a modern development of the Romanesque, was impressive, but the structure was unique in another respect: steel was used in the construction, a new departure which was to influence the design of Toronto's future buildings. No less than 1,427 steel beams had been employed to support its seven storeys. A circular wrought iron stairway with bronze newels rose from the basement to the top floor. The handrail, carved from five-foot long blocks of solid cherry wood, formed a continuous curve from the first to the seventh floor. Two elevators of the latest design and incorporating all safety features serviced every floor. The Board of Trade occupied the top story, and the remaining eighty-six offices in the building were designed for tenants. They were finished in black ash with floors of Georgia pine; most had open fireplaces, although the building as a whole was steam-heated. An elaborately decorated restaurant occupied the east wing.

The dominant feature of the Board's own premises was the Great Hall, used as a trading floor. It was a huge fourteen-sided room, fifty feet in diameter and thirty-two feet high, finished in quartered oak and lit by seventy electric lamps and forty-two gas lights. Here members met each business day to obtain the latest trade information and conduct transactions in grain and produce. This hive of dignified business activity was a carry-over from the days of the old Corn Exchange, and while it remained for some years a focus of many members' interest, its importance gradually lessened as trading methods changed and Toronto's dominance in the grain trade declined. For some time, too, there had been a feeling among members of the Board's Council that a preoccupation with day-to-day trading was inappropriate to the discharge of the organization's broader functions.

It was soon apparent that the new quarters would become a financial burden. On 5 April 1893 a form of Life Membership was created for a fee of $200, increasing to $225 after 1 July, and ninety-three members promptly availed themselves of it; these produced sufficient funds to liquidate $13,000 of floating debt. At the same time the annual fee of all other members was increased to $17, which was higher than fees charged by comparable organizations in other cities and considered to be at its top limit. By 1895 tenants were finding their prestigious accommodations too expensive and were being lured away to other new and less costly locations. The Board lowered its rental charges to meet the competition, but expenditures were coming dangerously close to revenue and it was clear that the heavy interest on the mortgage and debenture debt was more than it could bear. The Council gave the financial situation close attention and described it fully to the holder of the first mortgage bonds, the New York Life Insurance Company, and to the holders of the second and third bonds, who were for the most part members of the Board. A delegation finally went to New York and after prolonged negotiation prevailed upon New York Life to reduce the interest on its $249,000 first mortgage bonds from $4^3/_4$ to 3 per cent for a period of ten years, provided the holders of the second and third bonds would agree to reduce their interest from 5 to $2^1/_2$ per cent for the same period. For the most part, there was ready agreement to this plan. It was estimated that a saving of $8,675 a year could thus be effected and it was confidently expected that, with a strong and steady effort, the Board would be able to meet all its obligations.

But after only another year the Council was dismayed to find bank indebtedness at $12,443 and overdue interest payments amounting to $4,825. In spite of every effort, including the increase in members' annual fees, the Board could not make ends meet and a second expedition to New York was undertaken, again with a successful outcome. New York Life agreed to a further reduction in the interest rate on their mortgage bonds from 3 to $2^1/_2$ per cent. Holders of the second and third bonds were asked to place their securities in the hands of a trust created for the purpose, with interest suspended for a period of ten years, or until such time as the Board found itself able to resume payments. They really had no choice, and the Council gave assurance that it recognized a moral obligation to honour all its debts.

The Board continued to expand its activities and grow in membership support, but it could not solve the financial problems brought about by its ambitious building venture. The Board of Trade Building was sold in 1905, to the evident relief of the Council, and the Board continued to occupy its premises under a lease arrangement negotiated with the new owner on terms it considered reasonable. Members who held second and third mortgage bonds lost in this transaction, and the Council for many years suffered acute embarrassment since they had no way ot discharging their 'moral obligation'. The members were fully aware of the circumstances: most of them showed remarkable understanding and forbearance and simply wrote off their loss. A few voluntarily remitted their debentures and discharged any claim. The outstanding bonds were eventually declared legally inoperative, but for half a century afterwards certificates would return to haunt the Board, rediscovered among the dusty records of a deceased member.

It is difficult to understand how the Board allowed itself to be drawn into this venture except on the grounds of an inadequate or inaccurate assessment of costs and revenues. Men of high repute in the business world sat on its Council and they had readily available the best possible advisory assistance of others fully experienced in real estate, property management and general finance. There is no evidence that the project was undertaken with anything less than complete confidence and enthusiasm. A speculative spirit was certainly in the air, but the Board itself had repeatedly warned its own members and the public against the follies of improperly secured investment and over-extended credit.

An interesting innovation in the Board's operations during this period was the establishment of a so-called Gratuity Fund. This was referred to as 'a benevolent provision by members for the families of those of their number whom it may please Providence to call from among them' – in other words a form of mutual life insurance (although care was taken to avoid use of this term) whereby the subscriptions of participating members were used as a fund to provide survivor benefits on the death of such members. The scheme was submitted to a general meeting held on 16 November 1885 and approved; by-laws were adopted 29 June 1886 and shortly thereafter 806 of a total of 915 members had been enrolled as subscribers, each paying an annual subscription of $23. The amount of the benefit was to be calculated 'by taking such proportionate part of the gratuity of each year as the subscribing membership at the time of each death bears to the full membership of the Board.' In the first year the amount received by each beneficiary averaged $846; by the second year this had been increased by $100, and by 1890 the benefit had reached $1,273. The Fund was administered by trustees who reported annually to the membership. In the first four years of operation the families of thirty-six deceased members received benefits; the average age of those who died in this period was forty-eight. A larger than usual number of deaths in 1890 was attributed to 'the prevalence of la grippe.'

The fund appears to have served a useful purpose and provided an incentive to membership. Nevertheless, by 1895 considerable revision was necessary to put it on an actuarily sound basis. A review committee was appointed which submitted its recommendations to the membership the following year, the principal change proposed being the conversion of a uniform assessment to one based upon age. The recommendations were approved and put into effect, although it was clear that the plan thereby became more costly to the average participant and to that extent less attractive. It was agreed that the Fund's affairs should be kept under close scrutiny and further adjustments made from time to time when necessary to maintain financial soundness and a sufficiently attractive relationship between costs and benefits to those participating.

Thereafter the conduct of the gratuity plan became increasingly worrisome, and in 1897 application was made for authority to wind it up and distribute its assets. This being granted, securities held to the face value of $91,800 were advertised for sale by tender and sold to the North American Life Insurance Company at a premium of $332.76. Each subscriber received a return of $125, and under the terms of the provincial Act authorizing the winding-up the balance of $16,608 remaining was to be held for distribution in June 1903. During the life of the Gratuity Fund a total of $164,215 had been paid out to 567 beneficiaries constituting the families of 123 deceased members (4.6 dependents per member). Despite its relatively short operation it was generally well regarded. A major factor in the decision to wind up the Fund was the enormous amount of staff time involved in its administration.

# 3
# The Nineties

By the 1890s Toronto had achieved a significant level of maturity. No longer merely a provincial town in a remote British colony, it was an established city of some consequence in an ever more self-reliant Dominion. Many of its citizens were native-born and possessed a sense of local attachment that their immigrant fathers, seeking a foothold in the new land and retaining predominant loyalties to 'the Old Country', had rarely felt. The physical city was a substantial entity; its buildings, solidly constructed to withstand the rigours of the Canadian climate, in many instances nevertheless displayed considerable architectural grace. Increasing freedom from the mere mechanics of existence had developed cultural and recreational activities, and the numerous wealthy families had created their own social milieu, not unlike that of the Old World.

On the surface it appeared a staid and sober city. Photographs of the time show its citizens – even the children – sedately going about their affairs in surroundings still wholly free of the bustle of motor traffic, and even in summertime heavily clothed from top to toe. Curiously, they were always hatted; it seems to have been considered improper, if not indecent, to appear outdoors without a head covering. Sundays saw most of the city's 190 churches full, and Sunday laws were rigidly enforced; not until 1897 were the street cars permitted to run, after a public referendum on the issue. There was an underside to all this, of course. No city, and no port-city especially, is free of crime and violence, and Toronto had its full share. From the earliest days insobriety had been a major problem, and in the 1890s it remained the chief concern of the 260 stalwarts who constituted the police force. A police constable received $60 a month for his services.

The city had absorbed a number of adjoining towns and villages and by 1898 comprised 16.2 square miles. Total assessment in that year amounted to $130 million, and at a rate of $2.15 per $100 valuation produced taxes totalling $2.75 million annually. The value of building permits issued each year was averaging about $2 million. Property was expensive, commanding up to $2,000 per foot frontage in the best retail districts. The frontage costs for wholesale warehouses varied from $500 to $700 per foot, for factories $80 to $100 and for residential properties in the fashionable area $125 to $150, or in the suburbs $15 to $20. Rentals varied commensurately; for a six-room house in a modest district a normal rental would be eight or nine dollars a month. The mortgage rate was 5 per cent on good security, up to about one-half the market value of the property.

Many streets were still paved with cedar block, laid many years before, but the surface was not satisfactory and it was being gradually replaced by asphalt and vitrified brick. In the residential districts the sidewalks were mostly plank, but concrete was beginning to take over. A municipal authority in 1897 rated New York and Toronto as the two cleanest cities in North America, but rapid growth had produced sub-standard, even shoddy, construction in some parts of the city. By 1898 the Board of Trade was advocating replacement of sub-standard structures by permanent and more dignified works and buildings, and suggested that the city assume some responsibility for controlling the kind and quality of permitted structures.

The city was well served by its public transportation system. In 1891 the Toronto Railway Company, operating over sixty-eight miles of track, obtained a franchise giving it a thirty-year lease of the right-of-way over the principal streets. Between 1891 and 1894 the whole system was electrified, and by 1898 the company was operating four hundred street cars, employing a thousand men and each year carrying some 25 million passengers. Under this arrangement the city annually received $800 per mile of track plus 8 per cent of gross receipts, which in 1896 amounted to some $140,000. The standard fare was five cents, or six tickets for twenty-five cents, and with free transfer privileges the ride was considered a bargain. A proposal to extend the street railway to the Island was dropped in the face of vigorous opposition from the Board of Trade.

Six daily newspapers not only provided news and gossip but also played a considerable part in the community's political life. They were *The Mail and Empire*, *The Globe*, and *The World* in the morning and *The Evening Telegram*, *The News* and *The Star* in the evening; *The Mail and Empire* and *The Globe* sold for two cents and the rest for one cent a copy.

Wholesaling was still Toronto's biggest enterprise, turning over an estimated $300 million worth of merchandise annually. Manufacturing output had grown from $11.5 million in 1881 to more than $66 million by 1898, and it was unusually diversified. There was no dominant industry, and this proved to be advantageous since it permitted adaptation without serious dislocation as market conditions altered. To encourage the establishment of new industries the city was offering a ten-year period of tax exemption and other inducements, a practice the Board of Trade condoned but felt should not be necessary. A reputation for good retailing was maintained and the department stores of Messrs Timothy Eaton and Robert Simpson dominated this field. The T. Eaton Company, with 1,800 employees in 1898, was Canada's largest retailer.

The harbour was an exceedingly busy place and the arrival of 2,207 vessels, 674 of them under sail, was recorded in 1896. For many years coal was the principal cargo entering the harbour. There was an active lake passenger service: the Niagara River Line, with three vessels, operated four trips each way daily between Toronto and Niagara-on-the-Lake and Lewiston; a Toronto to Hamilton service likewise offered four trips daily, and every weekday a ship left Toronto on a direct run to Montreal, a trip that took from twenty-eight to forty hours.

Fourteen chartered commercial banks served Toronto, seven of them with head offices in the city. A bank report for June 1897 states that their total capital was $45.3 million, reserves $18.8 million, notes in circulation $21.3 million, deposits $150 million and total assets $242.2 million. The thirty savings and loan companies with offices in the city possessed assets of over $130 million. Toronto had also become the Dominion's main centre for life insurance operations, the transactions of which amounted to some $45 million annually.

The 1890's also witnessed the rapid growth of two major stock exchanges. In 1869 the Toronto Stock Exchange had still been almost entirely concerned with the shares of banks and loan companies; the nearest approach to an industrial stock was that of the Toronto City Gas Company. The volume of business increased and in 1878 the Exchange was incorporated with twenty-one charter members. At first sessions were held in the offices of the members. In 1885 a room in a building on the northwest corner of King and Victoria Streets was acquired to provide permanent premises. Trading was carried on during a 'call'; when the members were seated at their desks the secretary called out the stocks in their order on his list and each was dealt with separately. These quarters were occupied for fifteen years, by which time membership had increased to thirty-four and a seat cost $4,000. Upon completion of the National Trust Building the Exchange operated from the board room, which had been designed for the purpose. In the meantime the 'call' had been eliminated, the ticker tape made its appearance, telegraph facilities were provided, telephones installed and a clearing house had been formed. By 1902 a record trade of 1,600,000 shares had been achieved, not including bonds and mining stocks. For many years the latter were traded 'on the side'; they were not listed at regular sessions, but were dealt with at special sessions held twice a day.

On 1 May 1898 a Mining Section of the Board of Trade was formed by the Members of the Toronto Mining and Industrial Exchange to provide a more convenient medium for trade in mining securities. Interest in the mines had greatly increased; Canadians were investing, foreign money was beginning to flow in and the new Section was soon recording trade at a million shares a month. In 1901 application was made to the Ontario government for an extension of its powers to permit dealing in shares other than those of mining companies and for an appropriate change of name. Supplementary Letters Patent were granted authorizing general trade in stocks, bonds and debentures and operations were carried on under the name The Standard Stock and Mining Exchange Limited, although it became commonly known as the Stock and Mining Section of the Board of Trade. It was a regularly constituted stock exchange possessing all the privileges enjoyed by any other exchange. Sessions were conducted on the Board's trading floor beginning at twelve o'clock noon each business day. The Standard Exchange later broke away from the Board to set up operations on its own and it eventually became part of the Toronto Stock Exchange.

The city's administrative structure had undergone some changes. In 1891 the old division into thirteen wards, with three representatives to the council from each, was abolished. The city was divided instead into six wards, each electing four aldermen, and the mayor was returned by a vote of the city at large. The city sought legislation in 1902 to reduce to three the number of aldermen from each ward and provide for the election of four controllers by general vote. The Board of Trade at first had some reservations about the advisability of this arrangement on the grounds that few men with the necessary time and qualifications for Board of Control service would submit to the elective process. It finally agreed to go along with the plan until a better system was found; the city's application was supported and the legislation was obtained and given effect the following year. Civic elections were held annually.

The Board of Trade frequently expressed its dislike of Toronto's system of local government, mainly because it established a purely political administrative process which to the businessman was always suspect. For greater efficiency, it recommended a separation of the legislative and administrative functions, and it contended that the city should operate under its own special charter rather than general provincial legislation. The municipal machinery was obviously not working properly and the Board thought that the business community had a right, indeed an obligation, to find out why and seek remedies. One of the major faults, it claimed, arose from the reluctance of businessmen to become involved in civic affairs; according to the Board, the operation of a city was based on principles similar to those necessary to run a commercial enterprise, and the Board implored its members to work towards bringing about a basic reform of the administrative structure. 'It is not enough,' Board President John Davidson exploded in 1892, 'that questions of policy or executive management be left to the aldermen ... why should the ratepayers of Toronto entrust the direction of its affairs to men whom no bank or business house would dream of employing in a like capacity? ... It is the ward politicians, the ringsters, and the nominees of societies who exercise the rule over us, and we are paying for their domination through the nose.'

The Board came under some press criticism for 'seeking to run the city,' but its officers were undaunted and in November 1891 a delegation waited upon the Ontario Premier, Sir Oliver Mowat, urging him to establish a commission to look into the whole question of municipal taxation. The Board itself undertook to prepare factual material as a base for the commission's study. In the period 1881–91 annual civic expenditures had grown from $15.22 to $23.52 and net debt from $71 to $89 per head of population. The Board considered it 'an outrage that the expenditures for all purposes in the city should exceed the amount required for managing the affairs of the whole Province of Ontario,' and that taxes were at rates that 'few can pretend to justify or excuse.' Nothing was done about the commission, however, and a few years later the Board was again drawing attention to the city's rapid growth, the inadequacy of water and other services and the need for regulations governing the erection of buildings. A big city was being managed by 'a village system of municipal government', and a whole new municipal charter created by provincial legislation was needed, followed by enlightened policies for the future which all citizens could support.

Civic expenditures for what it considered unproductive purposes were deeply resented by the Board as adding to an already heavy tax burden. It lost no opportunity to fulminate against the iniquitous personalty tax and produced a survey showing that Montreal's system, a tax on the rental of business premises, was not only more equitable but produced just as much revenue. Amendments to the Assessment Act proposed by the provincial government in 1899 were opposed as patchwork; what was needed was a comprehensive revision based on a full study of existing inadequacies. Constant agitation led to the appointment of the Ontario Assessment Commission in 1900. The President of the Board, A.E. Kemp, appeared before the Commission in October of that year and recommended complete abolition of the existing method of personal assessment, pointing out its defects and claiming that 'if it were fully enforced there would be no sizable business in Toronto.' He added that 'the theory of the present law is that all capital invested in manufacturing should for municipal purposes be taxed, and taxed not like many other investments on its income or profits, but on the principal ... Industrial progress has been possible only by the connivance of municipal officials in the systematic violation of the law.' He recommended the substitution of a tax based on the rental value of property, and the Board's position was supported by the Canadian Manufacturers' Association. The politicians were reluctant to change their ways, and several years passed before the Board won this battle.

The city's general health was rated as good, with a death rate in 1896 of 15.18 per thousand. The principal causes of death were tuberculosis, pneumonia, cholera and diphtheria. Incomplete statistics showed 2,592 deaths from tuberculosis in the province of Ontario in 1892, and in the United States it was estimated that more than 100,000 died annually. The disease cost the American economy $500 million each year, and competent opinion held that a well-directed expenditure of one-fifth this amount could wipe it out in one generation. W.J. Gage, a member of the Board of Trade who later became its president, offered a very generous contribution in 1894 toward a hospital for the exclusive care of consumptives, and the Board backed him with a public plea for immediate action 'toward the prevention of this most prevalent and fatal of all diseases.'

For many years the Board had pleaded for improvement of Toronto's water supply. Its contamination by the city's sewage dumped in the lake was undoubtedly a big factor in the prevalence of certain contagious diseases, but until the late 1880s few Ontario communities had done much about clean water supplies or waste disposal. By the end of the century things were much better: Toronto's water intake had been moved almost three miles out into the lake, regular sanitary inspections had been instituted, and a Health Department and Board of Health were functioning with considerable effect.

The President of the Board of Trade in 1901, A.E. Ames, scolded the members for taking insufficient pride in their city. He told them he believed 'there are no more modest people living, as regards their own city, than are Torontonians ... the city, with the start it already has, is capable of being made notably the most beautiful city on the continent, but it cannot be made so haphazard.' He recommended that expert services be retained to prepare a comprehensive plan 'for the beautification of the city' under the supervision of a committee made up of Board of Trade representatives and other citizens. Funds would be set aside out of taxes to implement the plan, and legislation sought establishing a permanent commission to administer them. Progress could thus be made continuously toward defined objectives. His plea for action while there was still an opportunity to secure lands for public parks and squares was to echo down the years with ever-declining hope for an adequate response.

There was a feeling at this time that the city, with a population estimated in 1897 at 235,000, had developed too rapidly and was over-extended. Many small retail shops were placed in a precarious and, in some cases, superfluous position by the extensive operations of the two big department stores. Trade patterns were changing, too, as manufacturers' agents from Europe and the United States arrived and directly affected the traditional operations of the big wholesale houses, for so long a dominant element in the mercantile community.

Manufacturing activities were rapidly expanding: in 1897 one-third of the total value of building permits issued was for factory buildings and warehouses; existing facilities were operating at full capacity to meet demand. This was attributed in large measure to mining and farming development in the west and to expanding markets in Great Britain for agricultural products. Canadian exports in this general category rose from $37 million in 1890 to $77.5 million in 1898 and hence there was an accelerated demand for agricultural machinery, much of it produced in Toronto plants. One of the foremost of these was the Massey Manufacturing Company which was founded at Newcastle in 1847, moved to Toronto in 1879 and by 1890 employed 575 persons. Among Toronto's other manufactured export items were pianos, heating appliances, bicycles and rubber overshoes. The Board of Trade wanted more industry, particularly cotton mills, sugar refining facilities and rolling mills. It noted that supplies of iron and steel products entering from the United States were supplanting those formerly supplied by Britain.

The Board of Trade was by now firmly established as an institution of consequence in almost every realm of the community's interests. The Hon. George Raines, at its annual dinner in 1894 attended by the Governor General, the Earl of Aberdeen, went so far as to say: 'What the church is to religious life, the school to intellectual development, organizations of this character are to the activities of business life. They develop the hand, brain and conscience of commercial life; they are sensitive to immorality and profligacy in business and political life, and ultimately stand for the integrity and conservatism of a community.' In structure, the Board consisted of a president, two vice-presidents, a treasurer and a Council of fifteen, all elected by the members and serving voluntarily. A twelve-man Board of Arbitration dealt with commercial disputes, appointees of the Board served as examiners and inspectors of grain, flour, hides and leather, and representatives served the Harbour Commission and the Industrial Exhibition. There were nine Trade Sections in 1898, each conducting semi-autonomous operations in specific commercial fields; efforts were made to encourage the formation of such groupings. A Call-Board Committee had responsibility for the conduct of operations on the trading floor.

In 1897 President Edward Gurney complained that the Board's extensive interests were imposing too heavy a load upon the Council, which until then had been wholly responsible for the consideration of current issues and the subsequent determination of relevant policies. The Council also took any action that might be decided upon by the Board such as making representations to the government or other authorities. He recommended that committees be established in all of the Board's main areas of concern and endeavour and his recommendation was promptly acted upon. By the following year six standing committees had been set up and went into operation: the Railway and Transportation Committee, the Committee on Freight Rates, the Committee on Legislation, the Committee on Insolvency Legislation, the Committee on Membership and the Committee on Tourist Travel. Shortly afterwards committees were appointed on Municipal Taxation, New Industries and Technical Education. The committee system worked extremely well and it remained a basic element in the Board's operation, new committees being formed or old ones disbanded as dictated by circumstances.

Over the years the Board ranked among its officers many of the city's chief businessmen. Some found the extra work onerous, particularly those occupying the presidency, and the 1902 President, A.E. Ames, was somewhat apologetic that progress had not been as great as expected due to his and his associates' inability to deal with all the issues demanding attention. 'I feel that perhaps this kind of thing will be done much better in this country in a generation or so,' he remarked, 'when we shall have grown men whose personal requirements have been provided for by the previous generation, and who will themselves be disposed to secure their largest satisfaction in rendering service to the public.' Time proved him wrong; the principal office continued to be held mainly by men who remained actively engaged in their own businesses, held directorates in private corporations and often gave much of their time to other community enterprises. Administrative functions were discharged by a secretary and a clerk. Edgar A. Wills, who had held the secretarial post with distinction since 1883, resigned in 1901 and his place was taken by Paul Jarvis, whose tenure was brief. F.G. Morley was appointed Secretary in 1904.

Scarcely a year passed without the Board making its voice heard in a plea for proper bankruptcy legislation. Over a period of time provincial legislation had been shaped to a form the Board considered reasonably satisfactory, but a federal statute was needed to give businessmen security in commercial relationships that overlapped provincial boundaries. In 1892 a joint delegation of the Toronto, Montreal and Hamilton Boards of Trade presented its case to the Ministers of Justice and Finance, and shortly afterwards a Bill was in fact drafted. Nothing more happened until 1894 when, after further representations to the Federal cabinet, Sir Mackenzie Bowell introduced a Bill in the Senate which generally conformed with the wishes of the Boards of Trade. Again, however, the legislation failed to pass. Year after year the Board recorded its frustration and pleaded reasonably and patiently for comprehensive laws to deal with insolvent debtors. That there was genuine cause for concern appears from the number of business failures:

*Failures in Toronto*
1892    159, with liabilities $1,528,000
1893    180, with liabilities $4,117,000
*Failures in the Dominion*
1892    1,682, with liabilities $11,603,000
1893    1,781, with liabilities $15,690,000

Not until 1920 did the government finally yield to the pressures of the Boards of Trade and other commercial organizations; a Bankruptcy Act was finally given effect as of 1 July of that year. In general principle it followed the English Act of 1914, and the Toronto Board soon after its enactment was able to pronounce it 'satisfactory in application.'

In the arbitration of run-of-the-mill commercial disputes the Board had been performing a reasonably satisfactory service for its own members, but it was felt that its usefulness could be improved if its powers were extended by authority conferred by the city council. This arrangement had been put into effect and was working well in England, where a London Court of Arbitration functioned under the joint auspices of the London County Council and the London Chamber of Commerce. The matter was taken up promptly by Sir Oliver Mowat, the Ontario Premier, and The Boards of Trade General Arbitration Act, 1894, was passed conferring the powers sought. The Board quickly instituted the necessary procedures and the system proved to be a satisfactory method for the settlement of differences between those who wished to submit their problems to arbitration, whether members of the Board or not. The only drawback was the absence of power to enforce compliance with the judgments rendered. In 1892 the Board successfully settled disputes which had arisen in the milling trade between Toronto and Newfoundland, and the view was then expressed that there was 'every prospect, in the near future, that Newfoundland will form a part of the Dominion of Canada.'

With regard to general legal processes the Board was concerned about the high public cost of litigation and in 1894 recommended that judges be empowered to compel plaintiffs under certain circumstances to secure the costs of actions when instituting proceedings, on the grounds that 'the whole process of law should be cheapened, expedited and simplified.' Representations were made in 1899 to extend the jurisdiction of Division Courts to permit them to deal with cases involving larger sums, again to increase efficiency and reduce the cost of litigation.

The high cost of fire insurance was a common source of complaint at this time. The rates were considered unjustifiably profit-oriented, unwarranted in view of the city's compliance with all protective requirements and, if persisted in, likely to lead to insurers placing their business with United States firms or even to the inauguration of a government insurance scheme. In other areas surveyed by the Board, it was noted that proper statistical records were not being prepared and made available to businessmen. The Board recommended in 1897 that the government set up a separate office in Ottawa to collect information filed at various centres and co-ordinate it into regular and up-to-date reports. A careful eye was also kept on developing mining activities, and in 1899 a resolution was adopted recommending, in view of the large production of gold and silver, that a government assay office and mint be established to permit domestic production of the country's metallic currency.

Under prevailing legislation the charters of all banks were due to expire in 1891, and there was concern about what action the government might take in establishing new conditions to control banking procedures. In 1887 the operations of two banks had been suspended as a result of questionable practices, and businessmen were nervous that new legislation might weaken or unduly extend the existing system. Banking conditions in the United States had provided an object lesson. Interest rates there were running between 10 and 12 per cent and the general weakness of the banking system had caused much business uncertainty. Board President John Davidson commented in 1890: 'No one who has studied the causes of the collapse of the financial machinery of the United States during the recent panic can doubt that our superior system of banking is a matter for as much material satisfaction as our superior judiciary.'

It was felt that existing banks could adequately serve the needs of the commercial community for years to come; there was hence no need to grant new charters, and it was strongly advocated that stringent conditions be attached to any bank charter granted in the future. Guided by its Bankers' Section, the Board of Trade took the position that existing legislation needed review and adjustment rather than any drastic change. It recommended that to the extent possible the banks themselves be encouraged to arrange a system of absolute indemnity against loss rather than be compelled to hold gold or government securities, and further that new legislation not be laid down for a defined period, since this would result in disturbances when charters expired simultaneously, but be given unlimited duration with provision for periodic revision.

When the new Banking Act was passed in 1891 the Board took great satisfaction in its provisions, believing them to be admirably suited to the country's needs. The Board's Bankers' Section, as the only organized body of bankers in the Dominion, had keenly interested itself in the new legislation and was justifiably gratified in having achieved a new statute incorporating desired changes without materially altering a structure that had been proven sound. The motivating policies were conservative and they enforced caution and economy in banking operations. The Canadian system possessed the advantage of combining safety with sufficient elasticity to provide for the fluctuating demands of agriculture, trade and commerce. There were indications that the United States proposed to incorporate in its legislation some of the most important features of the new Canadian Banking Act.

The world economy suffered another serious setback in 1893. Board President D.R. Wilkie commented:

The panics that have followed one another in sharp succession uprooting credit, sweeping before them one industry after another, destroying confidence, bringing hundreds of thousands to poverty, attacking Australia and its antipodes irrespective of soil or flag, and finally settling down upon our nearest neighbour with dire results, are an object lesson to Canada to avoid public and personal extravagance, to avoid the borrowing of foreign capital for use in non-productive investments, to avoid fostering illegitimate enterprises for the benefit of the few, and to depend for success and fortune upon the gradual but sure development of her own resources upon straight economic lines. We have much to be thankful for – we have escaped the torrent of bankruptcy that has washed in vain against our borders, and today Canada stands eminent for its financial soundness amongst the nations of the earth.

Again and again the Board admonished businessmen to abstain from land and marginal stock market speculation and emphasized that financial stability could be preserved if individual business concerns would concentrate their efforts upon the prudent conduct of affairs within their own fields of enterprise. Severe depression continued and the year 1894 was one of unusual anxiety as the prices of staple commodities fell by as much as 33 per cent. During the year, rated as the most unsatisfactory since Confederation, both business volume and profits shrank and failures increased by 40 per cent; nor was the outlook for the future encouraging. The Board advocated retrenchment and economy as the only way toward a slow recovery and recommended a lowering of interest rates on deposits with both the banks and the government. It continued to deplore the high interest rates being paid by the government on the deposits, valued in 1895 at more than $44 million, in the Post Office and Dominion savings banks. Interest rates were high in comparison with those applicable in other countries and local businessmen were placed at a competitive disadvantage. A reduction, moreover, would encourage the employment of idle domestic capital in the development of the country's natural resources.

Some signs of gradual recovery were evident the following year, and the advent to power of the Reform Party in 1896, after eighteen years in opposition, was greeted with cautious hope for fiscal measures which would lead to improvement in the nation's economic health. By 1898 the corner had been turned. Abundant signs of prosperity reappeared throughout the Dominion: exports increased to more than $144 million, bank clearings and the circulation of bank notes were steadily rising and in Toronto the pace of manufacturing operation was accelerating substantially. The improvement was attributed, among other factors, to the development of mining and agricultural activities in western Canada, and to new tariff policies which were leading to significant increases in free imports of raw materials for industrial processing.

One blessing more than any other for which Toronto businessmen were thankful was the soundness of their banking system. In the 1893 collapse banks in the United States had fallen like leaves while those in Canada had withstood extraordinary pressures and maintained their credit unimpaired. With the return of prosperity several Canadian banks increased their capital by large amounts to meet the demands of business. The satisfaction with the Canadian banking system so frequently expressed by the Board of Trade's Council may have been somewhat influenced by the fact that so many of its members were themselves bank directors. By 1899 bank clearings in Toronto were $504.9 million, still some way behind Montreal's $794 million.

Acting on the recommendation of its Bankers' Section the Board in 1888 supported efforts to establish a bank clearing house. Such a facility had been put into successful operation in Montreal, and a similar organization in Toronto was regarded as a means of compiling statistical information on trade fluctuations and by its daily clearings would provide valuable business indices for year-to-year comparisons. A Bankers' Clearing House Association was created in Toronto in 1891; one large bank initially abstained but joined later to make the roster complete. The Bankers' Section offered its encouragement to the incumbent of the chair in political economy created by the University of Toronto in 1889. This field of study had been advocated by the Board of Trade as a service to the mercantile community in the belief that the University had for too long been preoccupied with the production of doctors and lawyers.

The Board did not at first look with much favour on the proposed introduction of legislation to control combines. When the matter was under consideration by a special committee of the House of Commons in 1888, the Board said it could see no reason why persons 'should not arrange among themselves fair and reasonable prices at which special clearly defined lines of goods should be sold at general terms of credits and discounts.' When combines legislation was passed by Parliament the following year the Board gave the matter some further consideration and discreetly decided to take no further action. It was, however, disturbed and annoyed by the proliferation of 'bucket shops' in Toronto. These illegal brokerages were operating with scandalous disregard for ordinary business ethics and almost complete freedom from regulatory restraint; they were not only mulcting the citizens of hard-earned money but were casting an unfavourable light on other wholly respectable businesses. The Board's agitation to root out 'this system of gambling' met with speedy success through the enactment in 1888 of provincial legislation instituting a system of controls.

When the Ontario legislature in 1899 proposed to introduce a workmen's compensation plan modelled after legislation recently put into effect in Great Britain, the Board strongly advocated deferment until the implications could be fully studied and, as a result, the Bill was withdrawn. Objection was not so much to the principle involved as to the inadequacy of the legislation and to the uncertainty, ill-will and high costs therefore likely to be encountered in its application.

The products of Ontario mines were beginning to assume a place of some importance in the province's economy and businessmen had become alert to their potential. Copper and nickel mining had begun in the Sudbury area around 1887; four years later three companies were in operation, employing 1,000 men and processing 500 tons of ore a day. In 1890 a Royal Commission appointed to study the mineral resources of the province had reported in terms that gave promise of a glowing future, but the Board of Trade was of the opinion that the provincial government was not acting as vigorously as it might to stimulate development. It suggested that qualified geologists be appointed to undertake more intensive and comprehensive field work, that the results of this work be made generally available in published reports and that adequate assay facilities be established in the mining regions to permit rapid assessment of ore qualities. Until then it had been necessary to send most ore samples out of the country for proper assay.

In December 1890 the Council and some other Board members visited the Sudbury mines and works on the invitation of the Canadian Copper Company and with the co-operation of the Grand Trunk and Canadian Pacific Railways. This was the first of a long series of trips by Board of Trade members into the northern part of the province to see for themselves what was going on in a field of endeavour which was to have increasing impact on the shape of Toronto's financial and mercantile development. Upon his return President Davidson said, ' ... I find it difficult to keep within bounds of moderation when I contemplate the possibilities of those northland nickel riches of ours, and since my return from Sudbury I have greater confidence than ever before in the great future for this Province and this City of Toronto, if we but use our opportunities wisely and strike while the nickel is hot.' What was not immediately clear was the exact extent of the market that might exist for all the nickel that could be produced from an ore body then estimated at 650 million tons. There was encouragement in a report made to the Secretary of the United States Navy advocating the use of nickel-steel as armour plate on naval vessels; this was seen as a substantial potential market, with possibilities for later extension in Europe.

Since the Board wanted Toronto to benefit directly from the growth of a mining industry, it advocated the establishment of processing plants on the waste lands bordering the east shore of the bay. Considering Ontario's virtual monopoly in nickel, it seemed only common sense to create local smelting and refining operations and thus reap the benefits of increased labour employment and higher export prices for a finished product. The same arguments were used in urging the development of a Canadian iron and steel industry. All necessary raw materials were available and it was confidently expected that British capital could be attracted; only initiative and enterprise were needed and perhaps some government leadership. It was true that the government was paying a bounty of $2 per ton on native pig iron and admitted mining machinery duty free, but this was not considered sufficient to stimulate the huge effort required to set up industries of the scale visualized by Toronto's enthusiasts. The Board's advocacy was obliquely met with the creation of iron smelting facilities in Hamilton, which it supported by recommending the duty-free admission of its coke supplies and machinery not produced in Canada.

Toronto was becoming the centre of activity for trade in the shares of mining enterprises and, as some of these were of a very dubious character, established business interests were concerned about the possible effect on the generally sound and sensible business life of the community. Board President Gurney remarked in 1897 that 'the atmosphere is so full of mining stock certificates that it is difficult to breathe.'

In 1890 the Board was again expressing concern about another of the province's natural resources – lumber. Tremendous inroads had been made into the readily accessible stands of good timber and supplies of the kinds and qualities most in demand had long since been seriously depleted. The Board called for government action which would institute effective measures of conservation and a program of reforestation.

Canada's trade was still amost entirely with the United States and Great Britain. In 1895 exports exceeded imports for only the second time since Confederation:

| | |
|---|---:|
| Imports from the United States | $  54,635,000 |
| Imports from Great Britain | $  31,132,000 |
| Total Imports | $  85,767,000 |
| Exports to the United States | $  41,298,000 |
| Exports to Great Britain | $  61,857,000 |
| Total Exports | $103,155,000 |

Increased trade with Britain had been a major objective of the Board for a long time, and the whole question of devising a system to foster trade within the Empire, including special schedules of preferential tariffs, was to occupy the Board's attention as a major issue for nearly half a century. Successive presidents were fond of referring to the fact 'that this Board was the first organized body to give public expression of approval to the principle of preferential trade within the British Empire.'

The Board's sustained effort in this field was doubtless motivated in large measure by hard-headed self-interest: for a healthy economy Canada had to have export markets. Trade relations with the United States had often proved unreliable, whereas the countries of the British Empire, although at a greater distance, offered an immense market with congenial political characteristics. The Empire then encompassed one-quarter of the world's land mass and one-quarter of its entire population. But there was more to it than that. Toronto had always been known for its strongly pro-British sentiments; most of its citizens, or their parents, had been born in the British Isles, which were still regarded affectionately as 'the Old Country'. Sentiment, and a genuine belief in the Empire as a force for good in the world, played a part in the effort to strengthen the relationship with bonds of trade. After an Intercolonial Conference in Ottawa in 1894 Hugh Blain, the Board's President, reported that the views expressed 'left no room for doubt as to the absolute necessity for maintaining intact a united British Empire as the dominant force in the civilization and enlightenment of the world.'

The ardent pro-British sentiments of Toronto citizens were demonstrated with the outbreak of the South African War in 1899. A Canadian contingent was quickly mobilized and sent on its long voyage to support British troops in the field, and the Board of Trade recorded a patriotic resolution favouring the mobilization of a second contingent 'to assist in putting down the insurrection' and any other steps that might be deemed necessary; it also advocated that Canada assume responsibility for all the costs of these efforts. The Board saw this as the fulfilment of an obligation toward a mother country that had assured and assisted in Canada's peaceful development, and quoted Lord Rosebery approvingly to the effect that the British Empire was the greatest secular agency for good known to mankind. These considerations led to some thinking about Canadian defence policy. The Board's President in 1899, A.E. Kemp, told the members it was time Canada saw to its own coastal defences and made an effective naval contribution, and he further proposed the establishment of a regular army of 10,000 men, independent of the militia, ready to serve in any Empire emergency.

No opportunity was lost to foster the idea of Empire unity. A strengthened Empire was seen as a bulwark to Great Britain and a contribution to world security. Some kind of Empire Federation was visualized, with an Imperial Colonial Council comprising representatives of all participating countries in which Canada would show her maturity by assuming a fair share of responsibility. Basically the Toronto Board's hope was 'that the Empire may become a commercial Empire; that a market may be established which no nation can take away.' The Board had unshakable faith that a British consumer would always favour a British product; moreover, it continued to be nervous over the unpredictability of trade relations with the United States and unsure about the general economic stability of that country.

The proposal to enter into a reciprocal trade treaty with Britain came to the fore after the failure to negotiate a new reciprocity agreement with the United States, and it was urged more strongly after the United States began to erect its protective tariff walls under McKinley. It was felt that Britain would probably react favourably, and Lord Salisbury was quoted as having said in 1890 that the only reason for having secured large slices of Africa was the anticipation that before very long the only part of the world that Britain could hope to trade freely with would be the part covered by the flag, and from that part he would have to exclude the self-governing colonies unless something was done to make the conditions of trade with them equal. A year or two earlier, at the instigation of the Prince of Wales, an Imperial Institute had been formed with a governing body made up of British and colonial representatives, and an Imperial Museum had been opened in London in which was maintained a display of the products, both agricultural and manufactured, available from the colonies. A leading British proponent of the idea of a better integration of the various components of the Empire was the Colonial Secretary, the Rt Hon. Joseph Chamberlain.

But Britain was in a difficult position. She could grant preferences to colonial goods only by abandoning her free-trade principles, applying tariffs against foreign goods and renouncing certain trade agreements, notably with Germany and Belgium, which were binding upon the whole Empire. There was, however, some disillusionment in Britain over free trade. When the policy was adopted it was expected that other nations would follow suit and British products would find their way into foreign markets on terms as liberal as those she herself offered. It was beginning to appear that what she had was free imports, not free trade, as one nation after another erected hostile tariff barriers.

The Toronto Board was optimistic that obstacles could be overcome, and when in 1891 it was announced that a meeting of Chambers of Commerce and other organizations would be held shortly in London for the discussion of common problems, the Board appointed its delegates and briefed them, confident that practical methods for trade development could be worked out and statesmen found to implement them. At the London conference there was apparently complete agreement on the desirability of Empire consolidation, but little practical progress made toward a system of preferential tariffs.

The Canadian House of Commons showed its good will by the adoption of a resolution in 1892 which said, in effect, that if and when the Parliament of Great Britain and Ireland admitted Canadian products to the markets of the United Kingdom on more favourable terms than it accorded to the products of foreign countries, the Parliament of Canada would be prepared to accord corresponding advantages by a substantial reduction in the duties it imposed on British manufactured goods. At a further meeting of the Chambers of Commerce of the British Empire held in London in 1895 the Toronto Board submitted for consideration resolutions embodying its advocacy of a scheme of preferential trade between all parts of the Empire, making the point that it was not motivated by antagonism toward the United States but by a desire for a wider and more balanced trading base. The resolutions were warmly received, and it seemed that progress was being made.

In 1897 the Canadian government under Sir Wilfrid Laurier reduced the tariff by 25 per cent on incoming goods of British origin, and the Board of Trade felt it had achieved a significant victory. At the Annual Meeting the following year the President of the Board, Elias Rogers, reported to the members that

Since August last the British preference has been an accomplished fact, and the goods of the Motherland and several important colonies have now a substantial tariff advantage in Canadian ports. Whether or not this preference ripens the feeling in Great Britain in favour of preferential treatment of the products of the Empire, we have the satisfaction of knowing that Canada has heartily done her share toward promoting an inter-Imperial trade.

Although Canada's goods remained without preference in the British market, her unilateral reduction of tariffs on British imports was said to have 'warmed the hearts of the British consumer as nothing else could have done,' and there was an improved acceptance of Canadian products. The

Board subsequently resumed its efforts to achieve a full-scale system of Imperial preferences, but it was not until 1919 that Britain adopted the preferential principle and allowed a tariff differential in favour of specified commodities produced in the Empire. This eventually led to the negotiation of reciprocal tariff preferences between the members of the Commonwealth at the Imperial Economic Conference held in Ottawa in 1932.

Reducing tariffs was one way of increasing trade with Britain and the rest of the Empire; another was the creation of better means of transport and communication. Most Canadian exports to Britain travelled via United States ports, a process that added costs to the shipment and as much as three to five days to the journey compared with a departure from Quebec. The Board pleaded for a fast Canadian trans-Atlantic steamship service, subsidized by the government if necessary, which would not only move goods efficiently but also facilitate immigration and open up the 'immense fertile lands in Manitoba and the north-west.' Although the Board in 1888 noted with satisfaction the inauguration of Canadian Pacific's steamship services, it was resentful that these did not include what was for Toronto by far the most important service, i.e., from eastern Canadian ports direct to Britain. Four years later it officially recorded its opinion that 'a first-class Canadian fast Atlantic steamship service would materially increase the value of our European exports, decrease the cost of delivery of our European imports, largely augment the volume of our passenger travel, improve our foreign and postal service, and otherwise be of great national importance.' The Board's position was supported by organizations in a number of other Canadian cities. Apart from the direct benefits, it saw that the Atlantic route, when linked with a trans-Canada railway system and steamship services from Vancouver to Japan, China and Australia, could make Canada a world highway between Europe and the Orient. By 1894 Joseph Chamberlain was promising an Imperial subsidy of £75,000 per annum if a service were organized. The Dominion government had indicated its willingness to provide a $750,000 subsidy, and accomplishment of the project within a couple of years was confidently anticipated.

The debate as to whether Canada's economic future lay in closer trade ties with Britain or with the United States was still going on in the late 1890's, although the Toronto Board had long since made up its mind. It was distrustful of the 'whimsical legislation' of the us Congress which had 'awakened Canadians from some of our dreams of Commercial Union of one kind or another, and made us see that in no large way can we allow the destiny of Canada to be dependent on the complaisance of our good cousins.' The Board thought, in fact, that Canada had probably erred in orienting its rail and water transportation toward the American market, and that its efforts would have been more productive if greater emphasis had been placed on developing an east-west system. In any event, the inequality of Canada-United States trade, as evidenced by a balance of $220 million in favour of the United States between 1874 and 1893, suggested the desirability of re-assessment. As a further means of improving British Trade, the Board in 1897 was advocating the establishment of an inspection service to ensure quality maintenance in Canadian exports, and the establishment of a Canadian commercial, as distinct from diplomatic, office in London.

Attention was also being given at this time to the development of trading relations with the West Indies and Australia. A direct steamship service to Australia on at least a monthly basis was being urged, together with the negotiation of a customs tariff agreement which would encourage reciprocal trade and the appointment in Australia of a permanent Canadian commercial agent. The Pacific telegraph cable project also won the Board's enthusiastic support as another means of drawing the Empire together and as a step toward an around-the-world Empire cable system. When Britain stalled on an initial agreement made through the Imperial Pacific Cable Committee for a sharing of the costs, A.E. Kemp pressed the matter directly with Prime Minister Laurier and Postmaster General Mulock in 1899 and probably influenced resumption of government action. In that year the Imperial, Canadian and Australian governments jointly contracted for the establishment of the cable connection, and the Board of Trade, expressing its gratification, hoped that this would lead to a full British Empire cable system free of dependence on any foreign linkage. The Board urged the Prime Minister to ensure that Canada was ably represented at ceremonies marking the inauguration of the new Commonwealth of Australia in 1901 and suggested that the occasion would be a propitious one for advancing the idea of reciprocal preferential tariffs.

In the matter of improved communication facilities the Board had long interested itself in postal rates and services. Beginning in 1884 it proposed the lowering of the general postage rate from three cents to two cents per ounce to conform with the American rate structure. The effect of the difference in rates was to encourage Canadian firms to have material intended for Canadian distribution printed and mailed in the United States; some mail was even being taken to American centres for delivery in Canada. The rate of postage for city delivery at two cents per ounce was also considered excessive. To compensate for reduced revenues under the lower rates proposed, the Board advocated the abolition of the practice, then in effect, of free newspaper and periodical deliveries. No opportunity was lost to propound these ideas and partial success was achieved with the adoption of Imperial Penny Postage in 1898 which made the two-cent rate applicable throughout the Empire. It was observed that 'but for the resolute action of Canada and the Hon. Mr. Mulock, the move for Imperial Penny Postage would have remained unsuccessful for years.' Upon his return from England after the negotiations leading to the adoption of Imperial Penny Postage, Mr. Mulock was paid a warm tribute by the Board for his 'brilliant achievement.' The Board continued, nevertheless, to urge a one-cent rate for local deliveries.

Railway building and operation continued to attract public attention. Increasingly aware of the potential resources and markets of the north, a Board of Trade delegation in 1892 urged the Dominion Government to provide further aid for the Nipissing and James Bay Railway. The Grand Trunk connected with the CPR at North Bay, and it appeared both logical and desirable to extend the line northward to tidewater at the mouth of the Moose River. This was seen as an essential communication link between the old and new sections of Ontario, thus uniting the province, and also as a step to prevent the newer territories from attaching themselves to Quebec for trade and commercial purposes. The Nipissing and James Bay Railway Company had secured a charter for the line, and when the Ontario and Dominion governments agreed to provide subsidies totalling $6,200 per mile for construction the Board felt that an important objective had been achieved.

The Board was interested in the development of any railway that possessed a reasonable measure of feasibility and gave Toronto access to new market areas. It opposed direct financial participation by the city of Toronto in railway construction, but generally had no objection to substantial subsidization by the Ontario and Dominion governments. About the road to James Bay it said, 'if this line of railway were once opened up, the trade of this territory would be largely tributary to this city.' It supported a line to Sudbury, and in 1898 sent two delegations to Ottawa to secure federal assistance for the Toronto and Georgian Bay Short-Line Railway. A proposed Ottawa, Arnprior and Parry Sound Railway was a different matter. This appeared to be designed to satisfy private interests, and its effect would be to divert traffic from much of Ontario away from Toronto to Ottawa and Montreal. The Board therefore opposed any government bonusing, and anyway it thought that the country through which it was to pass was almost useless for settlement and agricultural purposes.

But it was the Grand Trunk that principally roused the ire of Toronto businessmen. According to the Board's calculations the capital investment per mile of the Grand Trunk was $105,435, as compared with $51,480 for the CPR and an overall average in the United States of $63,421. It was felt that a realistic figure for the Grand Trunk should have been $40,000 to $50,000, and it seemed perfectly clear that a satisfactory return on such an enormously inflated capitalization simply was not possible. The road had been built, the Board contended, not on a basis of efficiency and earning power but in the interests of politicians, promoters and contractors, and the sad picture it presented was damaging the whole country's credit and repute. The Board of Trade was particularly incensed by the fact that the Grand Trunk's operations were administered from England, where local conditions were not understood. Decisions were delayed when issues arose; it was often weeks or months before Canadian managers were permitted or authorized to act. Moreover, there was deep suspicion that losses on American and through traffic were being charged against local revenues. When Sir Charles Rivers Wilson, the new Grand Trunk President, came to Toronto in August 1894, the Board placed five major recommendations before him. They urged that he establish a local board with power to make local decisions; inaugurate a first-class service between Toronto and Buffalo; provide better passenger cars; reduce the first-class passenger rate to two cents a mile; and begin the construction of the North Bay and Temiskaming Railway, for which Grand Trunk controlled the charter.

Farther afield, the Board considered it a prime necessity to build the Crow's Nest Pass Railway to foster mining development in and establish trading connections with British Columbia, which was showing signs of aligning itself with the United States rather than Eastern Canada. The completion of the Pass in 1897 was hailed as an accomplishment of national importance, and the Board took some credit for having been a major advocate. Coal and coke were soon flowing through to the smelters of Kootenay and refining costs were significantly reduced.

Inequalities in freight rates, particularly between Ontario and Quebec, continued to irritate Toronto shippers. The first-class freight rate from Montreal to Toronto was forty-four cents per hundred pounds whereas the rate in the reverse direction was fifty cents, and the Toronto Board understandably considered this indefensible discrimination. Through rates from points of origin in the United States were in some cases so much better than the commodity rates available to Toronto shippers that the latter found themselves unable to compete in their own market. The situation was inhibiting Toronto's development both industrially and as a distributing centre. In 1893 the Board placed its case for rate reform before the Hon. Mackenzie Bowell, Minister of Trade and Commerce, and the Hon. George Foster, Minister of Finance, and by 1898 its agitation had produced some adjustment. But much more was needed and the Board always found itself frustrated when remedies were sought. The railways themselves were preoccupied with dividend earnings and were disinclined to negotiate, and the only official source of redress, the Railway Committee of the Privy Council, proved to be inadequate and unsatisfactory. Again and again the Board sought the appointment by the government of an independent commission of qualified and disinterested persons with full authority to deal with rates and any other matters of dispute arising between the railways and the users of rail services.

The proposal to deepen the channels of the St Lawrence River to provide an improved shipping lane from the Great Lakes to the sea had long been under discussion. The old nine-foot channel depth had seriously restricted use of the waterway, and in 1874 the federal government had committed itself to works which would establish a minimum fourteen-foot depth over the whole distance from Lake Ontario to Montreal, with locks 270 feet long and forty-five feet wide. But the work proceeded very slowly, and when in 1890 an impatient delegation representing the cities of Toronto, Hamilton, Montreal and Kingston went to Ottawa to obtain some indication of where matters stood, government officials could only estimate another three and a half years to completion.

At a Deep Waterway Convention held in Toronto in 1894, with the work still unfinished, the general consensus was that a fourteen-foot depth was not enough and pressure should be applied for a twenty-foot depth throughout. The Toronto Board recorded its disagreement, holding that nothing was to be gained at this stage by introducing a new concept, and moreover that vast expenditures were involved requiring judicious administration in keeping with the country's financial resources. It did agree, though, that the government was being unconscionably dilatory and that renewed pressure should be applied. Progress was piecemeal: the locks at Cornwall, for example, had been completed in 1882, whereas the approaches were not even started until 1893. The channel was obviously useless as a deepened waterway until all the works had been completed. Toronto felt very strongly the importance of the St Lawrence waterway and hoped it might lead to a revival of the lake trade, stimulate shipbuilding and compensate for a pattern of railway development which was tending to make the city a way-station rather than a main terminus. Deepening of the St Lawrence waterway was finally completed in 1899, and some relatively large vessels bearing cargoes originating in Great Lakes ports were then able to proceed down its full length and across the Atlantic without trans-shipment.

Concurrently with the St Lawrence development Toronto needed to improve its own harbour. Deep-draft vessels taking advantage of the new fourteen-foot channel simply could not enter Toronto harbour. The Dominion government had made available a sum of $50,000 for necessary harbour works as part of the overall waterway development, but the city had taken no action. The Board of Trade's Marine Section took up the matter directly with civic representatives in 1898, urging the development of the waterfront properties in accordance with a definite plan 'with a view to providing facilities and dock accommodations for the important Seaboard and Intercolonial trade which will arise upon the completion of the fourteen-foot canals.' It advocated 'improvements based on uses for navigation instead of solely for the dumping of refuse from streets and excavations from cellars.'

The Board and the Harbour Commissioners induced the city and the Dominion government to appoint engineers who would prepare a report on harbour development; such a report was in fact produced in 1900 but led to no immediate action. The following year the Board again urged the city to act with the government of Canada and take immediate measures to stop the build-up of deposits in Toronto harbour caused by silt from the Don River and inflow from the city's sewers, and to proceed with other permanent harbour improvements 'on a scale commensurate with the system of navigation connecting Lake Ontario with seaboard.'

Concern with the proper utilization of the waterfront extended beyond the provision of harbour facilities. As early as 1891 the Board had recommended the reclamation of one thousand acres of marsh on Ashbridge's Bay, east of the Don River, and the utilization of the land thus produced for both industrial and residential purposes, instancing the success of similar works in Boston's Back Bay area. Its proposal was accompanied, however, by advocacy that properties so created be kept out of the hands of mere speculators and profit-seekers. In January 1899 the Board submitted proposals to the city council for a reorganization of the Harbour Commission to give it more effective and broader powers. They were not favourably received. Vigorous representations to the same effect were renewed in 1910 and this time they resulted, after an overwhelming endorsement by the electors, in the passage of the Toronto Harbour Commissioners' Act in May 1911 embodying most of the Board's proposals and setting the pattern for future harbour management.

The Board of Trade's pressure for harbour and waterfront improvement was motivated by a desire to see Toronto placed in a position to avail itself of the tremendous opportunities opening up as a result of increasing trade and commercial activity throughout the entire Great Lakes region. A major objective was the creation of an all-Canadian route, including Toronto, for western grain moving to seaboard, and it was in pursuance of this objective that the Board enthusiastically took up the cause of the so-called Toronto and Georgian Bay Short-Line (or Air-Line) Railway.

Every harvest time there had been a scramble to accommodate grain being shipped to Europe. Various means of alleviation had been explored, including the use of Hudson Bay ports which had been found not feasible due to the long railway haul and short season. The Great Lakes and the St Lawrence were considered to be a natural waterway from the wheat-producing lands of both Canada and the United States; use of this route was competitive, open to all and would stimulate the development of the port cities on the lakes. In 1896 the Canadian Deep Waterways Commission pointed out that the bulk of the grain from Manitoba and the Territories regularly reached the Atlantic by an exclusively American route from Lake Superior and the Soo Canal through Lake Huron, the Detroit and St Clair Rivers and Lake Erie to Buffalo, which possessed excellent storage and elevating equipment. From Buffalo it went by either the Erie Canal or rail to New York for overseas shipment. The rail haul was a long one, although the New York Central had done everything possible to minimize costs and improve its services and equipment.

Under prevailing coasting laws, which stipulated that a ship's voyage must originate and terminate in the country of its registration, the transit from Duluth and Chicago to Buffalo was reserved for vessels of United States register, although these vessels, with capacities of up to 300,000 bushels, could also pick up cargoes at Port Arthur and Fort William along the way. Since Buffalo rather than Port Colborne in Ontario was the main destination, American ships enjoyed a great advantage; few Canadian ships were engaged in the service and the developing Canadian west was being made tributary to the eastern mercantile centres of the United States. Grain shipments via the Welland Canal, Lake Ontario and the deepened St Lawrence canals were inconsiderable, although there was hope that they would increase, thereby stimulating Canadian marine activities and securing an adequate return on the large investment represented in the St Lawrence waterway improvements.

To create a practicable all-Canadian route the chief obstacle was the relatively narrow land promontory between Georgian Bay and Lake Ontario. As early as 1837 an attempt had been made to establish a short-cut via the Trent Canal, but this was in places little more than a shallow ditch and enlargement to conform with the depth and lock characteristics of the St Lawrence system would have been extremely costly. The alternative canal route from Georgian Bay to Toronto, as advocated by the Board of Trade in 1855, had been fully investigated but its cost of construction had also been ruled beyond the country's financial resources. Another alternative, and one that from 1898 received the Board's support, was a direct railway connection between Georgian Bay ports and Toronto, with adequate equipment and terminal facilities at both ends. There were no serious physical problems and the distance, under seventy miles, was inconsiderable when compared with the 440-mile haul from Buffalo to New York. The fourteen-foot St Lawrence canals would accommodate vessels carrying up to 80,000 bushels of grain; they were built (at a cost of $60 million) and maintained by the federal government, and were open to use by both American and Canadian ships. Indeed, it appeared that the United States would make greater use of the system, if usage of the Welland Canal was any criterion: in 1897 American vessels carried 898,773 tons through the Welland as against 345,977 tons by Canadian ships.

Canadian vessels would thus be in a better position to compete with United States vessels for cargoes in Chicago, Duluth, Milwaukee and other ports, while the trade from Fort William and Port Arthur could profitably be transferred to Canadian ships under the coasting laws. The distance from Fort William or Chicago to Buffalo or Port Colborne was roughly 900 miles, but to the southern extremity of Georgian Bay only 550 miles. Total distances from Port Arthur or Chicago were:

To Montreal via the Welland Canal    1297 miles
To Montreal via the Short Line Railway    995 miles
To Liverpool via the Lakes, the Erie Canal and New York    4915 miles
To Liverpool via the Short Line Railway and the St Lawrence River    4125 miles

Taking into account the hazard and delays of the passage from Lake Huron to Lake Erie, it was felt that transit time could be almost halved, or capacities doubled, by shipping from Chicago to a Georgian Bay port and thence to Toronto. As Liverpool quotations determined the price of wheat, any shipping economies meant a greater profit to the producers.

The project seemed to offer nothing but advantages: it would relieve a seriously overloaded system; Quebec and Montreal would benefit as termini of the St Lawrence route; new trade would develop in return cargoes from Montreal and Quebec to Toronto and other lake ports (coal from the Maritimes, for example) and a cooler northern route would lessen grain damage. By establishing a barge service out of Toronto, freight cars could be shipped across the lake to Oswego, Rochester and Ogdensburg without unloading and continue on their journey to United States destinations. Last, but by no means least in the eyes of the Toronto Board of Trade, the inauguration of such a system would vastly enhance Toronto's position as an entrepôt, with all the subsidiary benefits of associated commercial and mercantile activity. The government, the Board contended, should build this 'portage railway' as part of its canal system to realize on its big investment in the St Lawrence. As to the cost, it was argued that 'if the cost of Government elevators be added to the cost of the railway and equipment the outlay both for interest and sinking fund will be more than covered by the saving on the cost of hauling our own western harvests alone, without taking into account the immense commercial advantages to be derived indirectly from the turning of traffic to Canadian channels.'

To support its case the Board referred to the change in the world's commerce and the new competitive factors introduced by the opening of the Suez Canal in 1869. This had brought the East into direct competition with the West by reducing a voyage of six to eight months to thirty days and had 'virtually destroyed the value of the sailing vessels formerly employed, and made it necessary to readjust the old methods and ancient systems of distribution to an entirely new situation.' A 75 per cent reduction in freight rates on grain had enabled India to enter European markets, and this competition was intensified by the entry as grain suppliers of some South American states. It was more important than ever before that Canada improve her competitive position, and one way of doing so was to improve her internal transportation system.

In April 1898 a special committee of the Board of Trade discussed the project with the Minister of Public Works and the Interior, and in June of that year the Board's representatives, with members of the city council and local members of Parliament, conferred with Prime Minister Sir Wilfrid Laurier and his colleagues. The delegation was encouraged by a sympathetic hearing and a promise that the matter would have full consideration, and also by the support that seemed available from Montreal. There is no evidence that the matter ever did receive the government's serious consideration and, if it did, the likelihood is that, as with the earlier canal proposal, the project was put aside as being just too expensive. After considerable initial effort the Board itself eventually dropped the subject, although its interest in creating an efficient Canadian route for shipments to seaboard never abated and reappeared some years later when it sought the deepening and improvement of the Welland Canal and further development in the St Lawrence.

Controversy arose in 1898 as a result of pressures being applied by certain interests to induce the federal government to grant permission to vessels of United States registry to participate in the Canadian coasting trade, principally by transferring grain from Fort William to other lake ports. The Board of Trade immediately recorded its objection to any such abrogation of time-honoured coasting laws, and was shocked to learn shortly afterwards that such privileges had been granted to American vessels by Order-in-Council. A delegation from the Board took the matter to Prime Minister Laurier personally and was assured that the concession had been granted for a limited period only and would not be renewed. Toronto interests were sensitive on such issues, since it was known that in the United States there was concern over the effect of the St Lawrence route on the traditional pattern of grain movements through Buffalo and over American railways to seaboard, and that influences were being brought to bear to secure all possible compensating advantages. Perhaps the Board's vigorous actions impressed the government, for the concession was in fact not renewed. Just a year later it was noted that assurance of continued protection was leading to a renewal of Canadian ship-building activity and an extension of the pattern of water-borne traffic. 'The surest way to build up a national marine,' said the Board of Trade, 'is to hold our own waters for our own people in the same way that other nations hold theirs.' Better utilization of the St Lawrence waterway was a prime objective, both to realize on the huge government expenditures it had entailed and as a means of developing the Canadian cities along its route. Tolls had become a serious burden, and to stimulate traffic the Board in 1900 recommended that they be abolished on grain shipments through the Welland and St Lawrence canals and substantially lowered on cargoes of lumber and coal.

The concentration of interest throughout this period in matters relating to transportation, both water and rail, was based primarily on the grain trade and sprang from the conviction that the Canadian economy still depended upon a healthy agricultural industry. Speaking to the Board's

Annual Meeting of 1891, President John I. Davidson observed that 'if the crops fail, all other interests, and notably trade and manufactures, become depressed. If they are bountiful every other business and industry is stirred into greater activity.' The creation of agricultural colleges and experimental farms was noted with approval in 1895, as was the gradual reorientation of farming from the traditional wheat and barley to meat, eggs, butter, cheese and fruit. The encouragement and subsidization of immigration was advocated to ensure the availability of farm labour.

It was about this time that the Board began to take a direct interest in education, particularly as it applied to preparation for industrial and commercial careers. In 1899 the Board's representatives conferred with the Minister of Education, and afterwards a special committee was appointed to bring together the views of businessmen on the kind of facilities necessary to provide sound technical education. Interest in this subject intensified and the Board later became closely identified with the work of Toronto's commercial and technical schools. In addition to regular schooling, the Board thought there should be special instruction available for adult workers so that they could adapt themselves more effectively to the developing technologies of the industrial system. A delegation went to Ottawa in 1901 seeking financial aid for such an undertaking.

Since the invention of the metric system in France in the late eighteenth century and its subsequent adoption in many countries, its introduction in Canada had been discussed from time to time but nothing had developed. The Minister of Inland Revenue in 1899 requested the Toronto Board of Trade to look into the merits of the system. The Board's Council came to the only possible conclusion: the system had manifold advantages, particularly in the field of international trade, but Canada would have to wait and see what Great Britain and the United States would do. The use of metric units was authorized in both those countries, but the system itself had never been adopted. The Council nevertheless believed it was wise to be prepared, and recommended the teaching of the metric system in the schools so that young people would have a reasonable acquaintance with it and be ready to adjust quickly if and when it was introduced.

# 4
# Empire Trade

The Board of Trade was responsible in 1902 for an event which was to have substantial future consequences. For some time it had felt the need for a better consensus on national issues, and an invitation was extended to all the Boards of Trade in the country to send delegates to a Toronto conference for the discussion of common interests. The Premier of Ontario made available the Legislative Chamber for the purpose, and the meeting, held 4–6 June, was attended by 156 delegates representing sixty-three Boards on the basis of one delegate per one hundred members. The advance submission of resolutions had been invited; they had come in great variety and were fully dealt with. In most cases generally acceptable conclusions were reached.

The subject receiving most attention was Canada's relationship with Great Britain. Part of the commentary on this question is of interest:

... we will never receive nor deserve full respect from Great Britain until either Canada takes steps frankly for independence, assuming totally the costs of her own defence, or quietly takes her place as one of the self-governing and self-respecting countries of the Empire, with full partnership in both the privileges and the burdens of Imperial concerns. It is an anachronism that England still furnishes the sinews for defence, and retains the domination over her associate countries in other than internal matters to the extent she does ... the effect from our taking steps to carry out this principle would be the increase of the stature of Canadianism ... we are too inclined to rest easy under the weak fallacy that an obligation does not exist if we do not acknowledge it.

Resolutions adopted at the conference advocated the appointment of a Royal Commission to investigate the establishment of preferential trade within the Empire; the lowering of postal rates on newspapers and periodicals moving between Great Britain and Canada; the establishment of a Canadian Commercial Depot in London; the appointment of Canadian commercial agents to serve in the principal cities of the world; a fast Canadian steamship service between Great Britain and Canada and a subsidized cargo steamship service to South Africa and Australasia; provision in the federal budget for the Dominion to participate in the defence of the Empire; the granting of power to Canada to enact its own copyright legislation; the appointment of a Railway Commission to deal with all questions arising between the common carriers and their users; the deepening of the canals between Montreal and Lake Erie and the improvement of key Canadian ports; the creation of effective means for the control and management of insolvent estates; the stimulation of immigration; and steps to introduce the metric system of weights and measures in Canada. A.E. Ames, President of the Toronto Board, supported by the representatives of the Boards of Trade of Montreal, Ottawa and Brantford, presented the resolutions adopted at the conference to Prime Minister Laurier prior to the latter's departure to attend a meeting of Empire Prime Ministers in London, and he gave them a careful hearing. One direct result was the implementation of the recommendation to promote Canadian trade with South Africa and Australasia by inaugurating a cargo steamship service under subsidy.

The greatest value of the Toronto conference was nevertheless held to be that it brought together businessmen from all parts of the country for a comparison of respective viewpoints. This could hardly fail to broaden their thinking and reduce tendencies to sectionalism. The event was in fact reported at the time as being 'the most important commercial gathering ever held in the Dominion.' No effort was made to convoke another such meeting until 1925, when a conference held in Winnipeg, again at the Toronto Board's behest, led directly to the formation of the Canadian Chamber of Commerce.

The Board never ceased to press for a more closely integrated British Empire, and on this issue it had found a champion in Joseph Chamberlain, whose Tariff Reform League had been established to promote a customs union of all nations within the Empire. Because of her free trade principles, however, Britain was prevented from entering into reciprocal trade treaties, even with her own colonies, who were obliged to seek trade alliances with foreign countries. In an address before the London Chamber of Commerce, Lord Salisbury said: 'We have nothing to offer other nations when making a commercial bargain because, by adopting free trade, you have deprived the Foreign Office of the weapons by which alone such bargains can be obtained.' At a meeting of the Trades' Union Congress the President of the British Board of Trade, T.C. Ritchie, reported that '... every European country of any importance, and also America, has for the past few years been increasing their export trade to a very large extent, while we have been going back.'

The Toronto Board of Trade was not particularly interested in entering into a debate on the theory of free trade vs protection, but felt that a moderate strengthening of commercial bonds might be accomplished by continuing effort and that this would lead ultimately to the much-desired goal of a great and united Empire. One medium it employed to advance this project was the Fourth Congress of the Chambers of Commerce of the British Empire held in London in 1900, attended by 524 delegates, sixty-five of them from Canada. The Toronto Board's delegation, led by A.E. Ames, had come carefully prepared with a resolution emphasizing the need for better commercial relations between Great Britain and her colonies and dependencies. It was debated for two days, longer than all other resolutions combined. There was opposition, and what the delegates later described as 'a flood of Cobdenite rhetoric,' but at length a resolution was unanimously adopted, namely

That this Congress urges upon Her Majesty's Government the appointment by them of a Royal Commission composed of representatives of Great Britain and her Colonies and India, to consider the possibilities of increasing and strengthening the trade relations between the different portions of the Empire, and that the Chairman nominate a representative deputation to wait upon the Prime Minister, the Secretary of State for the Colonies, and the President of the Board of Trade, and lay the question fully before them.

There was satisfaction not only with this outcome, but also with the fact that the President of the Toronto Board was invited to speak on the subject to members of Chambers of Commerce in a number of major trade centres in the United Kingdom. At the Congress's concluding banquet, presided over by the Rt Hon. the Earl of Selborne, Under-Secretary of State for the Colonies, Mr. Ames was the spokesman for the entire Canadian delegation.

As well as its primary concern for the commercial interests of the Empire, there was evident in the Board's attitude an increasing awareness of Canada's maturity and of the need for a comprehensive system 'which will admit of the local internal concerns of each country being administered within the country, and of Imperial concerns being administered by a body representing properly those portions of the Empire which right and capacity and common sense indicate should be represented.' President Ames told the 1901 Annual Meeting that '... the British Empire is not composed, and should not be considered as composed, of one great dominating country with dependencies ... Canada and Australia are entitled to a growing recognition as vital parts of the Empire, and not as dependencies – as being governors as well as governed.'

In the meantime the Board wanted a bigger market in Britain for Canadian products, particularly foodstuffs, pointing out that of the total British imports of grain and flour Canada supplied only $8\frac{1}{4}$ per cent, of meat and poultry $4\frac{5}{8}$ per cent, of butter $3\frac{3}{4}$ per cent, and even of wood, timber and pulp only $17\frac{1}{6}$ per cent. Rapid inroads into this market were being made by the United States, and in 1902 the Board joined with sister organizations and the Canadian Manufacturers' Association to point out the urgency of the situation to Laurier and members of his cabinet and urge a whole series of activities to correct it.

In the same year the Toronto Board approached the Hon. George W. Ross, Premier of Ontario, to solicit provincial support for the creation of a depot in London where Canadian products could be displayed. The Premier promptly complied by appropriating the sum of $5,000 for the purpose. After due consideration, the Board's delegation went back to express their thanks, with the qualifications that the sum really was not sufficient; would the Premier agree to their approaching the Dominion government and the other provinces with a view to raising $50,000? He agreed, and the Board, again in collaboration with the Canadian Manufacturers' Association, made a submission to Prime Minister Laurier in June 1902 urging 'the establishment of a Canadian building in London and the appointment of a Trade Commissioner who shall represent the growing manufacturing and exporting industries of Canada.'

The Fifth Congress of the Chambers of Commerce of the British Empire was held in Montreal in 1902, the first time outside England, and more than five hundred delegates attended. Once again the Toronto Board's delegation, led by W.F. Cockshutt, pleaded the case for the adoption of a sound and practical 'Policy for the Commercial Unification and Consolidation of the Empire.' Afterwards delegates toured the Maritimes, Quebec, Ontario and the west; the tour apparently impressed upon them the country's vast potential, and resulted not long afterwards in an increased flow of British investment capital. The inauguration of a system of Imperial preferences became the Board's theme at every subsequent Congress and considerable satisfaction was taken in the fact that its position was increasingly supported. But although Canada had shown its good will in 1900 by increasing its tariff preference on British goods to 33¹/₃ per cent, the goal of an Empire-wide preferential system still proved elusive.

By 1906 Canada's total of exports and imports amounted to $551 million. Most exports (51 per cent) were to Britain, and most imports (61 per cent) came from the United States: 85 per cent of the total trade was with these two countries. It was considered 'worthy of note that our Eastern ally, Japan, is reckoned among our important sources of supply, and although not as yet a large customer, may doubtless be considered one of promise for the future.' In the five-year period 1900–1904, the excess of sales to Great Britain was $320 million, while the excess of purchases from the United States was $310 million, 'so that we practically drew bills of exchange on Great Britain and paid most of them to the United States.' The Board of Trade did not like this state of affairs on the grounds that it had an adverse effect upon Canada's banking and political system.

The Seventh Congress of the Empire Chambers was held in Sydney, Australia, in 1909; Messrs. W.J. Gage and W.F. Cockshutt were the Board's delegates, leaving Vancouver on 13 August and arriving in Brisbane 5 September. In addition to accord on the question of improving Empire commercial relations, the Congress adopted a Toronto Board resolution which enunciated the principle that all parts of the Empire should be contributors on an equitable basis in Empire defence. The delegates brought back favourable impressions of Australia and foresaw a great future there for Canadian trade.

The Board's Empire orientation strongly influenced its attitude toward trade relations with the United States. Many in Canada still cherished the idea of a new reciprocity treaty, but by 1894 the Board had concluded that far too much significance was being given to this glamorous market of sixty million people; in fact for many years the balance of trade between the two countries had been preponderantly in favour of the United States and was likely to remain so. It therefore advocated 'the freest and largest measure of trade consistent with the welfare and national dignity of both countries,' but no long-term or unwarranted commitments.

Sir George W. Ross, then a Senator, addressed a well-attended general meeting of the Board on 3 November 1910. He referred to the pilgrimages made by Canadian delegations to Washington in attempts to negotiate reciprocal trading arrangements; all had proved unavailing, the effort had been given up and the initiative now lay with the United States. There the question was largely one of political expediency within the Republican Party: dissension already existed over the Payne-Aldrich Tariff Bill authorizing the President to impose a 25 per cent duty on the imports of any country discriminating in tariffs against the United States. He went on to say:

There still slumbers in the minds of leading Americans the idea that Canada will sooner or later, either from choice or necessity, become annexed to the United States. It is well known that the repeal of the [Reciprocity] Treaty of 1854 was intended to so embarrass Canada commercially as to force us into annexation.

The Hon. G.S. Boutwell, Secretary of the Treasury in President Grant's second administration and a member of Congress at the time of the repeal of the Reciprocal Treaty said: 'The fact of the annexation of Canada to the United States, whether the event shall occur in time near or remote, depends probably on our action on Reciprocity. Canada needs our markets and our facilities for ocean transportation, and as long as these advantages are denied to her, she can never attain to a high degree of prosperity. The body of farmers, labourers and trading people will favour annexation ultimately should the policy of non-intercourse be adhered to on our part, and they will outnumber the office-holding class, and thus the union of the two countries will be secured.'

... Canadians would resent any imputation of their loyalty ... and with equal force any advance for a treaty with the United States that openly or by implication suggests annexation.

Sir George discussed in some detail the dire consequences to Canada of any loss of control over its own affairs and pointed with pride to the fact that Canada had shown its mettle by solving its own problems after the repeal of the Reciprocity Treaty in 1866. Between 1898 and 1908 the commerce of Canada had increased 88.14 per cent, a rate of growth greater than that of the United States (55.19 per cent) or Great Britain (37.81 per cent) or in fact any other country except Argentina. The United States, moreover, was exhausting its own resources, and it was up to Canada to conserve hers and employ them with discretion. Reciprocity, he said, was a two-way deal, but all the high cards were in American hands.

A recent statement by United States Senator A.J. Beveridge was then quoted: 'There must be reciprocity with Canada. Our tariff with the rest of the world does not apply to our northern neighbour. That policy has already driven American manufacturers across the Canadian borders, built vast plants with American capital on Canadian soil, employing Canadian workingmen to supply trade. That capital should be kept at home to employ American workingmen to supply Canadian demand.' Sir George's address continued: '... if trade and loyalty are to be considered together it is the mother country that has the first claim upon us. In the face of a duty of 25.7 per cent on all the goods she sells us we are allowed free access to her markets, while the Americans exact a duty of 42 per cent for a similar privilege. Should we forget this?' Cries of 'No! No!' were heard from the audience.

After enlarging on the desirability of maintaining ties with Britain, whose capital investment of an estimated £300 million in Canada had been such an important factor in building the country, the speaker reminded his audience that any treaty with the United States would be subject to interpretation, and for his part he did not want to see 'any act of the Canadian people subject to interpretation at Washington.' He saw no present need for a treaty of reciprocity, but believed that the trade relationship could be adjusted as necessary by independent legislation in both countries.

The members of the Toronto Board of Trade showed themselves to be heartily in accord with the sentiments expressed by Sir George Ross. The following year the terms of a proposed trade agreement with the United States were presented to Parliament, whereupon the Board called another general meeting which again attracted an overflow attendance. A resolution in opposition to the agreement was moved by Sir Edmund Walker, seconded by J.W. Flavelle and carried by an overwhelming majority. Sir Wilfrid Laurier, speaking in the House of Commons, paid Sir Edmund the compliment of saying that the resolution contained in condensed form all the arguments with which Parliament had been dealing. The election of that year indicated clear support for the position taken by the Board of Trade, and the reciprocity issue faded away.

In 1900 Canada had involved herself in a trade dispute with Germany. Two years earlier Great Britain, at the request of the Dominion government, had abrogated a Treaty of Trade and Commerce between the British Empire and the Empire of Germany, whereupon Germany promptly imposed special tariffs on Canadian goods, presumably in retaliation for the tariff concessions granted by Canada to Britain. As a result Canada's exports of agricultural products to Germany almost ceased, although the imports of German manufactured goods continued to increase. Against German imports of nearly $7.4 million exports from Canadian ports amounted to only $2.2 million, and two-thirds of this amount represented the value of produce from the United States passing through Canada. Resentment was aggravated by the fact that Germany continued to admit

American agricultural products at low tariffs although American tariffs against German goods were double those imposed by Canada. The Board of Trade made representations to Laurier requesting retaliation by the Canadian government to redress the situation. After some delay a surtax was imposed on German imports. When it finally came the impost was unexpected and the Board had to ask for a three-month deferment to protect merchants who had made purchases as yet undelivered. It was granted. Not long afterwards the Germans proposed a conference on the whole question of tariff policy.

However, it was 1912 before a German trade delegation came to Canada led by Dr Gustav Stresemann, then President of the German-Canadian Economic Association (a body formed in Germany to promote trade between the two countries) and a deputy in the German Reichstag. On 26 October the group was entertained at a luncheon by the Toronto Board of Trade and the Canadian Manufacturers' Association. Stresemann declared that there was no hostile feeling harboured in Germany, either toward England or Canada. He maintained that a mutually beneficial increase in the exchange of products between Canada and Germany lacked only the establishment of closer and more friendly relations between the businessmen of the two countries. By an odd coincidence two members of the Board, G.T. Somers and W.K. George, were in Berlin on the very day of the Toronto luncheon as dinner guests of that city's Chamber of Commerce. On their return they also reported expressions of the kindliest feelings toward Canada, and particularly toward the Toronto Board of Trade. In their German travels Messrs Somers and George had been immensely impressed by evidences of Germany's industrial growth and by the great strides made in the fields of technical and industrial education. Germany was at this time making enormous efforts to expand its world trade, and more than one nation was becoming alarmed at the dominant position it was assuming. At the fifth International Congress of Chambers of Commerce held in Boston in September 1912 the German delegation was by far the largest; the first item on the agenda for this occasion was world peace.

The Toronto Board was also looking for new trading partners. Asiatic markets were opening up by 1905, and the Board urged Canada to take advantage of her favourable position in what it saw as a twentieth-century struggle for commercial supremacy in the Pacific Basin. In 1906 James D. Allan travelled to the West Indies as the Board's delegate to investigate trading possibilities there. Lines of communication were established and soon afterwards the federal government appointed a Trade Commissioner to this territory to facilitate trading arrangements.

Closer to home, the Board was pressing for more effective action to develop the latent resources of northern Ontario. In 1900 the Ontario government was urged to formulate positive policies which would stimulate interest in this vast and rich territory; public meetings were sponsored by the Board to generate press attention both in and outside the country, and efforts were supported to direct the flow of immigrants into the region. At this time the province included the long-occupied and settled lands in the south, 'New Ontario', which consisted of a recently-settled fringe comprising some million and a half acres, and an area beyond North Bay of perhaps sixteen million acres which was almost wholly unoccupied and only partially explored. It had long been realized that there was great mineral and timber wealth in the newer parts, but real excitement was aroused only after the province of Ontario decided to build the Temiskaming and Northern Ontario Railway and two old prospectors, McKinley and Darreagh, who had sub-contracted to supply ties for the line, in 1903 had the wits to secure an assay on rock blasted from one of the cuts and found it running at 3,000 ounces of silver to the ton. The assumption had generally been made that the T. & N.O. alignment would run through barren country, but after the first smell of silver, the rock used at some points as ballast in laying the rail was assayed at $3,000 a ton. Interest focused on the Cobalt area, and by 1905 the Board's President, James D. Allan, was reporting that 'results were surpassing the wildest hopes.' Two years later silver production was reported at over ten million ounces and gold at 3,810 ounces. Sudbury in the same year produced eleven thousand tons of nickel.

The Board applauded the provincial government for its initiative in undertaking the T. & N.O. Railway and recorded its support for an extension to James Bay. By 1907 the Canadian Northern Railway had completed its line to Sudbury, and to mark the occasion a Board of Trade party made a 'delightful excursion' to that city, also visiting Key Harbour and the iron deposits on Moose Mountain. Following an address to the members by J.L. Englehart, Chairman of the Temiskaming and Northern Ontario Railway Commission, another tour of the north country, this time with 150 participants, was undertaken in June 1911 under the supervision of R. Home Smith, Chairman of the Board's Ontario Trade Development Committee. The expedition was considered a lesson to the Board of Trade on what had to be done to supply the north with goods and services and generally contribute to its development. The Board reacted by immediately appointing a special committee on northern Ontario development under Home Smith's chairmanship, and it set to work with enthusiasm and considerable success to develop interest in this new territory and establish effective communications between business and political leaders in the northern and southern parts of the province. Fred W. Field was appointed a special commissioner to northern Ontario, and his reports and maps were widely circulated among the Board's membership.

The Board wished to dispel the feeling in the north country that Toronto's interest was exclusively in the profits to be made from the mines. Its opportunity came tragically on 11 July 1911, when forest fires swept the mining district, destroying Cochrane, Pottsville and South Porcupine with a high loss of life, and causing serious damage as far south as Matheson. Acting in conjunction with the city of Toronto, the Board at once set up a committee to raise relief funds, and in a short time a sum of more than $60,000 had been collected, together with supplies of clothing and other necessities contributed by both firms and individuals. A carload of food, clothing and medicines sent independently by the T. Eaton Company proved a big factor in the relief of immediate suffering. Most of the money collected was used to assist widows and orphans, and the direction of the Supreme Court of Ontario was requested regarding the use to be made of an $18,000 remainder. By judgment of the Court made on 17 October 1913 the surplus funds were divided equally to establish two hospitals, one near Cochrane and the other in the Porcupine mining division. The Board's committee accepted from W.S. Edwards the gift of a plot of land east of Porcupine Lake in the District of Sudbury as a cemetery for twenty of the sixty-eight victims of the holocaust whose bodies were either unclaimed or unidentifiable. A granite monument was erected with this inscription:

Erected by the Citizens of Canada, through the Northern Ontario Fire Relief Committee of the Toronto Board of Trade, to the memory of those who suffered and lost their lives in the great holocaust that swept this district, July 11th, 1911.

Such philanthropic effort was not new; in 1892 the Board had raised more than $10,000 from among its own members to relieve suffering after a fire in St John's, Newfoundland, and in 1900 a substantial sum was collected and forwarded to help victims of a disastrous fire in Hull and Ottawa.

In a somewhat different context, after the death of five firemen in a fire on the premises of Messrs P. McIntosh & Sons on Front Street the Board's Council decided that a permanent fund should be set up, from which the income would be used to assist the families of firemen killed in the execution of their duties. A committee was appointed under J.W. Flavelle which secured a grant of $25,000 from the city; a public appeal was conducted and it produced another $54,300. Trustees of the fund were appointed, including the President of the Board of Trade; the city Treasurer acted as administrator, and the money was used to afford relief as necessary.

An awakening of interest in forest conservation received the Board's warm support. The Canadian Forestry Association held its Annual Meeting in Toronto in 1909 with the Board acting as host, and a year earlier A.H.D. Ross of the University of Toronto's Faculty of Forestry had been the principal speaker at a Board of Trade general meeting. 'In the past,' he said, 'our forests have been our greatest source of wealth, and only slowly does it seem to dawn upon the public mind that their loss, without adequate restoration, will be the deadliest imaginable blow to our future progress and prosperity.' Referring to the current average revenue of $4.5 million annually from forest lands controlled by the federal and provincial governments, Mr Ross pleaded for comprehensive and immediate steps to preserve forest lands and control their use. He concluded: 'The evils which have overtaken other lands can only be averted by the adoption of a far-sighted, aggressive and business-like policy based upon an adequate, scientific and practical grasp of the whole situation in all its respects.' The Board took the position that the provincial government should act immediately on this advice.

Another of the Board's projects in the provincial field at this time was to have enduring consequences. Progress toward some of the larger objectives would clearly be improved if efforts were based on a wide consensus; this realization had prompted the Board to bring together its sister organizations from across the Dominion at the conference of 1902. In 1910 the Council initiated efforts to create a body which would represent opinion throughout the province. Preliminary meetings were held and plans drawn for an inaugural general session the following year of the Ontario Associated Boards of Trade. The session was held in Toronto's City Hall 21 and 22 February 1911, and proved a great success. The Toronto city council offered every co-operation and tendered a luncheon to the delegates, while the Toronto Board was host at a banquet held at the National Club. Issues of common concern were discussed and a great spirit of co-operation was developed, resulting, it was felt, in a consolidation of the aims of businessmen from all parts of the province. W.J. Gage, who as President of the Toronto Board in 1910 had had a good deal to do with preliminary arrangements, was elected the first President of the new organization, and warm appreciation was conveyed to the other Toronto members who had worked with him to achieve such an excellent result.

A second Annual Meeting was held the following year, again in Toronto; it was apparently less euphoric and devoted itself solidly to the affairs of the day. Among the subjects discussed were a program for development in northern Ontario, the improvement of Ontario waterways and harbours, especially the Welland Canal, and Chicago's application for authorization to divert more water from Lake Michigan into its drainage canal. Strong objection was taken to the latter proposal, as a menace to Canadian marine interests; the objection was conveyed to Ottawa, which in turn recorded opposition in Washington, and the Chicago application was disallowed. With the Toronto Board as the prime mover the new federation continued to meet annually, changing its name to the unwieldy Ontario Associated Boards of Trade and Chambers of Commerce and becoming much later simply the Ontario Chamber of Commerce.

There was an increasing awareness on the part of businessmen of the need to upgrade the qualifications of citizens, both native and immigrant to fit them to play their part more effectively in an increasingly sophisticated industrial and commercial system. The Board of Trade had strongly urged the provision of better methods of technical education years before, and in 1899 a report by a special committee on technical education had received wide attention. The Board had assisted in a revision of the curricula at both the Toronto Technical School and the Department of Commerce and Finance in the University of Toronto. Its efforts in both cases were aimed at providing practical instruction which would better equip young people to avail themselves of career opportunities in the business world. The establishment in 1873 of a School of Practical Science affiliated with the University of Toronto had been applauded and in 1910 the Board sought government legislation and funds to broaden its scope and improve its facilities. Representatives of the Board had conferred with the Minister of Education in May 1901 regarding the provision of technical and commercial instruction in secondary schools and rendered support in subsequent approaches to the Dominion government for aid in establishing suitable courses of instruction. In the same year James D. Allan, acting for the Board, visited schools in Chicago and returned with specific recommendations for the introduction of new training methods based on the Chicago models. 'Methods of business,' he said, 'are constantly changing but we do not change our methods of training to meet them. The explanation of this probably is that practical business men have had no part in the preparation of educational curricula, which have failed to recognize the necessity of an education that bears some relation to the present environment or probable future of the student.'

As Chairman of the Board's Committee on Technical Education in 1901, W.F. Cockshutt reported that the commercial courses at the University were not proving as successful as had been hoped due to insufficient support from manufacturing and commercial interests and apathy on the part of the University. Scholarships offered by the Board had not been awarded, and the offer was not repeated. Progress was being made, however, toward a new technical school, although the Board and others interested expressed keen disappointment in the city's reduced allocation for this purpose in its 1902 budget.

The establishment of a Toronto Board of Education in 1903 seemed a step in the right direction, and the Board of Trade bent its efforts to see that competent men were elected as trustees. As technical schools would come under the jurisdiction of the new Board of Education the Board decided to withdraw from direct participation in this field, although it did oppose the Board of Education's choice of location for the new technical school and, with others, took credit for its eventual siting in the residential western sector. The creation of this facility, at a cost of more than a million dollars, seemed assured by 1912, and the Board took much satisfaction in this culmination of its considerable effort, led throughout by J.D. Allan. The Central Technical School was opened on 1 September 1915, offering regular classes in the practical sciences and both day and night classes in industrial processes and technical operations. It almost immediately became one of the city's main centres of educational activity. Members of a Royal Commission on Technical Education visited Toronto late in 1910. The Board was requested to appear and its representatives used the opportunity to present an outline of the Board's attitude, efforts and recommendations in this field over the past thirteen years.

In the same year the provincial government enacted legislation to provide for instruction in certain mercantile and manufacturing fields, and the Board was requested to appoint four representatives on the Advisory Commercial Committee of the High School of Commerce and Finance. The appointees were Charles Marriott as chairman, H.D. Lockhart Gordon, Thomas Bradshaw and T.D. Bailey. The Board agreed to provide gold and silver medals annually for competition among the students of the new school. The inauguration of the commercial courses fully justified the Board's efforts and hopes: by 1912 there were three hundred day scholars and more than six hundred were enrolled in evening classes.

The question of copyright legislation was raised for the Board's attention in 1899 by W.J. Gage, a member of the Council and of the Board's Wholesale Booksellers' and Stationers' Section. The conditions under which Canadian publishers operated were eminently unsatisfactory and placed them substantially at the mercy of British and American interests. While there had been legislation of a sort in Canada since 1868 under which copyrights could be registered, the protection it afforded had never proved adequate and the jurisdictional position *vis à vis* Ottawa and London remained unclear. A number of efforts to improve the situation had proved unavailing. In 1895 Hall Caine, representing the British Authors' Association, came to Canada to confer with the Canadian Copyright Association and helped draft a proposed Bill, but nothing came of it. Delegates of the Toronto Board of Trade attending the Fourth Annual Congress of the Chambers of Commerce of the British Empire in London in 1900 had secured adoption of a resolution favouring the right of the colonies to enact their own copyright laws, and the Canadian government was showing some disposition to move in the matter, but again there was no effective outcome. Two years later a delegation from the Toronto and Ottawa Boards of Trade took up the matter directly with the Minister of Justice, whose oral assurance that it would receive serious consideration was the only result. There was in fact a long wait before any effective action was taken. The United Kingdom Copyright Act of 1911 at last provided a mode; a Canadian Copyright Act was enacted ten years later and finally came into effect on 1 January 1924, at which time Canada also subscribed to the Berne Convention.

Apart from considerations of simple justice, the Board's concern was to foster the development of an indigenous publishing industry and, as a supplementary benefit, to promote employment in the paper and printing industries and related trades. Writing about Canadian paper production in 1900, W.J. Gage said:

Twenty-five years ago, when the writer started in business in Toronto, the great bulk of our paper came from Great Britain and English travellers regularly visited the Canadian trade to supply our demands. Today Canadian paper mills can meet all our requirements, and some of them have their London offices. Before the close of the next twenty-five years it is not too much to expect that the great London dailies will be printed on Canadian-made paper and that travellers from the Toronto paper-makers and stationers will regularly sell to the trade of Great Britain in the interests of their respective houses.

Toronto had become the centre of English-language book publishing in

Canada, and in 1910 a Book Publishers' Section of the Board of Trade was formed, comprising representatives of all the major concerns. It became recognized in time as the spokesman for publishers throughout Canada and played an important part in securing better recognition for this industry.

The generation of electrical power from Niagara Falls and the possibility of delivering low-cost power to the city and its environs in 1900 promised to have a substantial impact on Toronto's manufacturing activity. The Toronto Electric Light Company was at the time the city's only power supplier; not only were the rates high, since it relied on expensive imported fuels in the steam-powered generating plant, but a low capacity severely limited its ability to serve large industrial users. Access to large supplies of cheap electrical power was expected to lower manufacturing costs and give incentive to the establishment of wholly new types of manufacturing enterprise. Sir William Siemens, the famous British electrical engineer, had been the first to suggest the use of the falls at Niagara as a source of electrical energy in 1877, and he had then estimated the productive capacity at some seventeen million horsepower. In 1896 Buffalo was the first city to receive power from Niagara, supplied by the Niagara Falls Power Company from its works at the American falls.

Practicability having been thus established, the obvious question was: Why should the much greater flow of the Canadian falls not be used to generate power for distribution among the communities of southern Ontario? In 1900 the Toronto city council authorized enquiries into the matter, and the Board of Trade appointed its own special committee to investigate and report. The members of the committee were W.E.H. Massey, President of the Massey Harris Company, as chairman, Elias Rogers, Wm Stone and A.E. Kemp. Their report of 25 April 1900 was rather curious. It took the position that steam was the most important power factor, notwithstanding the great advances made by electricity, the latter being 'a secondary force, a handmaiden or servant of steam or some other primary power ... [possessing] limitations which are seldom realized or understood.' Other power sources were reviewed, including the gasoline engine, from which 'splendid results are being obtained by the latest machines, the makers guaranteeing that a wine gallon of gasoline will produce a horse-power for 10 hours,' and compressed air, which was coming into use and might be applied to various purposes. Niagara was recognized by the committee as an important energy source 'close enough to lead us to hope that at some time in the not too distant future it will supply us with electric energy,' but the opinion was expressed that due to high installation costs, depreciation and other factors 'the majority of our leading factories would not readily change to the electric power, even under quite favourable circumstances as to price.'

In spite of this somewhat negative attitude, the committee suggested that the Board of Trade appoint a new committee to investigate the possibility of providing power for the city through one of the companies at Niagara Falls. A likely choice was the Ontario Power Company, which was about to begin operations and had already signified its intention of serving Toronto. The thought was put forward that the city of Toronto should control its Niagara power connection. Problems of transmission still had to be solved. The land distance from Niagara Falls to Toronto was more than seventy miles, and there was as yet little experience on which to base the design of power lines of such length. The committee thought it not impracticable to consider underwater lines across the lake, thus shortening the distance to forty-one miles.

Few doubted the desirability of feeding power from Niagara to Toronto's homes and industries, provided it was cheap power. The existing private electrical interests were strongly profit-oriented and showed little disposition to conduct their operations for anyone's good but their own, and the idea of public ownership began to establish itself firmly. The city of Toronto was balked by the Ontario legislature in efforts to secure authority to set up a municipally-owned utility that would supply the city with electricity, and by 1900 the issue had generated considerable heat. Battle lines were drawn between the private developers and the proponents of a public system, with the Ontario legislature, in the early stages at least, protecting the private interests. Substantial initiative in the organization of an action group to press for cheap electrical power from Niagara through a publicly-owned system was given by the Boards of Trade of Waterloo, Berlin (later Kitchener), Galt and Guelph. After an important meeting in Berlin on 9 June 1902, attended by representatives of all the concerned communities and addressed by C.H. Mitchell, a consulting engineer for the Ontario Power Company (later to become President of the Toronto Board of Trade and Dean of Engineering at the University of Toronto), a committee was appointed to work for the establishment of a government commission responsible for the transmission of electricity to the various municipalities. The latter would then be solely responsible for its distribution to local users. Toronto was represented on the committee by Alderman F.S. Spence and P.W. Ellis, the latter a member of the Council of the Toronto Board.

A complex campaign with strong political overtones ensued. The Toronto Board actively participated on behalf of public ownership and supported the city of Toronto in renewed, but unsuccessful, representations to the Ontario Liberal Premier, George W. Ross. Unremitting pressure finally led to an Ontario Power Act, a compromise measure by which the Ontario Power Commission was created under the chairmanship of E.W.B. Snider, with P.W. Ellis as Vice-Chairman, to undertake an extensive investigation of the whole situation. The advent of a Conservative government under James P. Whitney in 1905 quickly and radically changed the picture. By July an Order-in-Council had created the Hydro-Electric Power Commission of the Province of Ontario, with Adam Beck, member for London, as Chairman and P.W. Ellis and George Pattison of Preston his fellow commissioners.

The fight was not over, but the advocates of a public hydro system and cheap rates smelled victory in the air and pressed every advantage. Adam Beck was now the protagonist, and on 7 May 1906 he introduced a Bill in the Ontario legislature – An Act to Provide for the Transmission of Electrical Power to Municipalities – to create the Hydro-Electric Commission of Ontario as an administrative body and establish the conditions under which it would function. The Bill passed and received Royal assent on 14 May, and shortly thereafter the first three commissioners were appointed: Adam Beck, the Hon. John S. Hendrie, Mayor of Hamilton, and Cecil B. Smith, an engineer. So Hydro was launched; intimidating obstacles lay ahead – legal, political, technical and financial – but they were overcome and the first power from Niagara over the new system was delivered to Berlin on 11 October 1910. Toronto entered the system in March the following year and, as the lines proliferated throughout southern Ontario, demand increased once the low cost and labour benefits available were recognized.

The Toronto Board of Trade played a secondary but not inconsiderable role in the long controversy over the establishment of Ontario Hydro. As a strong free-enterprise organization one can imagine some soul-searching as the public ownership forces mobilized to crush the private interests which had secured concessions and committed themselves heavily to power development at Niagara. But the importance of an abundant supply of cheap power to the development of local industries and the overall benefits to citizens generally outweighed all other considerations, and the Board's influence was directed at every opportunity in support of the project. At both private and public meetings Adam Beck and P.W. Ellis were provided by the Board with forums for the presentation of their proposals, and Board representatives were prominently identified with most of the activities organized to forward the undertaking.

On two issues the Board took some pains to express its point of view. While recognizing that the public interest must be served, it felt strongly that the private developers who had launched substantial enterprises for power development at Niagara should be fairly dealt with on the assumption of rights by Ontario Hydro and should be equitably recompensed for properties acquired; and it advocated that in carrying out the works required for power generation adequate steps be taken to preserve the scenic beauty of Niagara Falls and its environs, possibly by a union of Ontario Hydro with the Queen Victoria Niagara Falls Park Commission. The latter, created in 1885, had been the target of much criticism for its collaboration with private companies in their development efforts, but to its credit the Commission had always insisted that any construction works in no way detract from the beauty of their surroundings. The Board wanted to make sure that this policy would be continued.

The Board retained some flexibility on questions of monopoly and public ownership. It came down firmly on the side of public ownership in the case of a utility like Hydro and, although in 1897 the Board had successfully opposed an application by the Bell Telephone Company for an increase in rates, it had done so not because it saw anything wrong with a monopoly in this type of service but because it wanted legislation to ensure that any such application was subject to proper review and control. It nevertheless took credit for saving Toronto users some $200,000 a year by securing a refusal of Bell's request. Again in 1902 the Board joined the city of Toronto in opposing an application made by the Bell Telephone Company for authority to increase its capital stock and secured a year's postponement of the required legislation to permit thorough examination. In 1914 a city of Toronto proposal to assume municipal ownership of the street railway system by purchase for a sum of $33 million met with strong Board of Trade objection, and the city withdrew the offer.

By the turn of the century Torontonians were beginning to become critical of their Industrial Exhibition. Although it was moving along year after year with reasonable success, the vigour of its early purpose had waned and through lack of innovation, due mainly to inadequate financial resources, it no longer seemed to be keeping pace with the times. The Board of Trade asked its representatives to the Exhibition to look into the situation using a special committee of members appointed for the purpose, and when their report appeared in 1901 it received much attention in the local press. It pointed out that the citizens had 'had this magnificent advertisement for twenty-three years for nothing,' and that now funds were needed for 'a pronounced forward step,' otherwise it would gradually lose importance. The report noted an attitude which was to become all too common in the future: 'Many citizens belittle the Exhibition as being "the same old thing over and over again".'

There was no doubt in anyone's mind that the Exhibition was a valuable asset, not only to Toronto but to the whole country, as a showplace of Canadian products and a means of promoting their sale in world markets. The Board of Trade gave its full support to a city by-law authorizing bonds in the amount of $133,000 to erect three new Exhibition buildings – a Manufacturers' Building, an Art Gallery and a Dairy Building – and it did what it could to encourage public support. In another attempt to lift the Exhibition out of its doldrums, the Board suggested in 1900 that the next year's operation should be broadened in scope by incorporating displays from all the provinces, with financial assistance from the federal government. This took a little time, but the 1903 Dominion Exhibition, as it was called, received support from the Quebec and federal governments, and its extensive displays of 'Made in Canada' goods and demonstrations of industrial processes not only attracted wide attention but were looked upon as an evidence of Canada's growing industrial strength.

Around this time it was realized Toronto had some potential as a tourist attraction. Heretofore visitors had come chiefly on business, but the Board of Trade suggested that efforts be initiated to attract people from nearby American centres in the belief that the city and its surroundings had much to offer and that such an inflow would produce useful revenue for the merchants and service industries. There was some doubt about the adequacy of hotel accommodation; the three best hotels, the Grand Union, Queen's and Rossin House, were basically commercial houses, not really designed for tourist business. Talk of a new one probably referred to the King Edward, which was in fact completed in 1903, and was for many years the city's principal hostelry. The Board worked hard over a number of years to stimulate tourist traffic and in 1911 induced the city to set up the Toronto Publicity Association for this specific purpose. Through lack of funds, however, the association was unable to carry out an effective program.

# 5
# Transportation

Of all the Board of Trade's concerns, the one that most consistently drew its attention from the earliest years was transportation. The aim was always to ensure for Toronto the place the Board felt it so obviously deserved in the country's developing network of rails, roads and waterways, and to preserve equity in rates and tariffs and other conditions affecting the movement of people and goods. In this it concurred with a viewpoint expressed by James Mills, Railway Commissioner, in an address to the Canadian Club of Ottawa in 1908:

... the problem of transportation ... is *the* problem of the country, for however abundant and useful the products of our soil and the livestock of our farms, however great the quantity and excellent the quality of the timbers in our forests, however varied and rich the ores in our mines, however ingenious in design and high-class in workmanship the output of our factories, they are all to a large extent valueless unless we have fairly efficient and not unreasonably expensive means of carrying them from the localities where they are produced to localities where they are wanted – to places where there are markets for them.

That efficient transport facilities were vital to Toronto is perhaps exemplified by its imports of coal alone: in the year 1903, a typical year, well over a million tons of anthracite and bituminous coals entered the city by rail and water carriers. In the same year 3,164 vessels arrived at the port of Toronto.

Conscious always of its competition with Montreal, Toronto felt itself at a disadvantage being so far removed from the CPR's transcontinental line, which carried the trade of northern Ontario and all of western Canada to the Montreal terminus. Toronto's only access to the line was via the Grand Trunk Railway to North Bay, and as compensation the Board of Trade urged the government to encourage the construction of a line from Sudbury through the Parry Sound district, thus affording the settlers in this new territory a direct Toronto connection. Such a line was in fact built shortly thereafter, and on 15 June 1908 the Board tendered a dinner to Sir Thomas Shaughnessy, CPR President, to mark the opening of this short-cut to the west via Sudbury, which 'practically places Toronto on the main line of the CPR and means a saving of eight hours between Toronto and Winnipeg.'

Although it had no particular love for the Grand Trunk, the Board supported the latter's 1903 proposal to build another trans-continental line, considering it necessary to open up northwestern Ontario and western Canada. At this time the Toronto-based and favoured Canadian Northern Railway was vigorously pushing its way west, north of the CPR. It was expected eventually to reach the west coast, and Canada would then have, assuming completion of the Grand Trunk, three railways running right across the continent. The entry of the Canadian Northern into Toronto in 1906 was marked by a banquet sponsored by the Board of Trade, and by 1909 this railway was operating a 4,700-mile system and had opened up vast territories between Lake Superior and the Rocky Mountains. It moved forty million bushels of wheat from the prairies to Port Arthur in that year and its earnings had grown to $12.8 million from a mere $60,000 in 1897. The Canadian Northern also had its headquarters in Toronto for its 'Royal Line' trans-Atlantic steamship service from Montreal to Bristol.

In 1903 there were 18,257 miles of steam railway lines in operation, and over that twelve-month period they carried well over 22 million passengers and 47 million tons of freight. Gross earnings were $86 million and expenses $65 million. In spite of the apparent size and health of railway operations shippers were complaining of freight congestion everywhere, and the Board of Trade felt itself amply justified in pressing for still more extensive services. On more than one occasion its representatives went directly to the railways seeking more energetic operational policies and additional freight terminals, and it pleaded unceasingly for the appointment of officials with power to exercise authority over railway administration in the Toronto region.

The Board claimed a great victory when the Board of Railway Commissioners for Canada was appointed in 1903. For many years it had strenuously and persistently sought the establishment of such a body and at last it had achieved, if not an end to disputes with the carriers, at least an efficient means whereby such disputes could be adjudicated. The Board of Railway Commissioners, appointed under the Railway Act, initially consisted of three commissioners and staff, and was empowered to deal with all railway operations. One of the commissioners, James Mills, described its functions:

The Commission is a Court of Record, with very wide jurisdiction in matters pertaining to railways and railway companies; it has all the powers, rights and privileges which are vested in a Superior Court, and powers much greater than the powers of any other Court in the Dominion. The findings of the Board on questions of fact within its jurisdiction are binding and conclusive; every decision or order of the Board is final; the Board is not bound by the findings of other Courts, and no order, decision or proceeding of the Board can be questioned or reviewed, restrained or removed by prohibition, injunction, *certiorari*, or any other process or proceedings in any Court. There is a right of appeal from the Board to the Supreme Court of Canada on questions of jurisdiction, and the Board may allow appeals to the same Court on questions of law, but the only body which of itself can rescind or vary any order, decision, rule or regulation of the Board is the Governor-in-Council.

Doubtless the reason for giving such extensive powers to the Commission was the hope that through it, by direct, simple and informal proceedings, shippers and others having dealings with railway companies, express companies and telephone companies, might have their disputes settled and get substantial justice without expensive litigation and the possibility of appeals carried from court to court; and the greatness of the power bestowed has imposed on the Commission the obligation to exercise due care, deliberation and caution in everything it does or refuses to do.

The Commissioners planned a session in Toronto soon after their appointment and the Board's Council offered its services to Board members by making presentations on their behalf in matters of general concern.

The Board of Trade, quick to avail itself of the new facility, scored what it termed a 'decisive success' after protesting the provisions of a proposed new schedule of express rates. In 1904 it also entered an appeal against discriminatory freight rates, pursuing its case for three years with so much vigour against strong opposition from the railways that the Board of Railway Commissioners conceded and a new schedule of tariffs was brought into effect on 1 January 1908. It effected savings of between 5½ and 21 per cent, benefited all shippers in both Ontario and Quebec, and removed inequities that the Board of Trade had been complaining about for years.

The Board of Trade, the Canadian Manufacturers' Association and other organizations joined forces and were successful after a year's argument in securing the Railway Commissioners' assent to the introduction, starting 15 July 1909, of an Order Bill of Lading and a Straight Bill of Lading as aids to shipping operations. It was no wonder that the Board felt after a few years' experience that the Railway Commissioners were 'fulfilling an extremely valuable function.'

Realizing the number and complexity of problems affecting the movement of goods, the Board's Council in 1912 established a separate Traffic Department under the general supervision of the Railway and Transportation Committee to deal with adjustments of freight and express rates, the provision of facilities for freight handling and the convenience and costs of passenger services. It also kept on file for the reference of members a complete set of freight, express and passenger tariffs. Thomas Marshall was employed as manager of the Department; under his direction it quickly assumed an important place in the Board's total operations and became the means for dealing with innumerable questions of both individual and general concern.

The Board raised with the Commissioners the big issue of what to do about the Esplanade across Toronto's waterfront. The barrier created by the railways' rights-of-way had been for years an annoyance to the citizens and to the Board of Trade in particular. From time to time the railways had indicated a willingness to participate in the construction of bridge crossings at some of the main streets, but no plan was ever developed and it seemed clear that nothing would be done until the issue was forced by a competent authority. The Board found the railways' unwillingness to deal with the problem hard to understand; it was seriously antagonizing a community that generated a very large part of their total business.

It was thought for a while that the waterfront situation might best be dealt with as part of a drive for the elimination of level-crossings throughout the city, and in 1904 the Board suggested the appointment of an independent commission to generate action on the basis of a comprehensive plan. Such a move had proved fruitful in Buffalo, and in other American cities formulas had been worked out for the joint financing of grade separation by the railways, the municipalities and the federal government. The advent of the Board of Railway Commissioners offered a more direct line of approach, however, and in 1905 the Board of Trade solicited its intervention and received assurance that the matter would be looked into. This action stimulated the city council to appoint a special committee, and it seemed that things were moving at last. Soon afterwards, the city asked the Board of Trade to undertake engineering studies, and the Board responded by setting up a committee under J.W. Woods with power to secure professional advice. Engineering consultants R.M. Berrian of Boston and J.W. Moyes of Toronto were retained; a plan of waterfront development was prepared and presented to the city council in 1907, which they accepted and forwarded to the Board of Railway Commissioners later that year. Its many provisions included the siting of a new Union Station on land earlier acquired by the railways for such a purpose south of Front Street and west of Bay Street, with the necessary approaches.

Almost entirely on the initiative taken by the Board of Trade, the Board of Railway Commissioners in 1908 issued an order directing the construction within two years of a four-track viaduct along the Esplanade with separation of the railway and street grades or other adequate measures for the protection of the public at all main street intersections. The order embodied virtually all of the features advocated by the Board of Trade; this was a triumph, and due tribute was paid to J.W. Woods and his associates, whose considerable efforts had led to this splendid result.

It seemed as though the railway viaduct was almost an accomplished fact, and indeed the grade separation of the segment between Bathurst Street and the Humber River was undertaken and the work completed by 1909. There were engineering problems to be overcome in the central sector but, more importantly, the railways were strenuously objecting to the extensive provisions of the Railway Commissioners' order. They appealed the order to the Privy Council of England in 1910 on the grounds that the Board of Railway Commissioners lacked jurisdiction but the appeal was dismissed and the order re-affirmed. Although the Commissioners then acted to secure compliance, the railways used every delaying tactic possible. They proposed a new alignment for the viaduct, which they thought would be cheaper to build, and in 1913 succeeded in negotiating a new agreement among all the parties concerned. It was ratified by the Board of Railway Commissioners, who set a completion date of 29 July 1919. The matter now seemed again to have been brought to a satisfactory conclusion, and the railways began purchasing the lands required for the new alignment south of the Esplanade between Yonge and Cherry Streets on the understanding that when all the necessary lands had been acquired and provision made for a 230-foot right-of-way, the Toronto Harbour Commissioners should have the right, by paying one-half of the amount paid for the entire property, to take over all the balance remaining for industrial and commercial development.

The Board's President was moved to remark at this stage that 'the viaduct fight has been one of the hardest campaigns for public rights in the history of Toronto, and the members of the Toronto Board of Trade should take pride in the knowledge that the initiative, continuance and final success of this great struggle lies to the credit of the Board.' However, his gratification in the outcome was premature. The Board maintained its viaduct committee under Mr. Woods to work with the city in pressing for continuation of the action begun, but the war and its aftermath interrupted progress and when it became possible to resume work in the early 1920s fresh arguments broke out.

Apart from considerations of safety and convenience, the railway viaduct was needed to permit effective development and use of waterfront lands. In 1892 a tripartite agreement had been worked out establishing the rights and privileges of the two railways – the Grand Trunk and the Canadian Pacific – and the city of Toronto with respect to terminal facilities on the Esplanade and along the waterfront. By 1910 the railway companies and private industrial concerns owned or controlled three-quarters of the waterfront lands between Cherry Street and the foot of Yonge Street, while the city owned the balance. In the absence of any overall plan or control, the area, including the harbour facilities, had seriously deteriorated and this prompted the strong action by the Board of Trade leading to the passage of the Toronto Harbour Commissioners Act of 19 May 1911. It repealed all previous acts and set up a five-man commission, three appointed by the city and two by the federal government, one of the latter to be named on recommendation of the Board of Trade. The first Chairman of the Commissioners was Lionel H. Clarke, who had been President of the Board of Trade in 1908; the other members were R. Home Smith, T.L. Church, and F.S. Spence, all appointed by the city, and R.S. Gourlay, nominated by the Board of Trade. The new Act extended and defined the powers of the Commissioners, and by the end of 1911 the city had conveyed to them for development, in fee simple, all its waterfront lands and properties, including Ashbridge's Bay and Marsh.

What the Board of Trade now wanted was a thoroughgoing plan for the whole waterfront, which it believed had been woefully neglected. It saw two thousand acres of land there as an undeveloped asset, the value of which would be enhanced if an improved route to the head of the lakes were opened up through a deepened Welland Canal, and lake traffic thus increased. In addition to these practical benefits, the Board envisaged a splendid boulevard along the twelve-mile lakefront, stretching from Woodbine Avenue to the Humber River, and the creation of some nine hundred acres of new parkland. With the creation of a new and safer western channel into Toronto Bay it also suggested filling in the old channel to provide an additional sixty acres of land which could be used for boulevard and park purposes. The Harbour Commissioners, fully in accord with this thinking, prepared a plan of development, and its first public presentation was to the members of the Board of Trade by the Board's representative to the Commissioners, R.S. Gourlay, on 15 November 1912. The plan called for the reclamation of the Ashbridge's Bay area to provide 646 acres of industrial land, the improvement of the inner harbour and dredging to a depth of between thirty-five and forty feet from Parliament to Bathurst Streets, the excavation of a ship channel forty feet wide, twenty-four feet deep and 6,800 feet long, the construction of permanent docks between Yonge and York Streets and a boulevard drive from the western entrance to the city with breakwater protection along the shoreline, the creation of park lands on both sides and restrictions to be imposed on sales of adjoining lands to protect the investment and preserve the beauty of the whole.

The city approved the plan *in toto*. With the approval of the Dominion government it agreed to spend $1,803,000 on the boulevard and $6,123,000 on the breakwater and other related works. Construction was to begin in 1913 and be completed in five years. The Commissioners' plan for the waterfront was as far as possible integrated with the Board of Trade's railway viaduct project, and in its totality the proposed development represented the consummation of the Board's advocacy over many years. In his report to the members in January 1913 the Board's President, G.T. Somers, said: 'Of the many pieces of public work for which the Board of Trade is responsible there is probably no other of which the members have such just cause to be proud as that which resulted during the past year in the splendid plans for the improvement of the harbour and waterfront made public by the Toronto Harbour Commissioners.' A glowing tribute was paid to E.L. Cousins, chief engineer for the Commissioners, who had prime responsibility for the preparation of the plan and whose work brought him considerable fame. Referring to deterioration in other parts of the city, Mr Somers drew attention to the ease with which urban development could destroy aesthetic values 'in the ruthless spirit of vandalism which is a standing reproach to the patriotism and public spirit of the past.'

The Welland Canal was obviously a key factor in determining the future use and importance of Toronto's harbour. First built by private interests between 1824 and 1829, it had been purchased by the Province of Canada in 1841 and deepened to accommodate vessels of up to nine-foot draft. After Confederation the federal government increased the depth to fourteen feet, but by the early 1900s it was clear that further works were necessary to permit passage of the larger ships then plying the lakes. In 1910 a greater volume of Canadian grain was still going overseas by way of Buffalo and New York than by water to Montreal, and this pattern being so firmly established the fear was that it would prove extremely difficult to change. Moreover, since the Erie Canal was being enlarged and deepened by the United States at a cost of some $100 million to facilitate ship movements to seaboard, the route was becoming even more attractive. A Great Lakes and St Lawrence Navigation and Improvement Association was formed, and in 1909 the Board of Trade's delegates joined this body in representations to the government advocating a further deepening of the Welland Canal. The following year the Toronto Board's Council organized one of the largest delegations ever to descend on Ottawa, comprising representatives from fifty Ontario municipalities and Boards of Trade, to impress upon the government the need for a new and improved Canal that would permit freight carriage without trans-shipment from the head of the lakes to Ontario ports. Prime Minister Laurier seemed impressed and gave assurances which permitted the delegation to hope that something would be done.

When the government changed in 1911 a new effort was necessary. Another delegation waited upon Prime Minister Borden and was again sympathetically received, although hostility to the Welland project, chiefly from railway interests, was now evident. Nevertheless, the Board received word from the Minister of Railways and Canals in 1912 that the necessary works would begin as soon as design plans had been agreed upon. Construction actually started the next year, but the enlarged canal was not completed and opened to navigation until 1930.

If Canada was to benefit as it should from her magnificent waterways, the Board contended that in addition to the improvement of harbours and canals the government should encourage shipbuilding. It proposed that this be done by direct financial assistance if necessary, and also by imposing on foreign ships restraints on their privileges in Canadian waters at least as stringent as those in effect in most other countries. This was consistent with the Board's bitter opposition to the government's abrogation of the coasting laws in favour of United States carriers in 1899. At that time Laurier had promised that 'no interference with the Coasting Laws of Canada would ever in future be made upon any condition short of a Special Act of Parliament.' But they were suspended again in November 1912, permitting the carriage of Canadian grain from Fort William and Port Arthur in American ships to Canadian ports, to the detriment of Canadian carriers and, it was thought, the country's best interests. Again the Board protested strongly.

Another irritant to shippers which the Board took exception to was the equal rights given to American shipping in the use of Canadian canals. These were granted on the understanding that reciprocal privileges would be forthcoming, but in practice, while American ships freely used Canadian canals, American canals (with the exception of the Soo Canal in Michigan) were closed to Canadian vessels. The favoured conditions under which American shipping operated throughout the St Lawrence–Great Lakes system were much resented, and both the American and Canadian governments were blamed for creating and maintaining the inequality.

Carrying people was as important as carrying goods. Toronto was already the hub of a considerable steam railway system, and as early as 1900 the Board of Trade saw the possibilities of a supplementary network of high-speed electric railways connecting the city with all the surrounding municipalities. The matter was discussed with civic leaders, the Board's major point at the time being the need to co-ordinate terminal arrangements for the two systems and possibly also to tie-in the street railway and thus establish a wholly integrated operation. Several privately owned electric 'radials' had been established, but the issue became a lively one after Adam Beck espoused the cause in 1910 as a natural extension of Ontario Hydro. After the war it escalated into a bitter contest during which the Board did an apparent about-face and earned an 'anti-radial' reputation.

Toronto's local transportation system, operated by the Toronto Street Railway Company under a thirty-year franchise terminating in 1921, had begun to come under severe criticism due to the deterioration of its roadbed and equipment and its failure to meet adequately the growing city's demand for service. There seemed, moreover, to be constant friction between the representatives of the civic government and those of the Street Railway Company. The feelings of citizens were not improved by a street railway workers' strike in 1902. A special committee of the Board of Trade had been appointed to attempt to avert it, but its efforts to mediate between employees and the Railway Company proved unsuccessful. After the strike had been in progress for a short time negotiations were resumed and the differences finally composed. The role of mediator in a labour dispute was not a new one for the Board, and while it expressed its willingness to serve in this capacity its stand was always firmly based on the need for each side to observe fully the terms of its contractual obligations. The Board was, in principle, still not well disposed toward public ownership, but by 1909 it showed signs of concurring in a growing public opinion that an adequate street railway system could be expected only if the municipality took over its ownership and operation on the expiry of the existing agreements. An incentive to public ownership had undoubtedly been supplied by the success of Ontario Hydro.

A committee appointed by the Board under the chairmanship of J.P. Watson took the position that better 'street control' was necessary if public transit was to be improved. It recommended that legislation be enacted to ban all but public vehicles from the central zone, defined as the area bounded by Church, Queen and York Streets and the waterfront, and that improved controls be exercised at street intersections. The committee noted the increasing concentration of industrial and commercial operations in the central area and the rapid development of the outlying residential districts, which made it essential to provide good transit connections between them. Such connections simply did not exist and it was felt that if the Street Railway Company was unwilling to provide them the city should do so. Underground lines were one suggested solution: these were believed to have many advantages, among them the opportunity they would afford of bringing radial cars into the central city. Their construction would be costly, but in the long term the committee felt that the outlay would be more than justified.

The spread of population and the advent of the motorcar were calling attention to the need for improved roads, and in 1911 a Board of Trade committee under W.G. Trethewey began negotiations which it was hoped would lead to a program of road construction in at least the older part of Ontario. The pioneer system of statute labour for road improvement was no longer good enough and 'farmers for several months of the year are placed in a position of practical isolation by the almost impassable state of the country roads.'

The Board wanted the city to seek legislation enabling it to spend money on highways adjacent to Toronto and was responsible for a by-law to this effect being put to the ratepayers at the January 1911 civic elections. It received a two-to-one endorsement. The city, the county of York and the province each put up $100,000 and in September some work was started under the administration of a commission appointed for the purpose. Good progress was made; Toronto and York each voted another $100,000 the following year, and the Board's committee noted that 'already an agitation is on foot looking to the construction of a paved road from Toronto to Hamilton.' Much satisfaction was taken in this development, since it was felt with some justification that Toronto and York were blazing the way towards a good roads system throughout the whole province. The values of suburban and adjacent rural properties were materially increased and it was not long before it became evident that the combination of a highway network and the automobile would greatly influence the general pattern of movement of people and goods.

The studies that led to the Board's action in the roads question raised a good many other questions about the shape the city was taking and the pressures that were becoming evident as a result of its physical growth and an increasing population. By 1912 the city covered an area of 33.09 square miles, an increase of 16.2 square miles in five years, and population had risen to 470,000. In that year alone 56 factories, 66 warehouses, 383 stores and 5,675 dwellings had been built, and total assessment, at about 60 per cent of real value, stood at close to $345 million. A reminiscence recorded by W.J. Gage at this time gives an indication of the rising property values:

In childhood, I often listened to the story told by my mother of how her father, in the revolutionary days, left home and kindred in the land to the south, made a long, weary journey to this country that he might find a new home under a new flag; how he at last reached the place where we now stand, and after some hesitation rejected a farm offered him that today would have as its boundaries Yonge Street on the east, and Queen Street on the south, selecting instead as his homestead a better farm some three miles north. As evidence of the changed values it may be of interest to you to learn that a portion of this rejected farm sold last month at the rate of $10,000 per foot frontage.

The city had managed to keep pace with a constantly expanding demand for services, and a committee of the Board of Trade's Council in 1906 worked with architects and others in revising a proposed new building by-law, which it was hoped would impose some necessary controls over new construction. But there was no effective regulation of the city's overall development, nor does it appear that the idea of such regulation had at that time even occurred to anyone. The Board's Council had recommended in 1905 the development of Toronto's natural assets by the 'adoption of a comprehensive plan embracing every feature that will bring into prominence the unrivalled system of parks, promenades, ravines and drives that for a small outlay could be secured,' but this action was motivated by an interest in attracting more tourists to the city. The Council took its usual course of appointing a committee to look into the matter.

W.G. MacKendrick and James C. Forman represented the Board at a National City Planning Conference held in Boston in May 1912 and on their return reported to the members that the occasion had 'convinced them that city planning is not a fad, but practical and necessary, and something that Toronto should adopt.' The Planning Conference was held in Toronto in 1914; the Board participated and extended hospitality to the delegates, but with the disruption of the war the idea of instituting the means for comprehensive urban planning in Toronto was apparently not pursued.

A list of the major civic developments sought by the Board in 1906 included an improved water supply and sewage disposal system, safe and easy access to the waterfront, better harbour entrances and docking facilities, adequate railway entrances, a new railway station, post office and customs house, and the reclamation of Ashbridge's Marsh to provide new industrial and warehouse sites. It foresaw a population of one million in twenty-five years' time, and considered it vitally important that due preparation be made, even though it meant some upward revision in tax rates. The Board accompanied these specifics with a call for street widenings and the adoption of a general program of beautification.

In 1903, and again three years later, the Board and other interests reacted strongly against a proposal to remove Toronto's meteorological observatory to Ottawa on the ground that it performed an indispensable local service; on both occasions the Minister of Marine and Fisheries was persuaded to back down and the observatory remained. At a Board meeting in April 1911 the opinion was strongly expressed that the city was being ignored by the federal government, and it was decided that something should be done to induce Ottawa 'to treat Toronto adequately in the matter of Government buildings, on the basis of the city's requirements and its position in the galaxy of Canadian cities.' A delegation comprising the mayor and the city council, all of the Toronto members of Parliament and representatives of the Board of Trade met with the Prime Minister, the Rt Hon. R.L. Borden, and his cabinet and seem to have made some impression. Soon afterwards the Ministers of Public Works, Customs, and Marine and Fisheries came to Toronto, acknowledged that there may have been some neglect and reported that federal works for the city had been recommended. Among these seems to have been the concept of a civic square, which had often been talked about, but the reference was still very vague.

It may not have been altogether fortuitous that about a year later the Board saw fit to arrange a dinner for Prime Minister Borden in Toronto. It was 'the largest event of its kind ever attempted by any public body in Canada' with 1,500 diners and 7,000 spectators, and was accounted a great success. In spite of numerous speeches, the President of the Board of Trade, G.T. Somers, expressed gratification at its conclusion by 11.10

p.m., 'in direct contrast to many similar dinners, which frequently drag their weary length into the hours of the following morning.'

In 1913 the Board recorded its great satisfaction in the inauguration of the Royal Ontario Museum. Created by an Act of the Ontario legislature the year before on a cost-sharing basis between the province and the University, the actual building was erected for a sum of $400,000. Professor C.T. Currelly was given direction of the Museum and made a notable contribution to its development. The need for future expansion was foreseen, and the land extending from the original site on Bloor Street to the corner of Bloor and Avenue Road was reserved for this purpose.

Although Toronto had access to unlimited supplies of water, its pumping, storage and distribution system had long been considered inadequate. A small break at the main pumping station which had threatened a water famine in 1903 finally impelled the city to introduce a by-law authorizing the raising of a million dollars by debentures to improve the system, and the Board of Trade, after several meetings to discuss the project, threw itself wholeheartedly behind it. The Board further recommended the installation of a separate downtown water supply system for use in combatting fires. As though to give emphasis to this suggestion, Toronto on 19 April 1904 suffered the worst fire in its history. It swept through 19.7 acres of the downtown area, where most of the wholesale houses were located, destroying ninety-eight separate buildings and the premises of 137 firms. The total loss was estimated at the time at $10.5 million, which was probably low; the insurance coverage amounted to some $8.35 million. The Board of Trade commended the insurance companies for the prompt manner in which fire losses were paid, without a single default, and had high praise for the resourcefulness shown by businessmen (many of them members of the Board) in meeting the emergency and re-establishing their various enterprises in a remarkably short time.

The rapid spread of the fire was undoubtedly due in part to an inadequate supply of water and fire-fighting equipment. The city's proposed million-dollar expenditure for waterworks improvements was not only immediately approved, but another $700,000 was added to fulfil the Board of Trade's request for high pressure mains in the business section of the city for fire purposes only. Soon afterwards the Board's Council appointed a committee to look into the causes of and possible remedies for 'the abnormal fire waste that occurs in this country,' which was not only in itself costly and disruptive but also led to excessive rates of insurance. The New York Journal of Commerce estimated that total fire losses in the United States and Canada in 1908 amounted to some $240 million, about ten times those in Europe. The Board concluded that improved safeguards in building construction and maintenance, a program of education at all levels and the appointment of a fire commissioner with extensive powers were needed to lessen fire hazards. The latter recommendation was met at last by the appointment of a provincial Fire Marshal in 1915, but the Board was still unhappy about the 'standing reproach' of continuing and unnecessary fire waste, and proposed that the city establish its own fire commission comprising representatives of the city, the underwriters, the Board of Trade and the Manufacturers Association. The proposed establishment of a firemen's union had been vigorously opposed by the Board of Trade in 1903 on the grounds that 'the Fire Brigade should not be hampered by any such entanglements.' The city council concurred and the matter was dropped, although it has not been recorded what the firemen thought about this.

An objective for which the Board of Trade had fought hard almost from its inception was finally attained in 1906 – the replacement of the personalty tax by a business tax. A comparison of the two systems upheld the Board's contention that 'while doing away with an inequitable and inquisitorial system ... no impairment of revenue would occur,' as the business assessment of 1906 amounted to $19.2 million against a personalty assessment of only $12.4 million the year before. Moreover, the greater part of the increase occurred in the wholesale district, 'and furnishes an effective reply to the statement so persistently repeated that the effect of the change would be to relieve the wholesale trade of its fair share of taxation.' The Board contended that there were still manifest injustices in the application of the new rates of assessment, but felt confident that over a period of time these could be satisfactorily adjusted.

General business in Toronto was proceeding at a brisk pace in the early years of the century: increases in bank clearings averaged some $85 million each year. Of Canada's thirty-four chartered banks in 1904, twenty had head offices in Toronto, and the fact that there had not been a bank failure since 1899 was considered a gratifying record. It was expected that by 1905 Toronto clearings would reach the magic figure of a billion dollars. Loan, investment and trust companies had in 1903 a combined subscribed capital of $53.2 million, while the reserves of life insurance companies against Canadian business amounted to some $102 million. Manufacturing output was estimated at between $65 and $70 million, up $14 million in thirty years, and the city maintained its position as the jobbing centre of Canada. There were 978 business failures in Canada in 1903, the lowest figure in ten years.

It was clear nevertheless that much of the country's prosperity was due to capital imported for railway building and the development of resources, and voices were beginning to be heard in the Board of Trade warning against incurring excessive indebtedness abroad and expressing the hope that Canadians would find it increasingly possible to finance their own enterprises. There were some old business hands who had been through recurring depressions and who earnestly advocated sound and cautious business practices and the avoidance of ill-advised extensions of operations, especially in unfamiliar fields. Their slogan was: 'Be bold. Be not too bold.' But reliance on outside capital had become a way of life; it was estimated that $240 million entered Canada in 1909 from the sale abroad of bonds, debentures and the like. While recognizing the value of new capital, the Board once again warned against taking undue advantage of the easy inflow and in the process damaging credit. Over-capitalization and the creation of paper wealth would handicap the earning power of Canadian assets and resources, encourage over-speculation and create inflation, and lead to a violent swing of the financial and commercial pendulum, as had been all too evident in the United States after their periods of greatest prosperity.

There was ample justification for this wary attitude on the part of Toronto's businessmen. Great prosperity throughout the country in 1906 bore the visible seeds of lean years ahead in high commodity prices, which were nearing the point of inflation, extraordinarily large national expenditures and a heavy capital drain for interest payments. The United States was already suffering from a sharp recession, and experience had shown that Canada followed about a year behind the American cycles. By the latter part of the year the financial situation in the United States had deteriorated to the point of causing severe hardship, and again the Board of Trade's Council was able to take satisfaction from the fact that Canada remained relatively unaffected due largely to the strength of its banking system; a premium was in fact being paid for Canadian bank bills to circulate in the United States. The pace of Canadian business activity in 1906 had caused such a large circulation of money that many banks were close to their limit; the margin for all Canadian banks was estimated at only $9 million. To provide additional capital new banks were being established, and some of the older well-established ones were seeking their shareholders' authority to increase their paid-up capital as necessary, an action which the Board of Trade applauded.

The tail-end of the business disturbance hit Canada in the latter part of 1907 and set manufacturers looking for operating economies and new markets, but it was short-lived and in less than a year improvement was reported. There were many who believed the experience to have been a salutary one since it caused a tightening of the reins and dispelled some of the boom-time euphoria. Certainly the foresight and good judgment of the financial institutions had contributed in no small measure to Canada's avoidance of a deeper depression. But there were other reasons for the rapid return to prosperity. Crops were good and prices were high; mineral and other resources were being developed, and both immigrants and foreign capital were pouring into the country. In 1909 it was calculated that the wealth in actual cash brought into Canada by settlers from the United States alone was at least $100 million.

Immigration was a lively issue. Railway building and the opening up of new lands in the west had brought in a huge influx – 50,000 new settlers in Manitoba and the Northwest in 1899 alone. By 1903 Canada had received a total of 128,364 immigrants including 41,793 from Great Britain, 49,473 from the United States and 3,709 from continental Europe, and in that year 9,377,561 acres of land had been acquired for settlement in the west. The CPR was advertising in 1907 that it had '14,000,000 acres of land for sale on easy terms in Manitoba, British Columbia and the new Provinces of Saskatchewan and Alberta,' and in an advertisement the following year designed to attract immigrants to Ontario the Hon. James S. Duff, provincial Minister of Agriculture, promised that 'in and adjacent to every town of Ontario there are good houses with lots of varying size which can be purchased at reasonable rates for from $3,000 to $5,000.'

The Board of Trade had generally advocated government action to stimulate immigration; people were needed to develop resources, and people, moreover, meant markets for the goods of Toronto merchants and industrialists. It had reacted with shocked indignation to legislation proposed in 1901 to restrict the importation and employment of aliens. However, a few years earlier the Board had made direct representations to the Prime Minister complaining about Great Britain's practice of shipping criminals to Canada. The objection had been channelled through Canada's High Commissioner in London and as a result assurances were received that the practice would cease. In 1911 the Board helped establish a Toronto branch of the Imperial Home Re-union Association, an organization set up to provide financial assistance for recent immigrants from Britain and thus enable them to bring their families to Canada. About the same time the Board advocated the inauguration of a farm colony system for convict labour and suggested that such a system might also be adapted to put to profitable use the skills and energies of ordinary unemployed citizens.

The Board of Trade's attitude toward the huge immigrant inflow became one of cautious approbation. The country was growing, and this was good, but by 1909 the Board was beginning to have some qualms about the quality of immigrants being admitted and recommended the adoption of reasonable control measures, or at the very least that certain educational standards be met before full citizenship rights were granted. Toronto itself was still an English-speaking city, and a 1910 article on the city noted that 'it was founded by English, Irish and Scottish people, and for many years there has been a constant influx of British immigrants. A foreign element has been added within the past decade, consisting largely of Russian Jews and Italians, but they are segregated according to their habit. One may walk the business streets for months and not hear a word of any language other than English.'

The Board's 1908 President, Lionel Clarke, spoke of the spreading socialist tendencies and of the efforts made by certain elements to foment antagonism between labour and capital. In his view the interests of the two were identical and it was essential to the progress of the country that harmony be maintained; Canada was still heavily dependent upon outside sources of capital, and any weakening of its internal structure would undermine confidence and quickly reduce the flow.

Prosperity had its penalties; a subject of general conversation by 1912 was the high cost of living, and its cause and possible cure were attentively examined by the Board of Trade. On the basis of a 1900 price index of 100, Canada's index a decade later stood at 115, the United States' at 119, England's at 109, and they were still rising. In Toronto beef was selling at the unheard-of price of 25 cents a pound, milk at $9\frac{1}{2}$ cents a quart, butter at 35 cents a pound and hard coal at $7.75 a ton. Rental of a six-room house was between $22 and $25 a month. A consultant economist retained by the Board saw rising prices as a world-wide phenomenon, brought about by an increase in the volume of credit money in proportion to the gold base on which it rested. The world's stock of money had thus increased more rapidly than its stock of commodities, and the price of commodities rose. Other causes were an increasing diversion to unproductive military purposes of national revenues that could be devoted to the production of commodities of value, and increased urbanization which was resulting in agricultural lands going out of cultivation and a reduction of farm-family self-sufficiency. In Canada the tax levied on imported foodstuffs had been imposed to protect the farmers, but the development of the packing and canning industries had led to substantial control over the prices paid to the farmers and tended to maintain prices to the consumer at or near those of imports, which were made up of basic price plus freight and duty.

The analysis indicated that in Toronto effective competition had been practically eliminated by powerful commercial interests who controlled the prices paid to producers and charged to consumers. It also criticized the retailing system, which was characterized by large numbers of independent operators and general inefficiency. Favourable reference was made to the co-operative societies of Britain, whose aggregate sales of $565 million in 1908 had produced profits of $55 million for distribution to their members. Rather surprisingly, some blame was placed on poor shipping facilities. Commenting that '... our navigation laws appear to have been drawn up with the idea of injuring American shipping rather than serving Canadian consignees,' and on the fact that Toronto had no public wharf or market, the Board's consultant saw the railways as virtually free from the competition of water-borne freight and thus enabled to maintain high rates which inevitably were reflected in ultimate consumer prices. The near monopoly position occupied by the railways in the movement of goods was held to be responsible for the absence of facilities and services capable of effecting many economies. These considerations legitimately concerned the Board, but with the economic chaos caused by the outbreak of war in 1914 the immediate issue of high prices became almost irrelevant.

The general business picture remained good through 1912, but by May of the following year there were again signs of gathering clouds. The first warnings appeared in the west; construction began to fall off, and banks and financial institutions were exercising great caution in real estate transactions. Business cycles seemed inevitable, resulting from expansion to a critical point followed by a decline when it began to appear that growth was proceeding too far and too fast. Policies of retrenchment were then adopted, leading to reduced production, tight credit and unemployment. There seemed no way of controlling this process, and the period of the cycle was lessening from ten years to about seven; on the other hand recovery was more rapid, due perhaps to improved capital accumulations and more readily available financial accommodation.

The most conspicuous and unpleasant feature of depressed business was unemployment. The Board of Trade worked with both the provincial and municipal governments to see what, if anything, could be done about it, and when the province in 1914 appointed a commission under Sir John Willison 'to enquire into and investigate all matters relating to the unemployment of labour,' the Board's President was named a member of the commission.

Throughout this period the Board was pursuing a course which conformed to a definition put forth by one of its presidents that a Board of

Trade was 'a peculiarly constituted body, having little specific routine work and depending for its usefulness upon keeping in touch with vital commercial questions and taking such interest in them as will be productive of good.' It continued to attract businessmen of high calibre from varied fields to serve on its Council and committees and its general membership steadily increased, exceeding the 2,500 mark by 1911. A report on Toronto a few years before had noted that 'its Board of Trade is recognized as the most important colonial Board in the British Empire and is unceasing in its efforts on behalf of the business interests of the city and of Canada as a whole.'

Time and attention were devoted unstintingly to issues considered of substantial concern to its members or the community, often involving general meetings of the members, studies by committees and the appearance of delegations before representatives of the government of the city, the province and the Dominion – including, not infrequently, the Prime Minister himself. Nor were efforts devoted exclusively to the big issues. Postmaster General Mulock, for example, was importuned to seek an adjustment of the postal rate on newspapers and magazines to Britain, which was twice the rate on such material directed to American destinations; the authorities were urged in 1904 to declare the use of trading stamps illegal, to redeem badly worn silver coinage then circulating in abundance, and to withdraw legislation imposing taxes on commercial travellers in Quebec and British Columbia. Perhaps its actions were not always disinterested, and from time to time it was the target of press criticism for the positions it took in public affairs, but its work on the whole was performed in an honest endeavour to promote the well-being of the community and the country.

Delegations of members under eminent leadership regularly attended the congresses of the Chambers of Commerce of the British Empire, usually held in London, and always vigorously promoted the Toronto Board's favorite project – the creation of a preferential trade agreement among the nations of the Empire. At the 1912 Congress the leader of the Toronto group, W.P Gundy, was honoured by an invitation to take part, with a half-dozen others, in a personal interview with the King. Toronto was further honoured by being chosen as the place of the Ninth Congress in 1915, but the war later postponed all such occasions.

A visit by a Board of Trade delegation to Chicago and Cleveland in 1910 to investigate procedures employed in the welfare field in those cities led to a proposal, later acted upon, that the city appoint a commission to classify and co-ordinate charitable operations in Toronto as a means of preventing both overlapping and gaps in the distribution of relief. In June 1914 a large group of members, accompanied by the mayor, the Board of Control and other civic representatives, made an excursion by chartered steamer to Detroit, Cleveland and Buffalo and returned much impressed by the progress evident there in programs of parks development. At the Board's suggestion the city set up a Citizens Boulevard Committee under the chairmanship of Sir Edmund Osler to explore the possibilities of improving Toronto's parks system by creating a boulevard of about thirty-two miles around the city which would start from and complete the waterfront works of the Harbour Commissioners. Work was begun, and some land was actually acquired by gift, but the project appears to have been abandoned.

The Board's various Trade Sections continued to be actively concerned with their own affairs and reported regularly to the Council. Some of these reports throw an interesting light on the conditions of the time. The Tanners Section, for instance, was deploring in 1905 the depletion of the hemlock forests and reported that, not long before, anyone who might have predicted barkless tanneries would have been considered a crank, whereas much of the leather for shoes was already of necessity being tanned by chemical processes. In the same year the Dry-goods Section conveyed the news that 'ladies' ready-to-wear goods now have great vogue, and in style and finish and make-up generally the Canadian makes can hardly be surpassed. Merchants throughout the country are now establishing special departments for ladies' ready-to-wear goods.' The Flour and Grain Section was seeking the appointment by the government of completely independent official weighers at all public grain elevators, and the Jewellers Section regarded itself, with considerable justification, as a barometer of prosperity: a thriving jewellery trade indicated a prosperous community.

The Board noted with gratification in 1902 an increasing demand for the services of skilled accountants as auditors for both public and private enterprises and in various other capacities. Largely because of this improved recognition the Institute of Chartered Accountants of Ontario had requested legislative authority to exercise the sole right to designate those entitled to use the distinctive title 'Chartered Accountant.' On the advice of its own Accountants Section the Board opposed the application on the grounds that it would create a combine inimical to business interests, and that what was needed were improved educational facilities to upgrade professional qualifications rather than an organization with essentially selfish purposes. The issue led to a good deal of controversy among accountants in which the Board declined to become further involved. It was at length resolved by a clarification of the professional organization's legal and administrative status, and the affairs of the Accountants Section of the Board, having become redundant, were soon afterwards wound up.

The Council had always sought a closer identification with the Board's work on the part of members, firmly believing that the soundness of its policies and the effectiveness of its actions were directly proportional to the breadth of the consensus it could develop throughout the business community. Following a review of its own structure and methods in 1910, the Board sent a delegation, comprising J.P. Somers, W.P. Gundy and the Secretary, F.G. Morley, on a tour of several cities in the United States to examine the operations of their Boards of Trade and Chambers of Commerce. They came back much impressed by the comprehensive programs being conducted by some of the major American organizations and the important positions many of them enjoyed in their communities. They recommended an expansion of the Toronto Board's activities and renewed efforts to increase membership.

Better channels of communication with the members were also considered desirable. For some time infrequent issues of the slim *Board of Trade News* had informed them of major events, and in 1911 it was decided to issue the *News* regularly in a more attractive format to keep members aware of the work going on in the Council and in the committees. The improved publication was highly commended and received gratifying attention from other organizations both in and outside the country. To encourage member participation further, the Council in 1911 established a Conference Committee of One Hundred. Its members were selelected from the widest possible spectrum of business interests and were to meet regularly to hear presentations on issues of the day, form opinions concerning them and convey their views to the Executive Committee and Council and thus assist them in determining policy positions. The Committee held its first meeting on 28 December 1911; invited participants were Sir Edmund Walker, President of the Canadian Bank of Commerce, Robert Falconer, President of the University, and J.F. Ellis, a former President of the Board. The Conference Committee met fortnightly at luncheon through 1912 but it was an unwieldy medium. Interest began to flag and when it became apparent that its intended purposes were not being achieved the Committee was gradually phased out.

The work of the Board had so increased by 1912 that an Assistant Secretary was appointed in the person of F.D. Tolchard. In addition to the top-level work of the Executive Committee and Council, eighteen committees involving 170 members held 161 meetings in that year and, as a result, substantial secretarial service over and above normal administrative duties was required.

The rented premises in the Board of Trade Building at the corner of Front and Yonge Streets were becoming inadequate and unsuitable for the Board's purposes, and consideration was given to a possible move. A committee under C.McD. Hay, appointed to look into possibilities, found difficulty in locating the kind of accommodation needed, but at length recommended that quarters be secured on the nineteenth and twentieth floors of the new Royal Bank Building on the northeast corner of King and Yonge Streets. This selection was considered ideal. A ten-year lease was accordingly entered into and the Board formally opened its new offices there on 29 December 1914. The Royal Bank Building was then the loftiest commercial building in the British Empire. The Janes Building had formerly occupied the site, and before that a row of retail shops. On the nineteenth floor were a spacious assembly room, a council chamber, market room, the Secretary's and Traffic Manager's offices and a large general office. The twentieth floor was devoted to luncheon and dining rooms with accommodation for 150, kitchen, lounge and reading rooms supplied with newspapers and periodicals, and there was a balcony which provided a splendid view of the city in all directions. Eight hundred visitors attended the opening ceremonies, and the speakers on this occasion included the Lieutenant Governor, Lt Col. J.S. Hendrie, the Premier of Ontario, W.H. Hearst, and Mayor Hocken.

An important innovation in the new premises was the provision of what amounted to club facilities for the members, the outcome of a feeling long held that there was a need to stimulate social intercourse among businessmen, and that by so doing a stronger feeling of identity would be created with their Board of Trade. The immediate popularity of the luncheon facilities and clubrooms seemed to justify this view.

On his retirement from the presidency in 1915 W.P. Gundy remarked that 'it might be well for the incoming Council to consider if we should not now commence to set aside annually a sum which at the expiration of our present agreement would enable us to occupy a building of our own.'

# 6
# World War I

With the outbreak of war in 1914 the whole world changed. A wave of patriotic fervour swept Canada, nowhere more intensely than in Toronto, with its strong British background and undiminished filial ties with the mother country. A first Canadian contingent of 33,000 men was soon despatched for action on the European front, and a second contingent was enrolled and in training by the end of the year. After visiting the Canadian headquarters on Salisbury Plains, Rudyard Kipling observed: 'It is not a contingent that Canada has sent, but an army – horse, foot, guns, engineers and all details fully equipped ... an entire nation unrolled across a few square miles of turf.'

The ordinary processes of business were profoundly disturbed. At the Board of Trade's Annual Meeting in January 1915 President Gundy noted that '... when on August 4 last year war was declared, every stock exchange throughout the world was closed – orders were cancelled, international currency became as so much waste paper, and the whole system of world commerce was disorganized.' Actions taken by the British government averted a financial crisis and re-established some measure of confidence which it was hoped might lead to the resumption of 'business as usual', but it was quite clear that in the realm of capital funding little help could be expected from London, Canada's usual source, for a long time. While this would slow development, there were many who felt it might jolt the country into greater self-sufficiency. 'It remains for us,' said Gundy, 'by wise economies and by increased efficiency and energy in every industry to inaugurate a new era in the economic progress of Canada.' Indeed, there were some bright spots in the generally gloomy picture. Germany, for instance, had sold goods valued at $35 million to Great Britain in 1913, and Canadian traders saw no reason why they should not avail themselves of the opportunity to supplant this business. The President of the Montreal Board of Trade felt that the country's affairs were fundamentally sound and that, although trade at the end of 1914 was quiet and in many cases restricted, there were important compensations which gave him undiminished confidence in the future. The serious business leaders were warning against unwarranted speculation and ill-founded ventures, and advocating in the strongest terms that efforts be concentrated in immediate legitimate concerns. It was essential to strengthen the national effort by avoiding wastage of resources and human energy.

While it was felt to be 'impossible to estimate the effects of an earthquake while it is in progress,' all factors in the changing economic scene were kept under close scrutiny. One of the more interesting phenomena was the general tendency toward economy: at the end of 1915 deposits in chartered banks amounted to $1,144,680,000, an increase of nearly $132 million over the previous year. Some economists foresaw great future benefits in such a mobilization of capital. The accumulation of savings was reflected in the over-subscription by more than 100 per cent of the first Dominion War Loan. The most surprising effect of the war was commented upon by J.W. Woods in his address to the members of the Board at their Annual Meeting in January 1916: 'Had anyone eighteen months ago predicted exactly what has since happened, he would have been set down as irresponsible. Who then believed that war would relieve an industrial situation that was most critical? Who believed that war, of all things, would bring prosperity to Canada? Yet such has been unquestionably the case, and the situation is not without danger.' The danger he foresaw was, of course, that the prosperity brought by the war was inflated and false, and that the inevitable readjustment at the war's end could prove painful. The transition from peace to war had been accomplished with surprising ease; the reverse process would be much more difficult and complicated.

By the middle of 1915 the full effect of the demand for munitions was beginning to be felt in Canadian industry; new industrial patterns were developing, and attention was being given as never before to the recovery and utilization of by-products. For example, Canada supplied 70 per cent of the world demand for nickel, which had increased 300 per cent since 1902; refining was being carried to completion domestically, and in other areas of production accelerating demand was leading to improved technologies and efficiency. There were serious shortages: cotton from the United States was in short supply and expensive; flax, traditionally obtained from Russia and Belgium, was simply non-existent; the demand for wool exceeded the world supply by 25 per cent; and dyestuffs had become scarce and costly. However, there was work for almost anybody who wanted it and wages were high; in Britain, where there was an actual shortage of labour, wages had in some fields doubled in less than a year and a half. In the full year 1915 Canada imported goods worth $471.8 million and its exports amounted to $781.8 million. Exports to Britain alone had increased to $361.5 million from $184.2 million the year before. In the same year the exports of the United States exceeded her imports by $1.75 billion.

The Board of Trade carried on all its traditional activities and embarked on new ones directly related to the war effort. Throughout 1914 the Executive Committee was in almost weekly session. In the early days of the war a committee was established under Arthur Hewitt to raise funds for the relief of the Belgians. Setting out with a $50,000 objective they collected $72,000; all expenses were borne by the Board so that every cent would be used for the intended purpose. The King of the Belgians cabled his embassy in Ottawa: 'His Majesty is profoundly touched by the generous sympathy of the Canadian people. You are requested to convey to the Board of Trade of Toronto the expression of the feelings of lively gratitude of his government.' A campaign on behalf of the Red Cross, led by J.W. Woods, Sir Edmund Osler and F.G. Morley, with 200 members participating, produced $550,975 in October 1915. Nine members, including H.D. Lockhart Gordon, K.R. Marshall and C.H. Mitchell, went into active service immediately upon the declaration of war. By the end of 1915 the number was 62 and by 1917 it had reached 85, three of whom had been killed in action. The Board remitted the fees of members on active service and sent them Christmas cakes. In the flurry of early patriotic activity a Board of Trade Rifle Club was formed and its 120 members drilled weekly.

With food shortages in 1916 and a real threat of world famine, the Board organized a War Production Club whose primary object was to induce city men to spend their vacations on the land. Its initial effort produced 1,500 volunteers for spring work on the farms, and over the whole year some 3,000 took part; many spent as much as three to six months in agricultural labour according to an arrangement whereby their regular employers made up any salary differential. Encouragement was given to the cultivation of unused land near the city, and vegetable gardens were dug for a thousand soldiers' wives. Members of Toronto's police force were organized to plough, plant, finance and care for over thirty acres of potatoes, giving a half or a whole day each week to the effort and sending the eventual crop to the city's hospitals and charitable institutions. The efforts of the War Production Club, under the direction of E.F. Trimble, attracted wide and favourable attention from other cities in both Canada and the United States.

Canada's growing stature as a supplier of men and materials for war and, as a result, her increasing presence in Britain, emphasized in the Board's view the need for more substantial representation in London. The premises then occupied by the Canadian High Commissioner at 17 Victoria Street were considered 'in no respect satisfactory, being inconveniently located, shabby in appearance, entirely inadequate in accommodation ... neither suitable to the necessities nor worthy of the importance and wealth of the Dominion.' The government was urged to take immediate steps to remedy the situation and purchase an Aldwych site proposed by Earl Grey. A special reason for strengthening Canada's representation in England was the expected influx of immigrants after the war. A committee under Lionel Clarke conferred with Prime Minister Borden and Premier Hearst of Ontario and advocated the exercise of some measure of control before would-be emigrants left their native country, the fullest co-operation between the federal and provincial governments and transport companies in dealing with the flow, and adequate attention to newcomers after their arrival to ensure rapid and effective adaptation to conditions in their new homeland.

The immigration question received a great deal of the Board's attention during the war years. From 1906 to 1916 2.5 million people entered the country, 402,343 in 1912 alone, of whom a million had come from Great Britain and 900,000 from the United States. They had helped to build the country and had contributed vastly to its prosperity and the Board was eager that the flow be maintained. The Board was nevertheless concerned that, with a lessening demand for manpower in agriculture, serious employment problems would arise unless selective policies were adopted and special measures employed for the absorption of the newcomers. The numbers arriving from Britain, too, were diminishing, and ethnic problems were foreseen. Soon after the war a Board of Trade deputation laid a number of proposals before the Minister of Education to provide special educational facilities for the foreign-born population, new immigrants and the illiterate. The establishment of a Bureau of Canadianization within the Department of Education was recommended to survey needs and existing facilities, introduce citizenship features in present classes, train special

teachers, standardize textbooks and generally act to secure public understanding and support. The Board, along with other organizations, offered
some direction and financial aid to carry out such a program.

Continued dissatisfaction with tariffs was evident, and the Board in 1915
put forward the suggestion that a tariff commission, along the lines of the
Board of Railway Commissioners, be appointed as a means of taking the
tariff out of politics and ensuring that rates were worked out on scientific
principles by disinterested experts. In other matters, a year's experience
with Workmen's Compensation brought mixed reactions from businessmen. It was looked on with some suspicion as a form of state insurance, and
the business of companies which furnished employers' liability insurance
was materially affected. The original legislation had been considered unsatisfactory and, although patched by subsequent amendments, still left
much to be desired; the Board's attitude was noncommittal. In 1915 the
Board renewed a plea for the enactment in Ontario of a Bulk Sales Act
similar to those operative in other provinces to prevent a person, partnership or company involved in winding-up procedures from disposing of
assets in bulk and pocketing the proceeds, leaving creditors in the lurch.
Such legislation would obviously work to the advantage of those carrying
on proper wholesale and retail operations and contribute to the health of
the commercial community. The effort was finally successful and the
Ontario government enacted legislation in 1917 to go into effect the following year.

Relations between the Board of Trade and the civic administration had
greatly improved to the point where mutual respect and a working relationship made possible a good deal of useful consultation and joint effort.
Appreciation was expressed of the co-operation received from Mayor T.L.
Church and particularly of his efforts to improve departmental management, as evidenced by the appointment of Thomas Bradshaw, a respected
businessman, as Commissioner of Finance. Nevertheless, the Board continued to deplore the absence of consistent business methods at City Hall
and believed that Toronto's municipal affairs needed a strong application
of new management techniques. There was no indication of how this might
be directly achieved; the city's government was established in a political
mold and few leading businessmen had shown any inclination to become
involved. One suggested approach was to set up an independent body to
keep the administration under constant scrutiny and issue unbiased reports
from time to time for public information. The Bureau of Municipal Research became this body, instigated and supported by the Board and other
like-minded interests. Its first director was Dr Horace Brittain, an able,

forthright and knowledgeable observer, and operations were begun in 1915. Never spectacular, the Bureau kept an eye on how the city's business was run and its findings, usually compiled as a dispassionate commentary, undoubtedly contributed to probity and efficiency.

A pre-war unemployment problem became during the war a problem of demand for labour exceeding the supply. Before the war's end there were 67,700 females employed in Ontario factories subject to government inspection alone, with untold additional numbers in service industries, offices and mercantile establishments. This was a new phenomenon and bred genuine concern over the conditions that would prevail with the return from overseas of the 400,000 men serving in the armed forces. A glimpse of the rehabilitation problem to be faced appeared as early as 1915, when there were already a thousand soldiers in convalescent homes in Canada, most of whom would have to be retrained for re-entry into civilian life. The Board of Trade suggested that consideration be given to the development of new enterprises to absorb women who had acquired a taste for wages and would not wish to drop out of employment. It further proposed the development of a comprehensive program of special training for ex-soldiers and the inauguration of a pension scheme to assist their resettlement. Such a scheme would have the desirable added effect of stimulating recruitment.

The reference to recruiting probably arose out of the conscription issue then being vigorously debated. Voicing a personal opinion, the Board's President J.W. Woods had no doubts at all on the question: 'I would like to put myself on record as favouring conscription in time of war. I am in favour of patriotic funds being raised by taxation, which would reach the major portion of our people. Existing conditions leave the burden to be borne by the willing, whereas the unwilling are those we should aim at reaching, both for fighting and paying.' At a general meeting held on 18 June 1917 the Board of Trade formally placed itself on record as 'in full sympathy with a measure which will provide for a compulsory selective system necessary to secure reinforcements for our Canadian divisions at the front. Further, that the Government be urged to secure the passage of the Military Service Act at the earliest possible moment.' The Act passed, but Laurier, then Leader of the Opposition, did not want its provisions to take effect until the people had had an opportunity to pronounce upon it by way of referendum. Prime Minister Borden, on the other hand, declared that a situation of national emergency demanded that the war be prosecuted with ceaseless vigour, that conscription was necessary and that national objectives could best be achieved by a coalition government representing all parties. The Board of Trade for the moment abandoned its usual non-political stance and came down strongly on Borden's side at this critical stage, considering it 'the imperative duty of every loyal citizen of Canada to use every legitimate effort to secure a return to power of the Union Government.' In the elections of December 1917 the Unionist or Coalition Government under Robert Borden was returned with a large majority, except in the province of Quebec, and the Toronto Board praised the great ability it displayed in the conduct of the war and in post-war reorganization.

Daylight Saving was another wartime measure supported by the Board, providing it went into effect uniformly across the Dominion. The government declined to introduce legislation despite what appeared to be a nation-wide demand in 1916, the year it was introduced in Great Britain. There it was reported to have saved 300,000 tons of coal in a year and hence materially aided the war economy; the Board, feeling that resistance in Canada was based on unreasonable prejudice, joined a renewed appeal for its adoption. Some local attempts to work to an adjusted time system in 1917 were unsuccessful through lack of uniformity, but in April 1918 a Daylight Saving Bill, strongly supported by the Board and many other organizations, finally became law.

In 1916 the sale and use of spirituous liquors was prohibited in Ontario. Since this action was represented as part of the general wartime policy of economy and restraint, it met with surprisingly little opposition; the Board of Trade took no public position in the matter. As early as 1864 the legislature of the United Provinces of Canada had passed a Temperance Act giving municipalities the authority to prohibit the sale of liquors on approval of a majority of the electors, and in the late nineteenth and early twentieth centuries some had acted under this local option. Agitation for nation-wide prohibition had led to the appointment of a Royal Commission in 1892, but it found a majority opposed and nothing was done. When a Prohibition Bill was put forward by the Ontario government in 1902 the Board of Trade's Council, after careful consideration, favoured stricter control of the liquor traffic but recommended a gradual approach, examination of the economic results and compensation of commercial interests directly affected. Noting that there was already an 'advance in sobriety which, comparing with conditions a number of years ago, is very marked,' the Board expressed some doubt as to the efficacy of sumptuary laws unless they were soundly based, acceptable to the great mass of the citizenry and rigidly enforced. However, it was also noted that '... there is no quality upon recognition of which any government may rely more confidently for support than courage in instituting and enforcing whole-some laws. Yet there is no quality, perhaps, which governments are more prone to under-rate.' Representatives of the Council conferred in the matter with the Premier and members of the legislature, and the question was considered of such importance that a general meeting of the members was held on 10 February 1902. A resolution was unanimously adopted generally embodying the opinions arrived at by the Council. It concluded, however, that if a prohibitory bill were passed it should not be given effect until a referendum had established its support by two-thirds of the voters or 51 per cent of the duly qualified electors. The Bill passed and the subsequent referendum showed that the citizens were not prepared for prohibition, and there the matter stood. The Board viewed this outcome with satisfaction and felt that the air had been cleared. But the prohibition of 1916 was imposed under highly unusual circumstances and ostensibly with different objectives, and while it may not have been popular it was accepted on the whole with good grace. It was not lifted until 1927 when a system was introduced which gave the province a monopoly in liquor sales as well as a tight rein at every level of production and use.

In spite of wartime shortages of manpower and materials the physical development of the city proceeded. The spread of population east of the Don River had long made obvious the necessity of a proper linkage over the Don Valley. Consideration given at various times to a proposal to join Bloor Street and Danforth Avenue led to the preparation of a bridge design and cost estimates in 1912 and, in the following year, to a by-law authorizing the issue of debentures for the project in the amount of $2.5 million. The total length of the required connection was almost a mile and two bridges were needed, one over the Don River itself and the other over the Rosedale Valley. The contract for the former was let in December 1914 and for the latter in February 1915: one stipulation was that provision must be made in the design of the bridges for the addition of a lower deck to accommodate a possible future subway line. The Don bridge consisted of five spans: the longest was 281 feet and carried the roadway 125 feet above the floor of the valley. Work initially proceeded at a good pace, but in 1916 there was some official feeling that with the world in chaos such major construction should be deferred. The Board of Trade joined the city in pressing for completion, objections were withdrawn, and the work was finished. The Rosedale section was officially opened by Mayor T.L. Church on 18 October 1918.

In the spring of 1914 work began on the harbour and waterfront development which had been instigated primarily by the Board of Trade.

Because of the war, activity was at first limited to the creation of new industrial lands and the improvement of the eastern terminals, but the government gave assurances that operations would continue until the entire plan had been implemented. By 1918 some 900 acres of new land had been prepared for commercial and industrial purposes and 229 acres already leased. A year later improvements to the central harbour had been carried out, the 2,000-foot breakwater between Sunnyside and the Humber River completed and a 3,000-foot boardwalk built in the Sunnyside parklands. The Harbour Commissioners were actively promoting industrial establishment and capital investment in the lands under their jurisdiction.

Completion of the harbour plan was, however, impossible until the question of the Esplanade railway viaduct across the waterfront had been resolved. Negotiations between the railways, the Board of Railway Commissioners, the city and the Harbour Commissioners had been going on interminably, with the Board of Trade playing an important role as liaison and critic; from time to time it seemed that a solution had been reached, only to have a new element enter into the discussions and throw the dispute wide open again. After the war the integration of the Grand Trunk and Canadian Northern into a national railway system with its attendant complex realignments so occupied the attention of the Railway Commissioners and railwaymen that the viaduct question was for a time simply put aside. In the meantime the construction of a new Union Station on the Front Street site was undertaken. The structure itself was completed by 1921, but it could not be used until the viaduct issue was settled, railway grades established and the actual rail entrances to the station built. An application on behalf of the railways to use the station by entering at existing rail levels was turned down by the Commissioners, and there the new Union Station stood – beautiful and empty – for many years.

The creation of a national railway system, begun in 1917 and concluded in April 1923 with the final consolidation of two complete executive staffs, formed the largest publicly-owned railway in the world. It had been, as the Hon. George P. Graham, Minister of Railways and Canals, remarked, 'the most gigantic task ever faced by any railway president in the world.' The amalgamation was regarded favourably by the Board of Trade, although it cautioned that its success depended upon wise management, public support and freedom from political interference. However, the Board had always resented the fact that neither the Grand Trunk nor the Canadian Pacific had officers with powers to make administrative decisions in Toronto, and hence it felt a much closer affinity for the Canadian Northern, which had its home base in the city. Upon amalgamation, Toronto appeared almost certain to lose its one railway headquarters to Montreal; this change was resented, in view of Toronto's importance as a rail centre and the fact that one-third of the Canadian National Railway's milage would be in Ontario and one-half of Canada's total freight tonnage originated in the province. Sporadic efforts to achieve for Toronto what was considered to be its rightful place in the changing railways picture culminated in a strong Board of Trade delegation, including Thomas Bradshaw, C.L. Burton, R.W. Eaton, E.H. Gurney, Vincent Massey and Sir James Woods, waiting upon Sir Henry Thornton, the CNR President, in December 1922 in an attempt to convince him that the national railway's head office should be in Ontario's capital city. Nothing happened, and the effort was renewed the following year with the support of other Ontario Boards of Trade. A decision was then made: Toronto would not get the system's head office, but it would be the headquarters for the central region, extending from Port Arthur to Rivière du Loup and Monk in Quebec, and would include all Canadian National's lines in the United States.

The war profoundly affected Canada by developing a sense of self-reliance and nationhood that had never previously existed. The nation played a proud part in the fighting and had been able, from a relatively weak economic base, to maintain reasonable stability at home, contribute powerfully to Britain's needs and, in the process, develop its own strength and confidence. By the war's end total foreign trade had doubled and the export of manufactured goods had increased 400 per cent. Canada had produced almost a billion dollars' worth of munitions: Ontario was responsible for more than half and Toronto for quantities valued at some $175.2 million. The end of hostilities would clearly bring about a severe let-down, and it was the concern of governments and responsible business organizations to foresee the problems and prepare to meet them. The great strides made in industrialization pointed the way, and it seemed logical that a stable prosperity should be created and maintained by the systematic development of natural resources and the application of the new-found manufacturing prowess to convert exports from predominantly raw to manufactured, or partly processed, commodities. There was now a domestic market of over eight million people and, with effort, new overseas markets could also undoubtedly be found.

The enormous cost of the war had created a situation demanding close attention and enlightened fiscal policies. Under the direction of Finance Minister Sir Thomas White, five war loans had been floated, each of them heavily over-subscribed. The total amount produced amounted to $1,350 million on loans bearing interest at 5 and 5½ per cent with maturities between 1925 and 1937, thus creating cumulative obligations extending almost endlessly into the future. It is of passing interest that Canadian contributions to voluntary patriotic funds during the four war years amounted to another $104 million, of which over $20 million had been raised in Toronto.

The Board of Trade's Council saw many of the problems ahead quite clearly and devoted much time both during the war and long afterwards exploring possible solutions. In 1916 J.W. Woods represented the Board at a conference in Ottawa called by Sir George Foster, Minister of Trade and Commerce, to consider the post-war expansion of European markets, and he subsequently headed a commission which spent four months touring Great Britain, France and Italy to assemble data on which meaningful assessments could be based. In June of that year Mr Woods acted for the Board at a British Imperial Council of Commerce held in London, along with delegates from the United Kingdom, Australia, New Zealand, India, Ceylon and China, to discuss new trading patterns and commercial practices likely to develop when the war was over. The federal government was urged to extend its Trade Commissioner Service to countries where Canada as yet had no representation. To ensure the availability of qualified personnel for overseas posts a committee fully representing industrial and mercantile interests drawn from the memberships of the Board of Trade and the Canadian Manufacturers' Association was appointed to work with the University of Toronto in the creation and maintenance of a chair in economic geography.

Greater government encouragement to the development of native resources was advocated. Gold was an important factor in meeting national liabilities. Coal to the value of $55 million had been brought in from the United States in 1917 and effort was needed to supplant much of this from domestic sources. To forward these and similar aims it was necessary to stimulate the application of new scientific advances to extractive and industrial processes and create research facilities, as the United States, England and Japan had done when their supply of many vital commodities from Germany had been cut off by the war. The Canadian government in 1916 had appointed an Honorary Advisory Council for Scientific and Industrial Research to direct and assist research efforts, but it was the Board's recommendation in 1917 that the government should take immediate steps to establish an organization which would actually undertake basic research and develop technologies for application in Canadian industry, employing graduates from Canadian universities, and supplement this by improving the research and post-graduate opportunities in those universities. The issue was pressed in succeeding years, and the formation of a National Research Institute and a Canadian Bureau of Standards was specifically advocated. The position taken by the Board was fully supported in a report tabled by a committee of the House of Commons in May 1920. It recommended the establishment of a research organization to establish standards, devise methods for improving industrial processes, develop natural resources, utilize waste products and perform other related functions. The Board gave the report its full support and urged other organizations to do likewise, but the government was not then ready to act.

A parallel interest of the Board was the expansion of facilities providing technical education to bridge the gap between the primary schools and employment. Toronto had a fine new Technical School, but the Board believed its functions could be improved by closer collaboration with industry to ensure that courses were continually adjusted to meet realistic needs.

It was always a question of what the government should and should not do: the Board complained in 1918 of the increasing flow of legislation affecting all citizens, particularly businessmen, and the lack of sensitivity of most people toward the restraints imposed upon them by measures ostensibly designed to meet wartime exigencies. It was essential, the Board insisted, that there be direct and alert intervention to 'purge current legislation of provisions that burden and hold back productive enterprise.' It was especially necessary to alleviate the heavy load of wartime taxation. Soon after the war ended the Board petitioned Ottawa for the removal of the Luxury Tax and the Business Profits War Tax and their replacement by tax methods falling more equitably upon all classes of the community. Following a committee study of the tax question, a general meeting of members in May 1921 agreed to recommend not only that the Business Profits War Tax be removed but also that the special War Tax, as it affected sales and income taxes applicable to individuals (but not corporations or joint stock companies), be repealed and replaced by a turnover or sales tax on all commodities and a graduated income tax. Such taxes were to be clearly defined as 'War Taxes' and the revenues derived therefrom applied exclusively to payment of interest and reduction of the principal of the war debt as well as to payments of war pensions. A multitude of tax applications, such as the Stamp Tax on notes and cheques and the tax on receipts, were vexatious, and the Board consistently advocated their elimination and the adoption of a comprehensive system which would fall more equally on the community and, at the same time, produce enhanced revenues with less trouble and cost. Taxation had got out of hand and was threatening to curtail progress and inhibit enterprise. Addressing the shareholders of the Canadian Bank of Commerce at their 1922 Annual Meeting, Sir Edmund Walker remarked: 'You cannot on the one hand by unfair taxation strip those who have made or saved money, and on the other hand look to the same individuals for aid in new enterprises for profit.'

Besides a need for internal reforms, the end of the war also produced a change of attitude toward Canada's place in Empire and world affairs, reflected in an address by K.J. Dunstan, the Board of Trade's 1919 President:

The unexpected force exerted by the British Dominions in the actual determination of the issues of the war demonstrated the existence of a new factor in the affairs of the world. The Peace Conference, in admitting the Dominions to a distinctive share in its deliberations and decisions, and in according them a status of membership in the League of Nations and in the International Labour Organization, simply gave formal international recognition to this new fact .... The old political system of the world is disappearing; many of its constituent elements have been utterly destroyed by the catastrophe, while others lie helpless and exhausted. In the new order that must arise it is inevitable that these growing nations beyond the seas, with their capacity for affairs, their splendid resources, their freedom of outlook and their vigorous individualities, shall play a notable part. They cannot avoid the responsibility and it is their duty to prepare for it. So far as the constitutional relationships of the Britannic Commonwealth are concerned, they have for years been in a condition of development. That development is as yet incomplete, though the events of the war and of the Peace Conference have given a powerful stimulus.

What the outcome will be remains for the consideration of the special constitutional conference which under the decision of the Imperial War Conference of 1917 will be summoned as soon as possible after the war. But it has been publicly recognized ... that any solution must be based upon the principle of equality of nationhood, and that each nation of the Britannic League, while preserving its autonomy unimpaired, shall exercise its voice as to those external relations which involve the issues of peace and war.

There were other indications of the feeling that Canada had outgrown her colonial status and her unquestioning acceptance of Britain's parental role. Nothing suggested any significant lessening of loyalty and affection for the mother country, but it no longer seemed necessary or even desirable that Canadians, occupying a vast country populated by peoples from many lands, should be wholly guided by London in the management of their internal affairs or the determination of policies affecting relationships with

George Percival Ridout
was the prime mover in organizing
the present Board of Trade in 1844,
and was elected its first president.

King Street, looking west from Yonge, about 1865. Ridout's Hardware occupied one of the shops on the left.

Early meetings of the Board of Trade were held in this building, originally the Mechanics' Institute. By the time this photograph was taken in 1897 it was the Toronto Public Library.

The Council and officers of the Toronto Board of Trade in 1888. The following key identifies the men in the portrait: 1 Wm. Galbraith, 2 E.J. Davis, 3 Geo. A. Chapman, 4 J.N. Peer, 5 H.W. Nelson, 6 F. Barlow Cumberland, 7 Thos. Flynn, 8 G.M. Rose, 9 A.B. Lee, 10 W.B. Hamilton, 11 A.M. Smith, 12 E.R.C. Clarkson, 13 Edgar A. Willis, 14 W.D. Matthews, 15 D.R. Wilkie, 16 W.H. Beatty, 17 Robert Jaffray, 18 Joseph Harris, 19 John Laidlaw, 20 John I. Davidson, 21 R.W. Elliott, 22 John Macdonald, 23 S.F. McKinnon, 24 Wm. Stark, 25 John Earls, 26 R.S. Baird, 27 J.F. McLaughlin, 28 Jas. Stark, 29 J.L. Spink, 30 Hugh Blain, 31 H.N. Baird, 32 Edward Gurney, 33 Jas. Paten, 34 Wm. Ince, 35 W.R. Brock, 36 L.A. Tilley, 37 Elias Rogers, 38 Henry W. Darling.

Members of the Toronto Board of Trade and Corn Exchange in 1885, one year after the two bodies were amalgamated by Act of Parliament. The picture was taken in the Board of Trade premises in the Imperial Bank Building, at the corner of Leader Lane and Wellington Street. In 1885, Toronto was considered the grain exchange centre of Canada.

a

b

Horse-drawn streetcars and arc lights were features of Yonge Street, looking north from King, the city's centre, in 1890.

a The Board of Trade Building, on the northeast corner of Front and Yonge Streets, was the centre of the Board's activities from 1890 to 1914.

b One of the offices in the Board of Trade Building in 1897. It was the home of R.G. Dun & Company – and all-male.

A bird's-eye view of Toronto in 1907, from the tower of St. James' Cathedral.

a

b

a By the turn of the century, the railways had erected a barrier of tracks between the city and its waterfront.

b The level crossings on these lines – inconvenient and dangerous – were the target of a long Board of Trade campaign. This scene was at the foot of Yonge Street in 1907.

a

b

In 1912 the Board gave a formal dinner in Mutual Street Arena for the Prime Minister of Canada, the Rt. Hon. Robert L. Borden. The diners had an immense gallery of spectators.

a As part of its continuing interest in immigration, the Board helped families like this one, in 1911, to establish themselves in Canada.

b Groups of members regularly visited other parts of the province in tours organized by the Board. This was a businessmen's excursion to Northern Ontario in September 1922.

From 1934 to 1957, the Board was quartered in the King Edward Hotel on King Street.

Toronto's buildings were beginning to shoot skyward in the 1930s. The Bank of Commerce was the tallest building in the Commonwealth, the Royal York the biggest hotel.

Since 1957 the Board has occupied the top three floors of the Board of Trade Building, Eleven Adelaide Street West.

The opening of a Golf and Country Club in Woodbridge, on the city's
northwestern outskirts, in 1965 was a first for any board of trade.

Today's Toronto.

the rest of the world. The war had dried up the customary capital flow from Britain. By 1921 British purchases of Canadian bonds had begun again and made up 4 per cent of the total, but this was a far cry from the 60 to 75 per cent in the years prior to 1915; in the meantime, bond purchases in the United States had reached a high of 50 per cent and levelled off at about 33 per cent. It is noteworthy that of Canadian bonds issued to an aggregate value of $400 million in 1921, almost three-quarters were marketed through Toronto dealers.

That the new order of things was recognized in Britain appears from an address delivered in Toronto's Massey Hall by H.R.H. The Prince of Wales on 4 November 1919:

The welfare of the whole Empire is, after all, the big question for all of us, and it has taken a new shape since the war. Because of their wholehearted participation in the great struggle, the Dominions have entered the partnership of nations by becoming signatories of the peace treaties and members of the Assembly of the League of Nations. The old idea of an Empire handed down from the traditions of Greece and Rome was that of a mother country surrounded by daughter states which owed allegiance to that mother country. But the British Empire has long left that obsolete idea behind, and appears before us in a very different and far grander form. It appears before us as a single state composed of many nations of different origins and different languages, which give their allegiance, not to the mother country, but to a great common system of life and government.

These feelings were to receive their final expression in 1931 in the Statute of Westminister, which would declare the British Commonwealth of Nations a free association of autonomous Dominions and the United Kingdom, bound only by common allegiance to the Crown.

While these larger issues were debated, the Board of Trade continued to work in its more traditional fields. In the midst of the war, when Canada's supplies of lumber assumed vital importance, the Board reasserted its concern about the waste of forest fires and implored the provincial government to institute rigid and effective policies to control settlers' fires and extend the operations of forest rangers. Assurance was received that action would be taken. Just a year afterwards, on 29 July 1917, a devastating fire struck the Matheson-Cochrane-Hearst area, and was followed on 26 August by another at New Liskeard. There were 223 deaths and property was wholly destroyed over a vast area. The Hon. G.H. Ferguson, Minister of Lands, Forests and Mines, called a meeting of interests in Toronto, and a committee was set up under the chairmanship of the Board of Trade's immediate past-President, Arthur Hewitt, with Thomas Bradshaw as Treasurer, to solicit funds and goods for the relief of the survivors. Almost $300,000 was collected and in addition great quantities of clothing and food were assembled and shipped, enough to sustain some 7,000 people for several weeks after the fire. Grants of building materials valued at $150,000 helped erect nearly 750 buildings to replace those destroyed. When the emergency had passed, legal authority was sought and granted to retain surplus funds for immediate use in the event of future fires in the north; members of the existing committee were to serve as trustees. The fund was needed not long afterwards. Haileybury was virtually wiped out by fire on 4 October 1922; the Fire Relief Committee met within an hour of receiving the news and a special train with emergency relief supplies was on its way the next morning. After this latest alarm the provincial government decided to set up a permanent body to deal with similar relief administration. W.H. Alderson, the Board's representative, was appointed Chairman, and the President of the Board, D.A. Cameron, acted as Honorary Treasurer. In another charitable effort the Board collected and distributed more than $8,600 to assist indigent sufferers from the influenza epidemic of 1918.

The largely artificial socio-economic conditions bred by the war produced side effects. Labour unrest was one of the first: both the letter carriers and the police force struck in 1918, and in both cases the Board of Trade acted as intermediary in the negotiations leading to settlements. The following year the disorder spread and disastrous strikes in a number of important operations across the country prompted the Board to advocate a thorough re-examination of the principles underlying employer-employee relations in an attempt to establish conditions which would be recognized on both sides as just. It was also deemed necessary to create measures which would offer some relief to those who were unemployed and without resources.

The momentum of wartime prosperity carried through to the early months of 1920, when shortening inventories and a general scarcity of goods led to rising prices and a reaction in what was called the 'Overalls Movement.' Buyers began to resist high prices by curtailing purchases, and the movement snowballed with such unanticipated rapidity as to create market uncertainty, a sharp decline in business activity and the beginning of deflation. Economists saw the cure in a return to more judicious business methods, greater economy, curtailment of imports and a greater production of both primary and secondary products for export. The need for an improved understanding between management and labour again was emphasized. Remedies, however, were much easier to prescribe than apply; the situation worsened and by the end of the year there were twenty thousand unemployed in Toronto alone amid widespread gloom. By 1921 high unemployment and general business depression had become world-wide phenomena. European currencies were being devalued, leading to an increased flow of imports into Canada and the United States and reducing North American production. Industrial stagnation led inevitably to financial depression and commercial failures in Toronto alone increased from 78 in 1919 to 308 in 1921; the values of securities of all kinds were depreciating enormously. The world seemed to be sliding into an exceedingly dangerous trough, but before the year was out some bright signs were visible: interest rates were coming down, prices had started to decline and, surprisingly, some businessmen seemed to hope that labour would accept a modification in wage rates.

In the matter of wages the Board of Trade at this time strongly criticized a proposal of the city council to increase the minimum rate for those engaged in city contracts to sixty cents an hour to equal the rate paid to civic employees. The Board considered this move inopportune and unnecessary in view of a downward trend in prices; the city's sixty-cent rate was already higher than the general level and any upward pressure would tend only to increase unemployment and inhibit the anticipated return to normal activity. The city was prevailed upon to drop the matter, but the problem workers faced was clear when a weekly wage averaging between $24 and $26 was measured against the $24.02 calculated as necessary to sustain an average Toronto family each week in 1921. Either wages had to go up or prices come down; there was hope for the latter alternative, but how responsible business leaders could have expected in the circumstances to obtain willing acceptance of any wage rate reduction as a means of bringing prices down is difficult to understand. But they did.

As the end of 1922 some business improvement was noted, but it was being deterred by the unsettled state of Europe, a 39 per cent reduction in the flow of immigrants and a reduced flow of capital into new enterprises due, in the Board of Trade's opinion, chiefly to an increasing burden of federal and municipal taxes. Since high wage demands were not matched by enhanced production, Canada's competitive power in world markets was jeopardized and farmers' purchasing power, still a vital factor in the Canadian economy, remained depressed as a result of prevailing world prices for agricultural products. The sale abroad of securities with an aggregate value of $225 million had enhanced the value of the Canadian dollar: from a 4³/₄ per cent premium at the beginning of 1922, American funds were at par by August. Nevertheless, foreign trade was improving, exports exceeded imports in 1921 by $121 million and, with the notable exception of the prices of farm products, a general upturn was evident by 1923.

Throughout the period of post-war adjustment the Board of Trade gave preferred attention to the needs of returned soldiers. It gave strong support to a Housing Commission set up in 1919 to overcome a housing deficit estimated at some three to five thousand units. The Commission, comprising H.H. Williams (chairman), Allan Ross, Sir John Eaton, Sir James Woods and Frank A. Rolph, borrowed funds from the municipality at 5 per cent, purchased blocks of land and erected six-room houses under its own general supervision. They were to sell for between $3,750 and $3,900 on 20-year mortgages, and were intended primarily for the families of war veterans. In the first year 236 dwellings were to be erected and plans called for larger operations in the future if the project worked out as intended.

In December 1920 the Board was asked to devise a method of assisting the unemployed, many of them ex-service men, by setting up a fund on which they could draw for rent payments. A committee was appointed under Arthur Hewitt and it managed to put together almost $45,000 for this purpose. In the winter of 1920–21 the committee made 700 loans totalling $15,000 on easy terms of repayment and without interest, but the undertaking had been hastily arranged and many of the borrowers were soon in default. The committee reluctantly agreed to carry on the service the next winter when the need was even greater, but this time they were careful to respond only in cases of genuine hardship and to impose much stricter conditions of repayment.

When unemployment assumed alarming proportions in 1920, the Mayor brought together representatives of various interests to see what could be done. A Citizens' Unemployment Committee was established, with W.H. Alderson and F.D. Tolchard as Chairman and Secretary respectively, to explore new work sources and encourage businessmen to make their individual contributions toward alleviation. The following year the situation was worse and the Board's action to secure direct intervention by higher levels of government resulted in the creation of a Provisional Advisory Committee on Unemployment headed by the Premier of the province, the Hon. E.C. Drury. All interests were represented on the Committee; the Board's delegate was Charles Marriott. It came forward with a series of recommendations designed to correct some underlying causes of current difficulties, and at a general meeting of the Board in January 1922 Premier Drury, having previously secured the endorsement of the Board's Council, sought the members' co-operation in implementing them. The major ones were:

1 That manufacturers, wholesalers and retailers sell goods on hand at replacement prices.
2 That building contractors and builders' supply companies make a special effort to reduce prices to a minimum in order to encourage building and restore the building industry.
3 That banks and financial institutions allow all reasonable credits and decrease rates as rapidly as conditions may allow.
4 That farmers maintain reasonable production and prepare to make needed improvements and betterments.
5 That labour willingly take a reduction in wages proportionate to the progressive decrease in the cost of living, insofar as such a reduction has not already taken place.

The Committee may have been motivated more by hope than by any expectation of achieving its objectives, and there is nothing to indicate the extent to which its efforts were productive. The Board of Trade had already acted more directly by co-ordinating a Business Council of the Citizens' Repatriation League, which prepared a schedule of employment priorities to ensure preferred attention to veterans' needs, dealt with problems arising between employers and newly-employed veterans and recommended to the federal government the establishment of a Corps of Commissionaires as a means of giving employment to trained military personnel who might find difficulty in adapting to ordinary jobs in civil life.

Disabled ex-service men at Christie Street Hospital in 1924 asked businessmen to look into employment possibilities on their behalf. The President of the Board of Trade organized a study and produced a plan which was discussed with the Prime Minister and members of his cabinet. Their endorsement was followed by an Order-in-Council creating a Rehabilitation Committee of Toronto, with Melville P. White as Chairman and R.A. Stapells, the Board's President, as Vice-Chairman. The plan called for a technical assessment of each applicant's capabilities followed by his placement in suitable employment according to an arrangement whereby he was paid by his employer to the extent of his capacity and the federal government made up any difference to produce a living wage, placed at $32\frac{1}{2}$ cents per hour. Work on the plan began 1 June and by the end of the year 1,097 men had been registered, 162 placed and only 13 had required a government bonus. Some thought that features of this plan might be applied to solving the general unemployment problem. The work of the Rehabilitation Committee was carried on for three years, in which period 740 disabled veterans were placed in employment. The scheme not only ameliorated their financial situation; it restored their confidence in themselves and brought about a marked improvement in their physical and mental condition. The Committee was disbanded in 1927 and the work was carried on for some time thereafter by the federal government through its own departments.

When differences arose in 1921 between the city's Social Service Commission and the various agencies administering welfare, the Board, long anxious to bring about a more efficient handling of charitable and social work, put forward a number of suggestions. It wanted to see improved co-ordination of the work of the agencies, the adoption of more foresighted policies so that they would not be continually finding themselves in emergency situations and a complete re-organization and strengthening of the city's facilities for administering welfare. The city finally abolished the Social Service Commission and created a Welfare Branch within its Department of Health to take over its duties, at the same time instituting a number of reforms along the lines of the Board's proposals.

A confusion of charitable purposes led in 1921 to the establishment of a General Endorsation Committee of the Federation for Community Services to provide information about any organization soliciting funds from the public. The Board of Trade was represented on the Committee by Arthur Hewitt and H.L. Brittain, and it appears to have had some success in restraining unnecessary or ill-advised activities.

Since the beginning of the war the facilities of the Canadian National Exhibition had been taken over to provide winter quarters for troops and horses. Many thousands of men had been accommodated and the Exhibition had played an effective role in the mobilization of Canada's army and in organizing its movements prior to embarkation for overseas destinations. The Exhibition itself had carried on in its accustomed way, however, throughout the war years, embodying patriotic themes and providing both a diversion and a stimulant in trying times. An assessment of its function left no doubt that the decision to continue operations, in spite of difficulties, had been a wise one. The Board of Trade was one of the Exhibition's most ardent supporters and its services were called upon when, after the war, the city decided to set up a committee to review the CNE's plant and program and prepare a comprehensive plan for future development. A good deal of work was done, but it was 1926 before funds were authorized to build a new eastern entrance and undertake other improvements to develop this section of the grounds, as had been advocated.

Although the Exhibition had always concerned itself in a major way with agricultural interests, it was tending to become more and more an industrial and consumer show. There was a feeling that something new was needed to appeal more directly to the farmer and stock-breeder. In August 1919 a delegation, including representatives from the Board of Trade, appeared before the provincial authorities requesting a contribution toward the cost of a building to be used for an International Live Stock Show. At the civic elections of that year a by-law authorizing the allocation of a million dollars for the capital and operating purposes of such a show had been carried by a large majority, and when the federal and provincial governments each agreed to contribute $25,000 a year for ten years for such a purpose the Royal Agricultural Winter Fair Association was incorporated to organize and conduct a 'National Fat Stock Fair and Breeding Show' in Toronto. The building of the required arena was delayed when it became evident that the million dollars authorized was not enough, but the Board and others pressed for action and in 1921 the city awarded the contract – unfortunately not to the lowest bidder, because it was not a Toronto firm. This action immediately raised the ire of the Board of Trade as being wrong in principle; it took violent exception and the city council reversed its decision. Work then proceeded, the arena (named the Coliseum) was completed and the first Winter Fair opened at the end of November 1922. It operated for seven days, attracted an average of 20,000 people each day and was acclaimed an unqualified success.

At the end of the war the question of creating an appropriate memorial to those who had given their lives was widely debated. A consensus was reached at a conference of numerous organizations in 1919 to construct a broad thoroughfare from the new Union Station to a civic square to be created on land between the City Hall and Osgoode Hall, with a building as close as possible to the square housing regimental colours. The matter was taken under advisement by the city, but the eventual decision, strongly influenced by Britain's cenotaph in Whitehall, was to erect a simple monument in front of the City Hall as a memorial to all those who had died in service during the war.

# 7
# The Twenties

In the years following the war new problems faced the city and the Board of Trade. Automobile traffic by 1919 was beginning to build up on streets that possessed inadequate facilities for its accommodation. No funds were available for necessary widenings, nor did the city have authority to restrict the use made of land by its owners to permit a plan of future development and control. The Board of Trade recommended that the city seek legislation giving it the power to establish a 'homologated line' on designated streets defining the extent of future widenings and imposing limiting conditions on adjoining structures. Specific proposals were advanced by the Board in 1921 for the widening of Yonge Street from Heath Street north; there was some delay, but the city was at length persuaded of the wisdom of this move and by the end of the year had cleared the way for the work to be undertaken. As early as 1919 the Board was pointing out the need for establishing rules and designating lots for parking in the downtown area, and the following year new regulations were introduced after study by a special committee appointed by the city. It joined in advocating more stringent penalties under the Criminal Code for auto thefts and efforts to enforce the use of lights by all vehicles between dusk and dawn. The work of the Ontario Safety League was supported and as time went on an increasing awareness of the danger and inconvenience of unregulated vehicular movements on the principal thoroughfares led to a conference of representatives of the Board of Trade, the Canadian Manufacturers' Association, the Ontario Motor League, freight and express interests and others in 1926 and the organization of a Permanent Joint Traffic Committee under the chairmanship of the Board's President. It formulated a program of controls and submitted numerous recommendations for action by the city, one, for example, leading to the inauguration of a system of 'stop streets.'

On 1 September 1921 the thirty-year franchise of the Toronto Railway Company for the operation of street cars on the city's streets expired. The Corporation of the City of Toronto took over the service, appointing the Toronto Transportation Commission as the administrative medium. The Commission faced an almost complete rehabilitation of the system, and the consequent inevitability of a fare increase aroused much public criticism. The Board of Trade now strongly supported public ownership of the street railway system and the Commission's approach to its problems, and felt the adverse reaction to fare adjustment was wholly unwarranted. Within a year the Board was congratulating the TTC on the progress made in the replacement of tracks and introduction of new equipment, and on the expansion of the one-fare area from the seventeen square miles of the private franchise to thirty-five square miles.

Both during and after the war Adam Beck's proposal to construct a network of electric railways centring on Toronto, first put forward in 1912, was endlessly and hotly debated. In this grandiose scheme the municipalities affected would, in effect, surrender their rights to operate their own transportation systems to Ontario Hydro and the latter would assume responsibility for construction, maintenance and operation of the system, furnishing power at cost. There was at first great enthusiasm for the plan and by the Hydro-Electric Railway Act of 1914 Ontario Hydro was authorized to implement it under specified conditions of financing. The war intervened, however, and although negotiations continued and pressure was maintained, neither the federal nor provincial government was in any mood to offer direct financial encouragement to an undertaking estimated to cost in total something like $90 million. The Toronto Board of Trade, while fully appreciating the benefits of Hydro, was noting with some concern the growth of the system and the enormous investment it represented, against which no private enterprise could compete, and it wondered whether such a monopoly was indeed wholly in the public interest. Being aware also of the anticipated cost burden on the taxpayer, the city's loss of control of its own street railway system and the increasing role of motor transport, the Board opposed a 1916 civic by-law to bring Toronto into the proposed Hydro radials network, but it carried nevertheless by a large majority.

A protracted political battle ensued, complicated by the election of a

United Farmers of Ontario government in 1919 which found itself in an ambivalent position on the radials question. The leader of the new government, E.C. Drury, appointed a Royal Commission under Judge Sutherland to find the answer to the problem, and when it found itself unable to justify the radials scheme Drury refused to guarantee the necessary bonds. The strong pro-radials faction on Toronto's city council were not to be put off and at the 1922 civic elections the citizens were asked: 'Are you in favour of carrying out the Agreement with the Hydro-Electric Power Commission of Ontario for the construction of the radial railway to Bowmanville without the guarantee by the Ontario Government of the bonds of the Commission?' Again the Board of Trade expressed its reservations about the wisdom of such a course, but Adam Beck's vigorous campaigning on behalf of his brain-child had substantial popular impact and the electors responded affirmatively – this time by a very slim majority.

In August of that year the Board learned that the city council proposed to enter into an agreement with Ontario Hydro giving them the exclusive right-of-way for fifty years at one dollar a year on the only route available for radials along the eastern waterfront, with authority to build a subway up Bay Street to the City Hall. The Board's Council in a body waited upon the Mayor, requesting a copy of the alleged agreement and that action be deferred pending a referendum. The requests were declined. As time was running out the Board's Council then applied for an injunction to prevent the city of Toronto and the Harbour Commissioners (who did not favour the scheme) from entering into the purported agreement. An interim injunction was granted but was later withdrawn with an order for a speedy trial. The Board's Council was joined by representatives of other citizens' groups in another attempt to persuade city council to place the matter before the electors but the politicians were obdurate, refused to change their stand and ratified the agreement. The issue then came to trial and a judgment was rendered against the city, restraining it from entering into a radials agreement with Ontario Hydro without the approval of the provincial legislature. Premier Drury declined to authorize an agreement without a vote of the people; the issue was placed before the electors at the 1923 civic elections and was defeated. The outcome brought much satisfaction to the Board, which felt that its action – probably the most drastic it had ever taken – had preserved the city's waterfront.

It was a decisive defeat for Beck. The Toronto reversal led to a general collapse of his broad scheme for a Hydro radials system in southern Ontario, to which he had devoted so much of his great talent and energy, and he took it very hard. The point was not that the Board was against electric radial railway services on principle; it certainly had doubts about the extensive network proposed by Ontario Hydro, particularly in view of increasing motor traffic and an enlarged provincial road-building program and the fact that most lines of this kind in the United States were losing money, but it saw merit in the establishment of certain key services and urged the city to investigate the matter further. Both the Canadian National and Canadian Pacific Railways were interested and suggested three radial lines from the east, north and west using their right-of-way along the Esplanade viaduct to terminate at a common junction in Union Station and linking up there with the regular street car services of the TTC. This plan was well thought of for a time, but did not materialize.

The long battle for the grade-separation of the railways' right-of-way across the waterfront was resumed in 1922. Representatives of the city and the Board of Trade submitted a review of the situation to the federal government, urging that the viaduct agreement be carried out and the new Union Station brought into use with the least possible delay. With the formation of the national railway system the CNR had assumed the obligations of the Grand Trunk Railway under the 1913 agreement, and when the Board of Directors of the CNR had been appointed in 1923 the Board immediately brought the matter forward for its consideration. The Presidents of CN and CP, Sir Henry Thornton and E.W. Beatty, came to Toronto to confer with the Board's Executive and Viaduct Committees, after which Sir Henry personally inspected the crossings (it was the first time he had seen them) and agreed to a new study. Later that year CN's directors met in Toronto but made no announcement, but in November the two railways submitted a modified plan which the city agreed to consider. In the meantime the Harbour Commissioners were prevented from implementing their development plans by the uncertainty of the outcome.

The new proposal abandoned the idea of track elevation west of Church Street and substituted bridges at Yonge, Bay and York Streets, bringing the cost down from an original estimate in 1913 of nearly $34 million to $20.5 million. In a letter to A.O. Hogg, Sir Henry Thornton said: 'Permit me to assure you as President of the Board of Trade that the assistance of your organization has done much to bring the viaduct question to a head, and I earnestly hope that a decision will be reached which will prove completely satisfactory to the people of Toronto and the other parties interested in the matter.' Again the Board saw its goal in sight, presumably concurring in the new plan, which is somewhat surprising since it had previously insisted on a wholly elevated railway grade and wanted no part of a bridge compromise. However, the CNR was acting with good will and by January 1925 work was expected to start that spring and the opening of Union Station seemed only eighteen months away. Congratulations were extended to the Board's 'pioneers in the fight for grade separation' – Sir James Woods, Hugh Blain and Lionel Clarke. But the city council and the Harbour Commissioners rejected the railways' alternate plan and negotiations began once more.

This time the Minister of Railways and Canals, the Hon. George P. Graham, directed the chief engineer of his department to make an independent survey. This was done and a report was submitted 9 July 1924 recommending complete elevation of the railway lines with, however, some modest revisions which would bring the cost down to $28.5 million. The revised scheme was endorsed by the city council and the Harbour Commissioners on 11 July; an Act Respecting the Toronto Terminals Railway Company was passed by the House of Commons before the month was out, annulling the June 1909 Order of the Board of Railway Commissioners for Canada, the agreement of 1913 and all subsidiary amendments, and providing for the construction of a viaduct from Bathurst Street to Logan Avenue with an overhead bridge at Spadina and subways at York, Bay, Yonge, Jarvis, Sherbourne, Parliament, Cherry, Queen and Eastern. The whole undertaking was to be carried out to the satisfaction of the Board of Railway Commissioners and the entire cost borne by the CNR, the CPR and the city in proportions to be agreed on or, failing agreement, as directed by the Commissioners. All outstanding issues were settled at a meeting of representatives of the two railways, the city and the Harbour Commissioners on 7 November, were approved by the Minister and an order was signed by the Governor General on 18 November. An argument that had been going on for more than twenty-five years was at last settled with remarkable despatch.

The city of Toronto assumed a share of the cost amounting to $7.4 million, and the Board of Railway Commissioners' order for the commencement of construction was issued on 26 December 1924. Work was under way the following year and continued without interruption. In August 1927 Union Station, idle for so many years for want of rail approaches, was formally opened by H.R.H. The Prince of Wales, although the viaduct itself was still unfinished and a completion date had not been announced. It was in fact not wholly finished until December 1930.

The lack in Toronto of proper customs facilities had become a source of irritation. The old Customs House had been razed in 1919 and not replaced, and the Board considered this a shameful neglect of the country's biggest generator of customs revenues; it campaigned for years to secure adequate facilities, but it was 1929 before they were supplied in a new federal building on the south side of Front Street. The building extended eastward in an arc from Bay Street and, along with Union Station, created a beautiful façade from York to Yonge Streets.

By 1925 the Boulevard Drive had been built from Bay to Dufferin Street through the Exhibition grounds, and its extension through Toronto Island by bridging both the east and west harbour entrances was apparently contemplated. The Board of Trade recommended, however, that priority be given to the completion of harbour improvements east of Yonge Street and the development of industrial lands in this area. The construction of the CPR's enormous Royal York Hotel on the site of the old Queen's Hotel immediately facing Union Station, was under way, with completion expected in 1929.

The Toronto Board of Trade continued to promote vigorously the development of the Great Lakes–St Lawrence system as a water route from mid-continent to the sea. Traverse of the existing Welland and St Lawrence canals was limited to vessels of fourteen-foot draught and carrying capacities of up to 100,000 bushels of grain, whereas ships with five times that capacity were plying the upper lakes and unloading at Port Colborne or Buffalo. In June 1923 a party of 210, including representatives from other Boards of Trade, travelled down the St Lawrence and up the Saguenay River to gain some first-hand impressions and new outlooks on both shipping and power in this mighty water system. The Montreal Board of Trade, on the other hand, did not favour the creation of a deep channel from the lakes to the sea, contending that Montreal was a natural point of exchange; in 1921 it had signified its opposition to seaway proposals under discussion in Ottawa. Its position thereafter was somewhat equivocal and it was not fully reconciled to the St Lawrence Waterway project until the 1950s when the system's potential for power development outweighed other objections.

The Toronto Board supported the Canadian Deep Waterways and Power Association in its 1921 application to the Ontario government for a provincial contribution to its efforts to stimulate action and urged the growing importance of a deep St Lawrence channel as work progressed on the Welland Canal improvements; the two projects were obviously interdependent. In addition, power development on the St Lawrence would stimulate industrial establishment in eastern Ontario. Canadian and American engineers estimated that the creation of a twenty-five-foot channel to Montreal and the generation of nearly 1.5 million horsepower from the international section could be achieved at a cost of some $250 million.

The International Joint Commission advocated that a treaty be entered into by Canada and the United States for the joint execution of the project, and by 1925 representatives of the two nations were in consultation and the outlook seemed hopeful. Two years later tentative negotiations were still in progress and a resolution adopted by the Toronto Board urged the federal government 'to proceed without unnecessary delay to make arrangements for the early construction' of the waterway.

When an Act Respecting Bankruptcy was introduced in the House of Commons early in 1918 a special committee was appointed to examine its provisions and an exhaustive submission was made to Ottawa, followed by renewed representations when the Bill was before the Senate. Other interested organizations were urged to support the legislation, and passage of the Bill, with an effective date of 1 July 1920, ended a long campaign. Another Bill in 1923, An Act to provide for the Investigation of Combines, Monopolies, Trusts and Mergers, received similar treatment and was modified before passage to meet many of the Board's views. This statute conferred powers that were felt to be too far-reaching in their effects and it was feared they would create undue disturbance in the business field, but when the amended legislation had been in force for some time and there had been no prosecutions the apprehension of businessmen subsided.

The manufacture and sale of margarine, permitted by Order-in-Council under the War Measures Act, had been due to come under ban again at the end of the war; the Board, on the basis of conclusive evidence indicating continuing demand, petitioned the Minister of Agriculture to enact legislation authorizing its production and sale and succeeded in securing at least a temporary respite. Its manufacture and importation was extended to 31 August 1923 and its sale to 1 March 1924.

In 1920 the Board was represented at all hearings of the Board of Transport Commmissioners on an application by the Bell Telephone Company for a rate increase. It acknowledged the need for adequate financing but considered it essential that such need be sufficiently established and, even if it were, that increases should not be more than enough to assure payment of reasonable dividends, which it interpreted as not greater than 8 per cent per annum on the monies paid in by shareholders. A proposal to introduce a measured system was strongly opposed, any concessions granted to be predicated on retention of the flat rate method of billing.

Motion pictures and the advertisement of them roused the ire of Toronto citizens in 1920, and the Board saw fit to recommend to the Provincial Treasurer that stricter censorship be applied. The action led to an enquiry, a complete revision of the system and the appointment of a new Board of

Censors. The Board accepted an invitation to appoint representatives on the Motion Picture Committee of the Social Service Council of Ontario, and after a year or so expressed gratification that 'very decided improvements' had been achieved. A year earlier the Board had shown itself somewhat less puritanical by joining in an effort to provide some diversion for Toronto citizens on their traditionally gloomy Sundays. This resulted in the Sunday opening of the Museum and the Art Gallery, both apparently considered educational and sinless.

The Board remained dissatisfied with the city's assessment system; in 1920 it was investigating the practices employed elsewhere and endeavouring to induce the provincial authorities to draft a basis for municipal assessment which could be recommended for adoption across the Dominion. Concern, however, was not only with the tax base but with increasing tax rates. Between 1913 and 1922 Toronto's population had grown 19 per cent from 445,575 to 529,083, whereas municipal tax receipts in the same period had gone up from $8.5 million to $24 million, or nearly three-fold. The increase was due not only to increased assessment but also to new forms of taxation, and businessmen were seriously worried that the process, if allowed to continue, would jeopardize the city's growth and future prosperity as an industrial and wholesale distributing centre.

Federal taxes, too, were a heavy burden and seemed especially onerous in the light of rate reductions introduced in the United States. A Board of Trade delegation went to Ottawa in March 1923 to set a number of proposals before W.S. Fielding, the Minister of Finance, chief among them being the adoption of a turnover tax on all processed goods to replace the sales tax then in force; adoption of a graduated income tax; repeal of the Stamp Tax, and the segregation of revenues intended for the retirement of war debts. The last-named was motivated by a suspicion that a proportion of 'war taxes' was being used to meet debts of the railways, and this was resented on the grounds that the railways should be able to maintain themselves out of revenues. In proposing a graduated income tax with specified exemptions, the objective was to relieve the taxpayer of unjustifiable assessments and what were regarded as overlapping taxes at the municipal, provincial and federal levels.

So concerned were businessmen with the deterrent effect of current tax policies upon national growth that the Boards of Trade of Toronto, Montreal, Ottawa and Winnipeg jointly arranged a meeting in Ottawa in March 1924 to discuss the issues. It brought together representatives from Boards of Trade and Chambers of Commerce from across Canada, and at its conclusion a petition was submitted to Prime Minister Mackenzie King urging the government to curtail expenditures, both capital and administrative; convoke a provincial conference which would devise methods of co-operation and avoid duplication of effort; bring both staff and working conditions in the government service up to modern standards; eliminate the publication of unnecessary reports and reduce all government publications to a simplified form. The Boards and Chambers attending agreed to pursue these objectives locally, and the Toronto Board immediately made its representations to Ontario Premier Ferguson and to local members of Parliament and the provincial legislature.

An application to the Minister of Finance in 1922 led to an amendment of the Customs Act establishing more equitable conditions applicable to imports from countries with substantially depreciated currencies, although for some time afterwards complaints continued about the inadequate protection afforded by Canadian tariffs, illegitimate dumping and wholesale smuggling, all of which were depressing Canada's legitimate business. The Board reiterated its plea for the creation of a permanent and independent Tariff Board, and in 1925 collaborated with other organizations to form the Commercial Protective Association, comprising representatives of manufacturers, wholesalers and importers, in order to curb smuggling. The Association persuaded the government to strengthen the penalties in the Customs Act and employ additional preventive staff; these measures brought about substantial improvement almost as soon as they were put into effect. The next year the Board expressed its gratification over the formation at last of a Canadian Advisory Board on Tariff and Taxation whose function would be 'to enquire into and hear representations on all matters pertaining to the tariff and other forms of taxation under the direction of the Minister of Finance.' When the Customs Act was amended in 1921 to require all imported goods to be marked with their country of origin a Board delegation requested and obtained an extension of the time allowed for compliance to avoid imposing an undue hardship on dealers. Further regulations then issued were appealed so effectively that the entire legislation was withdrawn for reconsideration.

The flow of investment capital into Canada from Great Britain declined steadily after the war. Of Canadian bonds to the value of approximately $593 million marketed in 1924, 64.6 per cent were placed in Canada, 34.3 per cent in the United States and only 1.1 per cent in Britain. This was due of course to Britain's straitened economic condition, but there were signs of recovery and her early re-entry into the Canadian market was anticipated. The Board of Trade now looked somewhat askance at the growing practice of both the federal and provincial governments of raising their loans at home – a practice that probably grew out of the remarkable success of the War Loans. The Board felt that this withdrew from legitimate commercial enterprises the funds they needed for development, and that it would be preferable to seek capital abroad and leave Canadian funds available for the development of Canadian resources. Further evidence of the Board's concern for the rights of private enterprise was its disapproval of the federal government's intention, announced in 1922, to re-establish the Canadian Wheat Board. This was considered to be (except in time of war) a violation of the civil right of freedom of contract and an interference with normal commercial functions. The Board's position was upheld by the Minister of Justice, in whose opinion the reconstruction of the Wheat Board, with compulsory powers, was *ultra vires* of the Parliament of Canada.

Renewed attention was given after the war to the promotion of tourism. The Board recommended to the Ontario government in 1922 that it set up a separate bureau for this purpose and also concern itself with the adequacy of hotel accommodation throughout the province. In the same year a number of local organizations, including the Board of Trade, co-operated in the formation of a Toronto Publicity Bureau which, although its resources were limited, carried out a successful program designed to attract visitors to the city, particularly from the United States.

A special committee under C.L. Burton in 1923 prepared a brief on immigration policy which was submitted to the ministers concerned in both the provincial and federal governments prior to a Dominion-Provincial conference on the subject. The Board's advice was consistent with that of previous years, i.e., aggressive steps should be taken to stimulate the influx of settlers with, however, a screening process to assure that those admitted were assimilable, and adequate procedures should be introduced to ensure their effective absorption into Canadian communities. Some years earlier concern had been expressed over the importation of unwanted political ideas from Europe, but at the Board's Annual Meeting in 1925 the retiring President, R.A. Stapells, expressed his conviction that 'Sovietism and Communism are fast on the decline.'

Interest in the development of northern Ontario grew with the discovery and exploitation of new mineral resources. Trips to the mining country were organized frequently so that Toronto businessmen could make a more realistic assessment of progress there than was possible from merely observing the somewhat frenzied movement of mining shares, and the Board urged the Ontario government to make available more complete and reliable information about this huge and still relatively unknown territory. Representatives of the Board of Trade took part in the Ninety-fourth Annual Meeting of the British Association for the Advancement of Science held in Toronto in 1924 and assisted in arrangements for a subsequent visit to the mining country by many of the delegates. They were apparently much impressed, and it was believed that their enthusiastic reaction would lead to an increased flow of British capital into Canadian mining operations. A Northern Ontario Development Committee was appointed by the Board in 1924 to stimulate interest in that territory; one of its first activities was to bring to Toronto a group of businessmen from the north and arrange for them to confer with provincial officials and others whose support could be useful. This was a further effort to create understanding and confidence among those with common aims in the two parts of the province which still seemed in many respects to be so remote from one another. The next year a delegation of Board members toured extensively through the northern regions and these reciprocal visits, initiated by the Board and continued over many years, undoubtedly made an important contribution to provincial consolidation.

The Ontario Associated Boards of Trade continued to meet annually to deal with matters of common interest to its members. The main centres of southern Ontario provided the meeting places, attendance was good and discussion active. Subjects receiving special attention in 1921 were the desirability of establishing the greatest possible uniformity in the Companies' Acts of the Dominion and the various provinces, and the need for a review of all aspects of taxation to create a common ground for assessment and taxation throughout Ontario and equity with other provinces. In 1924 an attempt was made to broaden the scope of the Ontario Associated Boards of Trade, which had been largely a southern Ontario grouping, by an amalgamation with the Western Ontario United Boards of Trade and the Temiskaming and Northern Ontario Associated Boards of Trade and Chambers of Commerce. The idea of improving rapport between the two parts of the province was stimulated by an announcement from the Ontario Premier at that year's meeting of his government's intention to build a road from North Bay to Cobalt to give motor access to the north country.

Because of the war an interim meeting of the Chambers of Commerce of the British Empire was held in London in 1917 instead of the scheduled Congress in Toronto, but the Ninth Congress did take place in Toronto 17–23 September 1920. Delegates from all the major Empire countries met in Convocation Hall under the President, the Rt Hon. Lord Desborough. Resolutions presented by the Toronto Board favouring the establishment of a league of English-speaking people and reaffirming preferential trade within the Empire were adopted. A post-Congress tour took the delegates on a three-week circuit of cities in central and northern Ontario. The Ninth Congress also gave support to a proposal then being developed in Great Britain and the United States for the creation of an International Chamber of Commerce to provide a medium for the consideration of issues affecting the world-wide transaction of trade and commercial affairs and in particular to attempt to regularize the statutory conditions applicable to such transactions. A number of those attending the Congress subsequently travelled to New York for further discussion of the project.

At the Tenth Congress, held in London in July 1924, it was agreed to publish a textbook which would tell the story of the Empire for use in all the schools of Empire countries, but the British delegates declined to support a resolution favouring Imperial preference, feeling that Empire preferences would weaken her competitive position with the rest of the world. A compromise resolution was nevertheless adopted which affirmed belief in the observance of the most liberal terms of trade among Empire countries and vouchsafed support of any plan acceptable to Britain which, by promoting this object, would serve to develop and unify the Empire. Nor was everyone in Canada at this time enthusiastic about preferences. The Board's Tanners' Section, for example, was complaining about the influx of British leathers under preferential tariffs and abnormal exchange conditions, which was hurting Canadian industries. 'There is a growing feeling,' they said, 'among the business men and manufacturers of Canada that self-interest and not sentiment must govern our fiscal policy.'

Throughout this period the structure and operating methods of the Board of Trade remained basically unchanged. Its Executive Committee and Council and various standing committees continued to meet regularly to discuss the issues of the day, major and minor, and representations were frequently made to the competent authorities in what were deemed to be the best interests of business and the community at large. Internally, the Board was endeavouring to improve direct services to its members. An Information Department was set up in 1919 under F.D. Tolchard to deal with their enquiries and make available various publications and official reports for their reference. The Traffic Department under Thomas Marshall had from the start filled an evident need and its operations expanded year by year. It dealt with a constant flow of enquiry and requests for assistance from members on their individual problems, and in addition served in an advisory capacity to the Council on matters such as freight rates and classifications, radial and railway construction, carriers' liability, cartage services, legislation governing motor truck transportation – in fact, everything imaginable to do with the movement of goods and people.

The membership of the Board had increased to 2,685 by 1921, 35 of these being Life Members and 207 non-residents of Toronto. In addition to the Board's formal appointments to numerous organizations concerned in various ways with the city's welfare, and its increasing activities in an advisory or consultative capacity in civic affairs, virtually every member of the city's major commissions – the Toronto Harbour Commission, the Toronto Transportation Commission, the Toronto Hydro-Electric Commission – was a Board member. It had become not only large but also very influential. In 1921 F.D. Tolchard was appointed Secretary of the Corporation succeeding F.G. Morley, who had served for some eighteen years in that capacity and now became Adviser to the Council. Tolchard had been assuming increasing administrative responsibility since his return to the Board following wartime duties in Washington, where he had served, on leave of absence, as Assistant Director of War Supplies for the British War Mission.

The new premises in the Royal Bank Building were proving satisfactory: good use was made of the luncheon facilities which served between 250 and 275 each day. It was found convenient and time-saving to hold meetings of committees in private rooms during the mid-day period so that luncheon could be taken while discussion proceeded, and this practice was encouraged. As the Board was wholly responsible for the food service, the maintenance of a reasonably high volume was obviously important to keep costs down. The large Assembly Room was not much used for its intended purpose and in 1919 it was converted to a lounge where members could meet or relax. It proved extremely popular and the idea of providing members with services and accommodation comparable to those of the private and more exclusive clubs occupied an important place in all future consideration of premises requirements. With the expiry of its lease in 1924 the Board considered other possibilities but decided that its existing situation would be difficult to better and renewed its lease for a further ten-year period.

The various Trade Sections of the Board pursued their own affairs, often conveying data and opinion useful to the Council in establishing general policy. An Electrical Section was formed in 1915 to foster co-operation among members in this field, and a Lumbermen's Section, created the same year, gave initiative to the organization of an Ontario Retail Lumber Dealers' Association. Both the Tanners' and the Wholesale

Dry-goods Sections suffered severe shortages when imports were curtailed during the war and worked to develop domestic sources of fabrics and dyestuffs. An Advertising Club was formed in 1924 to foster better advertising and 'to promote just and equitable practices'; it also undertook to bring about co-operation among those engaged in the advertising field in assisting civic, philanthropic and patriotic endeavours. The Bankers' Section, an important affiliate of the Board since its early days, broke away in 1921 so that it could discharge its increased responsibilities more effectively as an independent organization.

When an Act to Amend the Copyright Act of 1921 was passed in 1923, the Board's Book Publishers' Section warned the Minister of Trade and Commerce that it would be dangerous to enforce the law before a copyright treaty with the United States had been negotiated. As a result the Minister took interim measures to protect Canadian copyrights until reciprocal arrangements could be made with the United States, and the next year arrangements providing full observance of each country's copyrights were worked out. Canada's adherence to the Berne Convention as of 1 January 1925, thus securing protection throughout the Copyright Union, materially strengthened the position of Canadian publishers. The Customs Department was also co-operating by adopting a screening process to prevent the importation of works whose circulation was, for copyright reasons, illegal in Canada.

A significant step to encourage active participation in the Board's affairs was the formation of a Young Men's Club in 1919. Organized under the leadership of Basil Tippet, who became its first chairman, the Club developed a program of regular dinner meetings to provide an opportunity for younger members to hear speakers on topics of current interest and to stimulate social intercourse. The objects of the Club were stated to be:

To promote good fellowship among younger members of the Board of Trade.
To educate members to a fuller realization of their responsibilities as members of the Board of Trade.
To pave the way to a better understanding of the City's social and economic needs.
To provide opportunity from time to time for the members to participate in public service work.
To make members better citizens of the Dominion of Canada and of the greater Commonwealth of British Nations.

The Club was strongly supported as serving a most useful purpose; its membership grew and it became a successful and popular feature of the

158 To Serve the Community

Board's total operation. With the passage of time the name Young Men's Club lost its appropriateness and in 1926 it became simply the Board of Trade Club. There remained, however, a need to capture the interest of up-and-coming young businessmen and in 1931 a new body, the Young Men's Section, was created specifically for members under thirty. Its basic purpose was to provide a training ground for relatively new entrants into the business field by furnishing instruction and offering opportunity for involvement in community affairs under the general supervision of the senior organization. It, too, grew and prospered, becoming affiliated with the world-wide Junior Chamber International organization and in 1947 changing its name to the Toronto Junior Board of Trade to conform with generally accepted usage.

# 8
# Toward a National Organization

While it had always considered that its prime responsibility lay with the city of Toronto, the Board had never regarded its mandate as a restricted one, and indeed its Act of Incorporation stated that its acitivities were to be conducted on behalf of 'the City of Toronto in particular and of the Province of Ontario and the Dominion of Canada in general.' Obviously the concerns of Toronto businessmen were directly affected by the legislation of the federal and Ontario governments, and to be effective it was essential that the Board's efforts should carry weight at these levels. That it had developed an impressive effectiveness in the broader jurisdiction was attested by the lines of communication it had opened up with both Ottawa and Queen's Park and by the successes achieved there in its attempts to influence legislative action. The Board's Council had nevertheless always considered a wide and co-ordinated base of business opinion as vital to carrying out a full program of work and making the greatest impact upon governmental authorities; this attitude had led to its leadership in the creation of the Ontario Associated Boards of Trade. But it wanted to go further and establish a body to speak for businessmen in Boards of Trade and Chambers of Commerce across the country. Its one effort in this direction in 1902 had been highly successful, but no attempt had then been made, or apparently even contemplated, to follow through by putting the conference held that year in Toronto on a regular basis.

A Dominion body had been organized in 1870 and it held its first meeting in Ottawa on 18 January 1874. According to S.B. Gundy, the Toronto Board's President in 1925, 'it contributed in large measure to the adoption for Canada of the fiscal policy which has since, in greater or lesser degree, been the accepted policy of this country.' There were a number of subsequent meetings, but the organization seems to have died a natural death by about 1880. Mr Gundy suggested that a new Canadian organization be formed, patterned after the Chamber of Commerce of the United States, which had been operative over the previous twelve years and was recognized as 'one of the most powerful business organizations in that country.' He proposed that a conference be held to consider the project, the idea of the conference being 'to subvert the spirit of sectionalism by a general discussion of Canadian problems, out of which would develop reciprocity of thought and principle.'

The Council in February 1925 directed a letter to every Board of Trade and Chamber of Commerce in Canada outlining the idea and seeking a reaction. The response was enthusiastic. The Presidents of the Boards of Trade of Vancouver, Montreal, Winnipeg, Toronto, Halifax and St John met in Montreal in September to develop a procedure and decided that a first informal conference should be held in Winnipeg in November. Letters of invitation were accordingly despatched and again the response was encouraging.

The Winnipeg Conference was duly held 16–18 November 1925, with 150 delegates representing Boards of Trade and Chambers of Commerce in every province. Toronto's delegation, led by President S.B. Gundy, was the largest. Sir Thomas White, Minister of Finance, led off the proceedings with an address on 'Canada's Present National and Economic Position,' and the event concluded with a banquet for 550 tendered by the Winnipeg Board of Trade which was addressed by E.W. Beatty, CPR President, on the subject of national development. It was the consensus of those attending that the occasion had engendered a great spirit of co-operation among the delegates, one of whom, A.M. Belding, was moved to remark that it was 'the second Confederation – the Confederation of mutual understanding and good will – the Confederation of mutual confidence and national unity .... The spirit of this Conference has convinced me that in the years to come it will be said of you who have assembled here that you, also, have builded better than you knew.'

S.B. Gundy was elected chairman of the conference sessions at which the subjects discussed included the national economy and taxation, Imperial trade relations and trade within the Empire, immigration and colonization, the St Lawrence waterway, scientific research in relation to industrial and agricultural development, the convening of a National Foreign Trade Conference, utilization of Maritime ports and a number of questions having to do with transport and communications. It was agreed to form a Dominion Board of Trade on a permanent basis and the Presidents of the Toronto and Montreal Boards of Trade, the London and Hamilton Chambers of Commerce and the Montreal Chambre de Commerce were named as a committee to prepare a plan of organization and financing and submit it for ratification to the other bodies concerned. This was done, and, general agreement on procedure having been reached, the first official annual conference of the new organization was held in St John, 19–21 October 1926. At the Annual Meeting of the Royal Bank of Canada in that year Sir Herbert Holt observed: 'I regard the inauguration of a Dominion Board of Trade as a movement of importance in promoting the growth of national sentiment. It is only by co-operation on the basis of a national economic policy, unimpeded by sectional appeals and prejudices, that we can attain that fuller prosperity to which the character of our people and our great natural resources entitle us.' A warm tribute was paid to S.B. Gundy for the vision and organizing genius he had displayed leading to the founding of the national body, and his election as its first president was a foregone conclusion.

The new organization was given the provisional name The Canadian Board of Trade, and to provide for the continuous administration of its affairs Wendell McL. Clarke, who had been Director of the Commercial Intelligence Service in the Department of Trade and Commerce in Ottawa, was named Chief Executive Officer, with offices in Montreal. C.L. Burton, First Vice-President of the Toronto Board, was the first of a number of sustaining members who undertook to contribute $1,000 a year toward the cost of maintaining the operation. The name finally decided upon was The Canadian Chamber of Commerce, and its initial year was successfully completed with the Second Annual Convention in Vancouver. Progress was steady, services were broadened and, by the Third Annual Convention in Quebec City in 1928, active membership had increased by 35 per cent and was still growing. Policies were being established on many important issues affecting the nation and the nation's business, the final determination of policies being a major purpose of the annual meetings held regularly thereafter in principal cities across the country.

Throughout these years the Toronto Board of Trade maintained a congenial relationship with the elected members of the city's government; its earlier distress over what it considered to be incompetence in civic administration appeared to have subsided. Representatives of the city and the Board had worked amicably together on a number of projects for social or civic betterment, and in 1924 the Board was even able to extend its congratulations to Mayor Hiltz and the city council for having achieved that desideratum of all citizens – a lowering of the tax rate. It refrained from any direct participation in the elective process for civic office, although it had frequently indicated a fervent hope that candidates possessing higher qualifications would offer themselves for public office.

The apathy of voters toward the municipal elections, then held annually on the first day of January, disturbed the Board's Council and many other conscientious citizens, since it frequently resulted in a plurality for candidates who had managed to acquire an active, though minority, following. Accordingly the Board undertook a campaign in the weeks preceding the elections of January 1925 to stimulate the citizens to exercise their franchise. Various media were employed to induce electors to 'Vote as you like – but vote!' The costs of the program were met by a special fund created for the purpose from moneys subscribed by members, mostly representatives of the larger corporations. The effort resulted in a gratifying increase in the total vote polled, and it was repeated the following year with, however, somewhat less effect. Campaigns, always with the same theme, were conducted irregularly for many years thereafter. Through the Ontario Associated Boards of Trade and Chambers of Commerce the Toronto Board encouraged its sister organizations to act similarly in their own municipalities and generally to become more directly involved in civic government. There was some doubt whether 1 January was the best day for Toronto's municipal elections, and in 1928 the Mayor requested the Board's opinion on a proposed change to a day in early December. The Board found itself not in favour, but when other interests were consulted it became evident that there was a considerable division of opinion. The question was put to the electors at the January 1929 elections and they voted heartily for the retention of New Year's Day as Election Day. A few years later another plebiscite was taken on the same issue; again the citizens voted against a change and the Board, which had consistently opposed a change, hoped that the matter had finally been settled.

Problems associated with the physical growth of the city were becoming more acute. The Board had long ago recorded its belief in the need for a civic planning authority, but when a Town Planning and Housing Conference in 1922 submitted recommendations to a special committee on this subject appointed by the Ontario legislature that municipalities be authorized to establish local planning commissions, the Board, after consideration, registered objection. It was considered improper that wide powers in such an important field should be conferred upon a commission which was not under the control of the municipal council. The Board contended that planning needs would be better served by an advisory committee appointed by the city council. Nothing was done, however, in spite of obviously increasing problems created by extensive new construction, higher population densities in the downtown area and a rapidly worsening traffic situation. Population had increased to almost 550,000 by 1925, and in that year alone buildings were erected to the total value of $25.8 million. In 1927 the Board decided on a course of its own and appointed an Engineering Section made up of qualified members who were to study growth patterns and advise the Council in matters of development control. A year later a Board of Trade delegation headed by the President, C.L. Burton, conferred with the Mayor on the need for a planning authority, and this led to action by the city council and the appointment of an Advisory City Planning Commission composed of businessmen and engineers. After a year's work the Commission in March 1929 produced a plan and recommendations for development in the central district which, with some amendment, was endorsed by the heads of the civic departments concerned. Implementation of the plan would involve substantial expenditures and the approval of the citizens was sought at the next municipal elections. It was not forthcoming. Apparently popular opinion was that if expensive development projects were to be undertaken they should embrace a much wider territory than the downtown sector covered by the present plan, and, after some debate, the city indicated its willingness to proceed on a broader front.

In the meantime the Board of Trade was proceeding on its own way, concerning itself for the time being more with improving the appearance of the city than with basic planning. It arranged a meeting of representatives of businessmen's organizations and service clubs to discuss, under the leadership of architect John M. Lyle, ways in which property owners might themselves contribute to making Toronto a more handsome city. Out of this discussion arose the idea, which for a long time had a strong appeal, of arcading the sidewalks on main streets, thereby extending the road surface and affording protection to pedestrians. Some thought was given to the suggested award of a medal or plaque to the owners and architects of new buildings deemed the most beautiful in each two-year period. The advisability of recommending a city by-law requiring the removal of overhanging signs was debated, but there was far from unanimity on this question. On the recommendation of its Retail Merchants' Section, however, the Board in 1928 proposed the enactment of legislation for the removal of signs by a specified future date and their prohibition thereafter, but there was still much opposition to such regulation and nothing more was done for many years.

When the proposed annexation of York Township was under consideration in 1928 and there was evidence of general opposition to any further annexations by the city, the Board took the position that some form of working relationship with adjoining municipalities was desirable to ensure orderly development and uniformity of controls, both of which would greatly facilitate what appeared to be an inevitable unification in the future. The Board's Civic Improvement Committee under A.E.K. Bunnell in 1930 gave much attention to this question and was led almost inevitably to the idea of creating a metropolitan area in which the adjacent municipalities of the region would be united under some form of common administration.

Much concern was evident at this time over the detrimental effects of the emission of smoke and gases on the health of citizens and the value of properties. A joint committee representing the Engineering Section and the Civic Improvement Committee was delegated to study and report on the subject, and information was secured on control measures being enforced in other cities. One possible solution looked on favourably at the time was the establishment of central heating plants.

To relieve traffic congestion in the central area, the city's Works Committee and the Chief Constable in 1930 wanted to prohibit all parking on downtown streets during business hours. The Joint Traffic Committee (on which the Board of Trade was represented) thought this was going too far and advocated a prohibition during rush hours only. A by-law to this effect was duly passed, but the city began to fear the effect it might have on business activities and held it in abeyance, finally succumbing to pressures from the Board, among others, and announcing an effective date of 31 March 1931. The Joint Traffic Committee had been working to good effect, making proposals to the city for through and stop streets, street widenings, one-way streets and other measures to relieve pressures and speed traffic movement, and a good many of them were adopted. The Committee observed with interest an experimental installation of automatic electric traffic signals in 1927 and concluded that such devices should be employed at all major intersections.

Progress was being made in the creation of a provincial roads system. George S. Henry, Ontario Minister of Highways, announced in 1926 that a material extension of the highways network was being planned and that the trunk road between Windsor and the Quebec border was nearing completion. Also, with better road surfaces and improved vehicles, the speed limit on provincial highways was increased from twenty-five to thirty-five miles per hour. By 1927 there were 938,540 cars and trucks registered in Canada, and registrations that year were greater than in any previous year. The automotive industry had become Ontario's leading industry in terms of product value. With the increasing volume of automobile traffic, accidents multiplied; insurance rates rose sharply and came under the scrutiny of the Attorney General, as did the question of compulsory insurance. The Board of Trade had doubts about making insurance obligatory, but urged that driving regulations be more strictly enforced and that heavier penalties be applied in cases of infringement. When an Automobile Insurance Rates Enquiry was instituted by the Ontario government in 1929, with Mr Justice F.E. Hodgins as Commissioner, the Board recorded its doubts regarding the advisability of introducing compulsory insurance legislation, as applied in Massachusetts, and favoured instead a safety responsibility law similar to that operative in the state of New York.

The Commissioner's eventual recommendations were along the lines of those made by the Board; implementing legislation was immediately introduced, was supported by the Board and passed by the legislature. It provided for the suspension of drivers' licences on conviction of offences involving expenses in excess of $100 and non-payment thereof, the reinstatement of licences to depend on satisfactory proof of financial responsibility. The Board worked with Mr Henry and other organizations in the establishment of a Highway Safety Committee to promote safer driving habits. It also took a prominent part in negotiations leading to the proclamation of the Public Commercial Vehicles Act, which came into force on 17 September 1928, and after some experience had been gained expressed its satisfaction that it was effectively regulating the operations of motor transports. Both the Canadian Chamber of Commerce and the Ontario Associated Boards of Trade and Chambers of Commerce supported the Toronto Board when it suggested in 1930 that the federal and Ontario governments co-operate in the immediate construction of a Trans-Canada Highway through northern Ontario. This was considered feasible under the terms of the federal government's contributory financial arrangement and would establish an important link between eastern and western Canada, in the process generating substantial – and by then much-needed – employment.

The grade-separated railway viaduct across the waterfront was completed in December 1930 to the great satisfaction of the Board, which had pressed for it unremittingly since 1899. Work begun in 1925 had proceeded without serious interruption and the final structure conformed in all respects to the agreed design, thus fulfilling all expectations. Harbour improvements had also been proceeding well and more than a square mile of land on the eastern lakefront had been reclaimed and made usable for industrial establishment and highway extension. However, this development had suffered a setback in 1926 as a result of internal differences among the Harbour Commissioners (characterized as 'disorder and friction') which apparently sprang from irreconcilable views concerning administrative methods, particularly in matters of finance. The situation was so serious that the Board of Trade suggested enquiry into the whole operation by judicial commission, and an investigation was in fact undertaken under Mr Justice Denton. The outcome was a reconstitution of the Commission which restored orderly procedures and permitted an effective resumption of normal operations.

In his address to the Board of Trade's Annual Meeting in January 1928 the retiring President, Brigadier General C.H. Mitchell, announced that commercial aviation had arrived and Canada, already far behind other countries, must take immediate steps to prepare for it. The federal government was taking the initial steps toward the inauguration of an aerial mail service, but there was as yet no fully organized commercial air service in Canada. Such services were being supplied in Europe and the United States, with scheduled passenger flights providing journey speeds of up to one hundred miles an hour. Britain was building two dirigibles for trans-Atlantic crossings, and an airport to receive them was under construction in Montreal. United States companies had been investigating possible airfields in Canada, and it was essential for Toronto to move into the picture quickly if it wished to retain control over air traffic and leadership in the general transportation field. There were local fields available for training purposes, but these were totally inadequate for the larger purposes envisaged, and the creation of the necessary facilities would require the co-operation and financial participation of the federal government, the municipality of Toronto and private interests. If appropriate action was taken, the possibility of goods being shipped throughout the province by air within two or three years was foreseen. General Mitchell soon found himself chairing an Airport Committee.

By the following year an air mail service was operating between principal Canadian cities as far west as Calgary and Edmonton, and the Toronto Board was urging the city to take the necessary measures to ensure the provision of adequate local facilities. Nothing was done. In a letter directed to the Mayor in January 1929 the Board again emphasized the need for prompt action, suggesting that the Harbour Commissioners be asked to give leadership to the project and that a civic committee be formed to study the whole situation. Again the city did nothing, but in the early summer the Harbour Commissioners on their own initiative submitted a proposal for the creation of an air harbour on the sandbar at the western entrance to the harbour. This was speedily approved and the sum of $100,000 was granted to permit the commencement of construction. When the Board of Trade was asked for its opinion on this development it expressed some reservations about the suitability of the site and requested its Aviation and Engineering Committees to observe the operation and report upon it from time to time.

The Airport Committee continued its studies and also worked to develop a wider appreciation among the public of the coming revolution in travel and transportation. The Harbour Commission's seaplane base was all very well, but in the Committee's opinion this should be considered a minimum facility pending decisions with respect to the establishment of accommodation for all types of aircraft and the provision of full airport services. On the Committee's recommendation the Board in 1930 urged the city council to acquire land northwest of the city, then available at a cost of some $400,000, which was suitable for airport use and would meet the needs of commercial aviation for many years, but again the city showed itself reluctant to come to grips with the issue. At the same time the Board was emphasizing the need to develop air routes connecting the various parts of the Empire and proposing subsidies by the federal government to assist in establishing regular commercial air services between Canada and Great Britain. The provision of customs services at Canadian airports was also advocated.

Although the days of railway building were long over, there was one unfinished link in the rail network which the Board had consistently advocated – the extension of the Temiskaming and Northern Ontario line to James Bay. It was therefore a matter for gratification when Premier Drury turned the first sod on 28 October 1921 to signal the start of construction on this final 200-mile lap from Cochrane to Moosonee. Twelve years passed before it was completed, establishing a total operating milage for the Temiskaming and Northern Ontario line of 609.3 miles from North Bay to tidewater and creating what enthusiastic Toronto proponents referred to as Ontario's first ocean port. While its importance as a line to the seaboard was questionable, it did give access to the resources of a huge northern territory, and this had always been a prime concern of the Board of Trade. Its delegations were travelling through the north country almost annually, bringing back glowing reports on the development taking place and the still untapped reserves of minerals, timber and power. A Northern Ontario Committee kept closely in touch with developments and acted frequently both to stimulate the interest of Toronto businessmen in the opportunities of the north and to bridge the gap which many northerners still felt existed between themselves and the centres of government and commerce so many miles away. Representatives of the Board were on hand for the opening of the Moosonee terminus in July 1933, and shortly afterwards tendered a dinner to George W. Lee; in recognition of his quarter-century of service on the Temiskaming and Northern Ontario Commission he was presented with an engraved cigar case made from northern Ontario silver.

The railway freight rate structure came under investigation by the Board of Railway Commissioners in 1926. The Board of Trade's representations to the Commissioners were mainly concerned with the maintenance of equity and the avoidance of rate adjustments to ease costs in other parts of the country by the imposition of higher tariffs in southern Ontario. The findings of the Commissioners, announced the following year, generally supported the Board's contention that the existing structure was fair and equitable and no important changes were introduced.

The proposed development of the St Lawrence Waterway continued to receive attention. A communication was directed to Prime Minister Mackenzie King in 1929 commending a proposal for an inter-provincial conference to agree on procedures, and at the Board's urging the Canadian Chamber of Commerce in that year adopted a resolution advocating full debate of the project by all concerned interests, both federal and provincial, with a view to evolving a policy which would 'carry the united judgment of the people of Canada.' The following year the Board secured unanimous endorsement by the Ontario Associated Boards of Trade and Chambers of Commerce of a resolution whereby each member of that body would 'strongly urge the Dominion Government to make appropriate arrangements for the construction of the enlarged St Lawrence Waterway and for the development of hydro-electric power from the St Lawrence between Lake Ontario and Montreal to be undertaken with the least possible delay.'

Since the depression of 1921 business had substantially improved and five years later all signs were indicating a complete restoration of economic stability and a new era of expansion. Railway earnings were up, banks were strong and showed an increase in commercial loans, government revenues were buoyant, construction was active, unemployment was negligible and wages and living costs were stable. The total assets of Canadian banks were nudging three billion dollars and bank clearings had increased from $513.7 million in 1900 to $5,196.4 million in 1926. Trade was good, with exports at $1.32 billion and imports of only $1 billion. By 1926 the country's population had reached the 9.3 million mark, and projections based upon densities in the United States indicated that Canada could eventually support a population of 126 million.

Wages in the building trades in 1926 ranged from thirty-five cents to $1.25 an hour for a forty-four-hour week; in the metal trades from fifty to ninety cents an hour for a fifty-hour week; and in the printing industry wages averaged $16.80 weekly for females and $36 to $42.50 weekly for males per forty-eight-hour week. A weekly budget for an average Toronto family worked out to $22.53, including rent and fuel, compared to a country-wide average of $21.41. A factor influencing living costs was seen to be the evolution taking place in distribution and merchandising methods, evidenced by the success of chain-store operations and a general tendency to eliminate the middleman; the idea was gaining acceptance that this principle might be applied to restore equilibrium between turnover and overhead, a primary concern in all industry and merchandising.

Canada greeted the Diamond Jubilee of Confederation in 1927 with a comfortable feeling of present prosperity and confidence in future progress. The Board of Trade was prominent in the arrangements to celebrate the occasion, and its float, given the honour of first place in the pageant parade on 1 July, bore the title 'The Child at the Gate' and symbolized Canadian youth at the gate of the future. The accelerating pace of business throughout the year was striking, but although it was welcome and enjoyed, there were a few who had been through enough business cycles to be apprehensive of the downturn likely to follow such an abrupt upward swing. British Prime Minister Stanley Baldwin, who spent three weeks in Canada in 1927 with the Prince of Wales and Prince George, later addressed a meeting of the Canadian Club in London and said: 'Canada has an enormous future, and, if it be not impertinent to say to Canadians, I would say: The future is with you; do not be in too much of a hurry ... I have often thought that it is as dangerous a thing to the morale of a nation to get rich quickly as it is to an individual.'

And Canadians were suffering from a get-rich-quick syndrome. Many were becoming aware for the first time of the country's great potential mineral wealth and were investing with more enthusiasm than perspicuity in mining concerns that had suddenly sprung into existence with glowing prospectuses. Three million shares were sold in a day on one exchange and many sober businessmen were showing uneasiness at the widespread evidences of reckless speculation; this feeling was aggravated by indications which began to appear of fraudulent dealings in securities. The Ontario legislature acted quickly on this issue and brought in legislation effective 15 May 1928 designed to protect the investor by the regulation of promoters, brokers and stock salesmen. Authority was established to register brokers and salesmen, revoke registrations and undertake any investigations that might be deemed necessary. The Board of Trade conveyed its highest commendation of this action to the Attorney General. On the whole, though, the country's prosperity seemed soundly based. Agricultural production, still Canada's backbone, was healthy, and the pulp and paper industry had achieved a dominant position, producing nearly two million tons for export in 1927, most of it going to the United States. Industrial operations were enlarging and diversifying and new power sources were being developed to meet their expanding needs.

For many years the Toronto Board of Trade had been concerned that industrial progress was not being backed by adequate research for the development of new techniques and processes. In a highly competitive world Canada could keep pace only if she could match the skills of other nations and the production economies they were achieving. The Board applauded the work performed through the National Research Council, but in 1926 it renewed an appeal to the federal government for the establishment of long-term policies, more extensive facilities and particularly for larger appropriations. It was rewarded the next year by a government announcement of a budget for industrial research amounting to one million dollars which would permit substantial enlargement of the operations in Ottawa and the creation of additional facilities in other centres. The federal government's participation in research activities had actually begun in 1916 with the appointment of an Honorary Advisory Council for Scientific and Industrial Research in response to a request by the British government following the creation of a similar body in that country. The Canadian Council was made up of fifteen prominent scientists and its purpose was to promote the utilization of Canada's natural resources, to devise methods for the improvement of technical processes in Canadian industry, to investigate standards and methods of measurement, and to work toward the standardization of the materials used by or the products of any industry requesting assistance. The Council had immediately found effective industrial research in Canada to be virtually non-existent; not only were facilities lacking, but trained personnel were not available, and one of its first objectives was to encourage the development of promising graduates from Canadian universities. It was not until 1928, when the funds were provided for buildings and equipment and Dr H.M. Tory was appointed as full-time President, that the National Research Council became completely functional. Work was begun in temporary quarters and new buildings created for its use were occupied in 1932.

The expanded activity made possible by the federal government's injection of funds for research purposes was followed in the same year by Ontario legislation creating the Ontario Research Foundation. Its purposes were similar to those of the National Research Council and its operations in an initial five-year period were to be supported by equal contributions, totalling more than $3 million, from industry and the provincial government. Sir Joseph Flavelle was named Chairman of the Foundation. This stimulation of research was wholly in accord with the Board of Trade's consistent advocacy, and through the Board's efforts both the Canadian Chamber of Commerce and the Ontario Associated Boards of Trade and Chambers of Commerce placed on record resolutions warmly commending the action taken by the federal and provincial governments.

The work of the Toronto Board itself in this field had been carried on through a special committee under the chairmanship of John A. Tory, brother of Dr H.M. Tory, and had consisted largely in efforts to create a public understanding of, and hence a more receptive attitude toward, a research program. It had worked in close collaboration with Dr Tory, Ontario Premier G.H. Ferguson, members of Parliament and officials of the University of Toronto, and its efforts undoubtedly made some contribution to the new impetus to research given by the two governments. Having succeeded in this undertaking, the Board directed its efforts to what it called 'economic' research, its initial objective being to establish means for compiling, housing and classifying business records to ensure the preservation of material of historic value and thus facilitate future research enquiry. Negotiations were begun with the University of Toronto.

A project to stimulate industrial establishment in the Toronto area was undertaken early in 1927 when representations were made to the city council urging definite and constructive action by the city to attract new manufacturing enterprises. Much of this work was being carried out by the Board itself and by the Harbour Commissioners, but there seemed an obvious need for co-ordinated services supplied by a qualified and full-time staff under civic direction. During much of the balance of that year the Board's efforts were diverted from this project by its participation, with others, in the revival of a somewhat parallel activity – a Toronto Publicity Bureau – but in 1928 it had become impressed more than ever by the need for a comprehensive industrial survey and the compilation of data which could be supplied to companies contemplating plant establishment or expansion.

Acting on behalf of the Board's Council, C.L. Burton conferred on several occasions with Mayor Sam McBride and presented a report which had been prepared on the procedures followed in other cities. The Mayor finally met with representatives of various interested organizations; a resolution was adopted approving the appointment of a Commission of Industry and Publicity for the city of Toronto, its operations to be independent of the civic government but supported by an annual grant from the city and the balance of funds required to be subscribed by the private business sector. An independent committee appointed to work out the details recommended that a Commission be organized under the Ontario Companies Act with administration by a board of directors of not more than twenty, one director to be appointed by each of the city of Toronto, the Ontario government, the Toronto Harbour Commissioners, the Canadian National Exhibition and the Toronto Transportation Commission, three to be appointed by the Canadian Manufacturers' Association and six by the Toronto Board of Trade. Management would be in the hands of an Executive Committee, which would be responsible, with the approval of the directors, for the appointment of an Industrial Commissioner.

In December 1928 these recommendations, with some adjustment, were accepted by the city council, which undertook to finance the Commission's operation by grants of $25,000 a year for the next five years. The Commission was incorporated before the end of the year and was functioning by March 1929. Of the fourteen original directors the Board of Trade appointed five: C.L. Burton (who was elected Chairman), Harry McGee, C.W. Rowley, J.A. Tory and F.D. Tolchard. The Board considered its work well justified when the Commission was able to report that in its first nine months it had brought twenty-one new industries to Toronto and was actively negotiating with a number of others. In the years that followed the Commission maintained a high level of operating efficiency and played a large part in the city's industrial growth.

Leadership was given by the Board to yet another undertaking at this time on the request of the Central Section of the Investment Bankers' Association, the President of the Stock Exchange and the Board's own Retail Merchants' Association. The request stemmed from the concern of these bodies over sales of questionable securities, and a meeting was convoked by the Board on 17 February 1928, with C.L. Burton presiding, to consider the advisability of business organizations setting up a medium which, by assembling relevant data, would permit an assessment of the bona fides of securities and other transactions. Information was available on the operations of Better Business Bureaus in Montreal and a number of United States cities, and it was agreed that there was a need for such an organization in Toronto. At a subsequent meeting in July arrangements were made to form a Bureau whose functions would be to promote honesty and dependability in merchandising and business methods, develop factual material respecting doubtful securities and assemble data relating to fraudulent schemes of promotion and misleading advertising. The Bureau was duly incorporated under the presidency of C.L. Burton, with representation from (in addition to the Board of Trade) the Retail Merchants' Association, the Dominion Mortgage and Investment Association, the Investment Bankers' Association, the Toronto and Standard Stock Exchanges and the Toronto Real Estate Board. Regular meetings were held, but it was decided to keep the operation on a small scale in the early stages and place it on a permanent and enlarged basis when experience had been gained and its scope more clearly defied.

The promotion of trading interests in a broad sense was a continuing activity pursued in a number of ways. On the invitation of the Canadian Trade Commissioner in New York, a Board of Trade delegation attended a Pan-American Commercial Congress held in that city in December 1925 and participated in discussions covering a wide range of issues affecting commercial transactions among the nations of the Western Hemisphere. A special welcome was extended to the Canadian delegates, and the latter conveyed an invitation for the next Congress to be held in Canada. The next year representatives of the Toronto Board and other Canadian organizations attended the Thirteenth Annual Foreign Trade Convention held in Charleston, North Carolina, where it was felt that a great forward step was taken in developing a better understanding of Canada's trade problems by the 1,200 influential American businessmen attending. They gave the Canadian delegation a hearty reception and a sympathetic hearing. The President of the Toronto Board, George Wilson, took advantage of the occasion to urge a lowering of American tariff barriers.

Some 3,500 Ontario citizens, including a strong group from the Toronto Board, took part in 'Cleveland–Canada Day' on 11 June 1926, an event initiated by Cleveland businessmen. Its outstanding success from the standpoint of publicizing Ontario (tourist traffic increased 20 per cent that summer) prompted an effort to bring about a program of reciprocal events of a similar nature. Officers of the Board attended a National Foreign Trade

Conference held in Detroit in May 1927; a special 'Canada Session' was programmed in their honour and arrangements were made for its perpetuation in future Conferences.

A delegation from the Board waited upon the Prime Minister in 1925 urging ratification of a Canada–Australia Trade Agreement which would introduce preferential tariff conditions as a means of stimulating trade between the two countries. The necessary legislation was passed shortly thereafter and was extended to include New Zealand. Action was taken the next year, but with less success, to bring about a similar agreement with the West Indies, and later efforts were directed to strengthening trade relations with British Guiana and Japan. In 1929 Canada's newly-appointed Minister Plenipotentiary to Japan, Herbert Marler, visited the Board and suggested the establishment of a Canadian showroom in Tokyo as a means of stimulating interest in Canadian products available for export.

The Board's principal interest, however, remained steadfast in its advocacy of a preferential trade agreement among the countries of the British Empire. By 1930 there was renewed public interest in this proposal and it was felt that the time had come for definite action. The Board's Foreign and Domestic Trade Committee under John M. Millar proposed, and the Council concurred, that steps be taken during the coming Imperial Economic Conference to appoint a commission, accredited by the various parts of the Empire, which would make a complete and comprehensive study of Empire resources and the conditions affecting intra-Empire trade development as a basis for a full report and recommendations to the several governments concerned. It further proposed that consideration be given to the formation of an Empire Trade Council 'for the purpose of promoting and fostering concerted action between and among the several governments and the trade and industrial interests of the Empire along sound, practical and permanent lines.'

The Twelfth Congress of the Chambers of Commerce of the British Empire held in London in May 1930 was attended by several hundred delegates from all parts of the Empire. The fifty Canadian delegates, ten of them from the Toronto Board of Trade, represented twenty Boards of Trade and Chambers of Commerce. The Toronto Board's intra-Empire trade development proposals formed the main item of discussion and the principles embodied in its resolution on the subject were adopted. The proposals were then placed before the standing Imperial Economic Committee, and while no immediate result was evident, or indeed expected, there can be little doubt that the initiative taken by the Toronto Board and the subsequent action following the Twelfth Congress of the Empire

Chambers of Commerce played a considerable part in the determination of policies at the Imperial Economic Conference held in Ottawa in 1932 which provided for a reciprocal exchange of tariff preferences between the member-nations of the Commonwealth.

The Twelfth Congress also marked the accomplishment of another of the Board's objectives. Six years earlier Charles Marriott had introduced a resolution advocating the preparation of a textbook dealing with the history, geography and resources of the Empire. It had been acted upon and the delegates were informed that such a book, *The British Empire Since 1783*, had been produced and published and some initial success had been achieved in securing its use by educational authorities. Efforts would be made to develop a regular course of study as a means of stimulating interest in and creating an awareness of a great heritage.

Internally, the Board helped its own members forward their direct interests in foreign markets. A Foreign and Domestic Trade Committee was formed in 1928 under the initial chairmanship of J.E. Birks and devoted its attention to policy issues and matters of broad concern. At the same time staff services were expanded to deal with an increasing inflow of enquiry about sources of Canadian products and also to assemble a library of commercial information and make advisory assistance available to members regarding their specific problems in the field of foreign trade.

If Canada was to sell its manufactured goods in overseas markets it was obvious that domestic conditions had to be maintained which would permit the production of those goods at prices that would make them attractive in a world growing ever more competitive. The Board of Trade always considered taxes an important inhibiting element in the effort to minimize costs of production, and hence prices, and it fought to obtain and preserve levels of taxation which were straightforward and non-duplicating, realistic in terms of providing for the proven revenue needs of governments and equitable in their application. Representations were made to governments from time to time appealing for tax modification, a particular grievance being the reluctance of the federal government to reduce or remove special taxes applied during the war. These had been accepted with good grace in the face of the financial emergency of the war years and those immediately following, but in the opinion of many businessmen the continued pressure for revenues had become unjustifiable and harmful to the economy.

At the Annual Meeting of the Ontario Associated Boards of Trade and Chambers of Commerce held in Kingston in November 1925 the Toronto Board secured acceptance of its proposal to approach the federal government for a number of reforms, most of them reiterations of previous advocacy. They included requests for:

a reduction in income tax to at least the rates applicable in the United States;
the exemption of income tax paid to other countries and paid to municipal and provincial governments on income also assessable by the federal government;
the exemption from income tax of carrying charges on non-dividend paying securities;
the averaging of incomes over a three-year period of persons, firms or corporations engaged in business;
repeal of the Corporation Income Tax;
repeal of the Stamp Tax on cheques and other documents currently imposed under the Special War Revenue Act;
removal of the injustice of taxing dividends in the hands of shareholders of incorporated companies upon the net profits of which income tax had been paid.

The federal Corporation Tax, always resented, amounted at the time to a rate of 10 per cent on all income in excess of $2,000 plus an additional 5 per cent of the amount of the tax payable with respect to any taxable income of $5,000 or more. Manufacturers were also required to pay a Sales Tax of 5 per cent on the sale price of goods produced or manufactured in Canada, with numerous exemptions.

The Minister of Finance responded to the representations by intimating that the federal government would be willing to consider tax relief measures if revenues permitted. As the total income from the federal Income Tax in 1926 was under $50 million, it was the Board's contention that its abolition was justifiable; capital would thereby be attracted to investment in productive enterprise to an extent that would create new revenue sources in other forms of taxation more than sufficient to offset the loss. While it was difficult to substantiate such an argument, the Board used as support for its contention an affirmation by the Treasury Department of the United States that every material reduction of the surtax in that country had stimulated business and resulted in an increased total taxable income offsetting in part, if not wholly, the loss of revenue from the higher incomes. Support of the Board's position by the Canadian Chamber of Commerce was obtained at the latter's Third Annual Meeting held in June 1928.

The next year a study of provincial taxation undertaken by the Board's Taxation Committee under C.L. Burton led to the retention of Dr H.L. Brittain, Director of the Bureau of Municipal Research, for the preparation of a comprehensive report on the rationale of tax imposition at the provincial level and its effect upon Ontario businesses. The outcome was the formulation of a number of proposals for reform, among them being a request for a reduction in the rate of taxation, the avoidance of double taxation by exempting dividends, avoidance of tax overlap and establishment of uniform succession duties between Ontario and Quebec, and a full review of the provincial legislation governing municipal taxation. These proposals were placed before the Ontario Associated Boards of Trade and Chambers of Commerce, but in the course of a full debate considerable difference of opinion became evident and the result was a resolution merely requesting the Ontario government to appoint a Commission to investigate the income tax in all its aspects with a view to its modification and, if possible, its ultimate repeal.

Although it had succeeded in securing removal of the obnoxious personalty tax, the Board remained dissatisfied with the form of municipal taxation replacing it, and in 1926 it petitioned the Ontario government to revise the Business Tax in such a way as to reduce it and base it upon a percentage of rental value or otherwise to create conditions for businesses in Ontario no less favourable than those in other provinces. It also pressed vigorously for repeal of the municipal income tax.

Taxation was a continuing but not overriding preoccupation of the Board; it was especially alert to all new legislation in this period in keeping with the belief, as enunciated by John A. Tory, the 1929 President, that 'there is a limit to the advantageous regulation of private business by statutory authority ... when this limit is exceeded disadvantage results not only to the business interests particularly affected, but to the general public interest which these businesses serve.' Objection was taken, for example, to redrafted legislation governing the conditional sale of goods introduced on the recommendation of the Commissioners on Uniformity of Legislation in Canada on the grounds that the new terms would weaken the protection afforded under the old statute, and the provincial Bill was withdrawn for reconsideration. Dissatisfaction expressed in connection with the provisions governing transient traders in proposed amendments to the Municipal Act introduced in 1929 led to a new Bill which was found more acceptable and passed.

A Bill to amend the Ontario Companies' Act, substituting the Provincial Secretary for a judge of the Supreme Court as the authority who would order a meeting of shareholders in cases of compromises or arrangements, was opposed and the offending clause was deleted. The inclusion in the 1928 Security Frauds Prevention Act of strict disclosure rules respecting the sale of any securities likewise met with disfavour as being too rigid and hence unenforceable: as a result of the Board's representations the conditions were ameliorated. Support was given in principle, at the instance of the Ontario Association of Architects, to an Ontario Bill creating an Architects' Registration Board to regulate the practice of architects and establish qualifications for those entitled to practise.

A House of Commons Bill requiring all corporations subject to the Railway Act to obtain approval of the Board of Railway Commissioners of the amount, terms and conditions of any issue, sale or other disposition of capital stock, other than the original capital stock, also came under fire. The Board contended that the Board of Railway Commissioners' proper concern was corrective legislation, not business management, and moreover that the new powers proposed for it were an interference with the normal function of private enterprise likely to prove prejudicial to the interests of the corporations concerned by restricting their access to available capital. The Board sought and obtained support for its position from organizations throughout the country, and Parliament amended the legislation under the strong opposition aroused.

At the request of the Federation of Chambers of Commerce of the British Empire for observations on unsatisfactory features of bankruptcy laws, the Board in 1930 undertook, with the advice of eminent counsel, a study of existing legislation which resulted in recommendations for a general simplification of procedures, the provision of safeguards against the improper making of receiving orders and a revision of the regulations applicable to the appointment and powers of trustees. The subject was one of long-standing interest to the Board, and the purpose of the Federation was presumably to create satisfactory statutory conditions with the highest degree of uniformity in the countries of the Empire in order to build confidence in future commercial relationships among them.

The effective development and utilization of the country's natural resources and the strengthening of the domestic economy were the underlying motives of most actions taken by the Board in the firm belief that thereon depended the prosperity of Toronto and Toronto's businessmen. To broaden the market at home and strengthen the labour force the Board consistently urged the government to formulate and implement well-defined immigration policies. It induced the Canadian Chamber of Commerce to establish a standing committee on immigration to work toward this end, and through its own committee sought improved co-operation between the federal and provincial governments; the latter would create demand by stimulating resource and industrial development, and Ottawa would regulate the inflow of immigrants to accord with the employment opportunities available. It was agreed that the time had come to place a strict limitation on the entry of farm labourers. The Board was disturbed by an announcement from the federal government in 1930 that it was going to transfer jurisdiction over immigration to the provinces and retain only supervisory powers, but the whole subject was relegated to the background when the government in the same year imposed a virtual prohibition against immigration as a consequence of worsening economic conditions and mounting unemployment.

In the matter of the improved utilization of Canadian resources, the Board had on a number of occasions raised the question of coal from known Canadian sources being made available for consumption in Ontario. It joined other Ontario organizations to confer with the Premier of Alberta in the matter in 1926, following which the federal government was petitioned to direct the Board of Railway Commissioners to investigate the feasibility in terms of cost of interprovincial coal movements. It does not appear that this petition was acted upon, and Toronto's coal requirements continued to be met by shipments, mainly water-borne, from United States sources and, to a minor extent, from the United Kingdom.

With the city's industrial and commercial growth there had been a corresponding decline in its concern for agricultural interests. The centre of the grain trade had long ago moved westward, and although there were many important manufacturers and brokers whose businesses revolved about farm products, and there had never been any doubt in anyone's mind that the general level of prosperity was profoundly affected by crop success or failure, the old feeling of close identification with the soil and its products was fast disappearing. Grain still moved through Toronto's harbour and cattle flowed increasingly to its packing plants, but the average citizen knew little about it and cared less. Many businessmen thought this an unhealthy state of affairs; Canada was still essentially an agricultural country, and if there were not a reasonable degree of understanding and co-operation between the farmer and the industrialist it was clear that neither could achieve their fullest potential. These considerations had led to the establishment of the Royal Agricultural Winter Fair in Toronto as one means by which not only would incentives be given to breeders and growers but opportunity would be provided for city-dwellers to learn something about the objectives and problems of their rural counterparts. Under the leadership of the Canadian Chamber of Commerce, the Toronto Board convoked a conference of agricultural, industrial and commercial interests in its premises at the time of the 1928 Winter Fair for the express purpose of establishing a closer relationship and a forum for the discussion of matters of common concern. It was judged a successful preliminary effort and plans were made to repeat and extend the occasion, but the good intention does not appear to have materialized.

At the Canadian National Exhibition an effort had been made to maintain some balance between displays of farm and factory products, but here too there was evidence of an increasing emphasis on industry at the expense of agriculture. The CNE marked its fiftieth anniversary in 1928 by opening a huge new Engineering Building – and incidentally achieving for the first time a two million attendance record. The following year saw the opening of the still grander Automotive Building, erected at a cost of more than $1 million and although the next big addition in 1931 included new horse stables as part of the agricultural complex, their occupants were more familiar with the show ring than the farmer's field. The Automotive and Engineering Buildings implemented a planned eastward expansion of the Exhibition grounds following the erection of a new entrance, the Princes' Gate, formally opened in 1927 by the Prince of Wales (later Edward VIII), who was accompanied by his brother the Duke of Kent.

Major objectives had been achieved in the fields of technical and commercial education; the Board continued to be represented on the Commercial and Industrial Advisory Committees of the Board of Education and attempted to ensure that school curricula were attuned to modern business methods. Effective 1 January 1928 the two aforementioned committees were amalgamated into the Advisory Vocational Committee of the Toronto Board of Education, the new body to consist of six representatives of the Board of Education, three employers engaged in commercial, agricultural or manufacturing enterprises and three employers of labour or directors of companies employing labour. The Board of Trade was made responsible for an appointment in the last category; its first appointee was J.D. Trees, and it has played a part in the work of the Committee ever since.

The tragic death in 1927 of Henry Maurice Cody, son of the Rev. Canon H.J. Cody, led a number of his friends to create a fund which would perpetuate the memory of 'this brilliant young Canadian.' Sir Edward Kemp, heading a committee of organization, was able in December 1928 to present to Sir Robert Falconer, President of the University of Toronto, a Declaration of Trust wherein the sum of $50,000 was to be administered to enable the University to grant fellowships of at least $1,500 annually and other scholarships at its discretion as the means afforded. Study was to be in the field of economics with specific reference to information useful in dealing with national problems involved in the development of Canadian

Confederation. The administrative committee named in the trust instrument included the President of the University and two others named by him, plus one representative each from the Toronto Board of Trade and the Canadian Manufacturers' Association. C.L. Burton was the Board's representative on the original committee and representation has been maintained.

An Empire Buyers' League was organized and sponsored by the Board in 1930. Its purpose was to educate the public regarding the need for and advantages of trade within the Empire, and it proposed to operate by enrolling members who would pledge to give first preference in their purchases to goods made in Canada; second choice would be Empire products, and foreign purchases would be made only if there were no alternative. A publicity campaign was organized and the support of other organizations secured, but the effort was not long sustained.

The Board also acted to secure support for a proposal originating in the Canadian Section of the Empire Press Union for the establishment of an intra-Empire news gathering and distribution service and the inauguration of newsletters dealing with both the economic and cultural aspects of Canadian life for use in the presses of other Empire countries. This was a project dear to the hearts of Board of Trade traditionalists; an exchange of news would help keep the family together and by so doing would contribute to a sense of security and to improved trading relationships. The Empire chauvinism of the time is illustrated in a remark made by Lord Beaverbrook, quoted with approval in the Board's *Journal*: 'Let us have throughout our world-wide Empire free trade, free commerce and a higher standard of living than our less fortunate neighbours can possibly enjoy, and let us protect these great benefits by means of tariffs against sweated imports from abroad.' It was not an attitude likely to endear the representatives of Empire to their 'less fortunate neighbours.'

The rapid development and huge impact of radio had led to the appointment of a Royal Commission on Radio Broadcasting whose report, issued in 1930, included a recommendation that the government assume ownership and operation of all radio broadcasting facilities throughout the Dominion. The Board's Council found itself sharply divided on this issue and decided to withhold comment until it became clear, through legislation, whether the nationalizing proposal of the Commissioners would be acted upon. A survey of the membership was made in an effort to establish whether there was a strong preponderance of opinion in the matter one way or the other, but the result proved inconclusive. Radio entertainment had become enormously popular, and there appears to have been considerable doubt that its quality would be enhanced by government control; there was some feeling, however, that a measure of control would sooner or later be necessary. An editorial comment in the May 1933 issue of *The Board of Trade Journal* foreshadowed things to come:

A new kind of 'sales appeal' has recently made its appearance via the radio, and a poor kind of appeal it seems to be. At the conclusion of certain programs the announcer says something to this effect: 'If you have enjoyed this program, please show your appreciation of the kindness of the sponsors by buying their products.' In other words, the radio audience is asked to purchase this or that brand for the reason that the manufacturer has given them so many minutes of entertainment.

This type of appeal insults the intelligence and rubs one the wrong way.

In 1938 the Board recorded its opinion that the Canadian Broadcasting Corporation should subsist wholly on licence fees and confine its activities to public service broadcasting, and that private broadcasting stations should be allowed to increase their power to permit more effective operation in the commercial field.

# 9
# Depression

A crescendo of economic prosperity in the last half of the 1920s came to a crashing close with the collapse of the stock market late in 1929 and Canada, with most of the rest of the world, plunged into the terrible depression which was to last through much of the next decade. Virtually every class of business was affected in some degree; the demand for goods and services declined and as the disease fed upon itself conditions worsened and even the strongest industrial and commercial enterprises were forced to adopt the most stringent measures of economy to preserve their corporate lives. The number of unemployed began to increase and then to skyrocket and as is always the case in such circumstances, the problem was most acute in the urban centres. Those without work in all the surrounding regions converged on the cities in the belief that the best chance of a job lay where in normal times there was the biggest and most diversified employment field.

A Joint Committee on Unemployment was formed in 1930 to which the Board of Trade appointed five representatives: C.L. Burton, C.E. Edmunds, H.C. Grout, J.A. Tory and F.E. Waterman. On the recommendation of this committee the Board directed letters to all its members requesting their co-operation by increasing their contributions to social agencies and avoiding lay-offs to the greatest extent possible, and the response was encouraging. Distress became so widespread that welfare organizations found it impossible to cope. Not only were their ordinary resources insufficient, but deficiencies of organization and coverage soon became apparent with the result that the city set up a Civic Unemployment Relief

Committee to co-ordinate their operations and deal with emergency situations as they arose. F.D. Tolchard acted for the Board on the Committee, whose work at least ensured that no hard-hit family was without food and shelter. The Board of Trade Club joined other Toronto service clubs in a campaign to find jobs or make work for those who suddenly found themselves unemployed.

The Board of Trade itself was not at first greatly affected by the depression. In 1927 a permanent member of the staff had been appointed for the first time to devote his time to calling upon prospective new members, and a noticeable membership increment had soon followed. In two years' time the number of members exceeded the three thousand mark, and there was slow growth even through 1930. Thereafter there was an accelerating decline, not because of any weakening of the Board's purposes or lessing of its activities, but simply because increasing numbers of businessmen could not afford the modest $25 annual fee.

Indeed, until the depression struck, the Board had been enjoying one of its most successful periods. An energetic Council had maintained a full program of work in almost every field of significant interest to the Toronto businessman: policies formulated and acted upon in a steady, if unspectacular, manner had resulted in a good record of accomplishment and heightened repute. Publicity was rarely sought unless it was felt that an issue was of such general concern that a public explanation was desirable; on the whole the Board was quite content to pursue its own course with scant newspaper attention. It was usually only when the Board played host to distinguished visitors, an increasingly frequent event, that it came into the public eye. Its dinners for the Rt Hon. L.C.M.S. Amery, Secretary of State for Dominion Affairs, and the Rt Hon. Lord Lovat, Parliamentary Under-Secretary for Dominion Affairs in the British government, were notable events, as was the entertainment of fifty visiting members of the Empire Parliamentary Association and a dinner at Hart House on 22 November 1928 for the Rt Hon. Mackenzie King on the occasion of the opening of the Royal Winter Fair. The Board was prominent in ceremonies attending the opening of the Royal York Hotel by the Governor General, the Rt Hon. the Viscount Willingdon, and had the honour of conducting the first major event in the hotel on 11 June 1929 – a luncheon attended by 1,400 guests tendered to Chairman E.W. Beatty and the directors of the Canadian Pacific Railway Company in appreciation of the new hotel's importance to Toronto.

By 1930 there were ten Trade Sections carrying on their own programs within the general framework of the Board: Book Publishers, Commercial

Travellers, Engineering, Lumbermen, Motion Picture, Oil Heating, Retail Merchants, Tanners, Wholesale Dry-goods and Flour, Grain, Malt and Hops. Soon afterwards, in 1932, a British Trade Section was formed, comprising for the most part representatives of British interests in Canada who felt that much could be done to stimulate trade and generally improve commercial relations between the two countries. This Branch, later re-named the British Empire Overseas Branch and then the British Common-wealth Branch, became an active force in Empire and Commonwealth affairs and was a prime mover in the development of a British Section at the Canadian National Exhibition. Premises alterations had been necessary to accommodate the staff, which had increased to twenty in addition to the thirty-one employed in connection with the dining and clubroom opera-tions. As of 1 January 1931 the title of F.D. Tolchard was changed from Secretary to General Manager 'in keeping with the greatly increased ac-tivities in which the Board has, during recent years, become engaged.'

Some concern was evident in 1929 over the appearance of competitive organizations with similar purposes, and the Toronto Board, supported by the Ontario Associated Boards of Trade and Chambers of Commerce and by the Canadian Chamber of Commerce, sought an amendment of the Boards of Trade Act to prohibit the use of the name Board of Trade or Chamber of Commerce by other than incorporated bodies. While such an action appears somewhat incompatible with the Board's avowedly free enterprise stance, it was in fact motivated by a reasonable wish to prevent the improper use of a respected name and to avoid an overlap of jurisdic-tions which could only lessen the effectiveness of any organization seeking to represent the total interests of its community. The Act was amended accordingly in 1932.

Canada suffered less severely than many countries in the early years of the depression, which had been brought about, according to a federal government report of the time, by an international race to increase produc-tion and capture markets, the breakdown of price control schemes and acute credit stringency. Production in Canada did decline by 20 per cent in 1930; nevertheless, business leaders retained a good deal of optimism and by the beginning of the following year saw signs of recovery which led them to believe that with good management and the active development of new markets the country would soon be back to normal. The Board's President, F.A. Rolph, referred to 1930 as

... a year in which a diversity of problems perplexed and often mystified business, but we have cause for rejoicing in that the conditions responsible for our difficulties were superficial and entirely temporary – they have not affected in the slightest the fundamental soundness of the country. On the contrary they have had a much-needed salutary effect upon trade and industry, out of which will undoubtedly come greater efficiency in production and distribution, a better appreciation of values, a strengthening of national sentiment and greater prosperity for all.

But there was little in the next few years to restore business confidence. Economic activity continued its steady decline and in 1934 Prime Minister R.B. Bennett was reporting world trade at 36 per cent of its pre-depression level. By that year, however, there were appearing some faint but genuine signs of steadying conditions: prices of some basic commodities had begun to rise, industrial production and employment were improving, and both domestic consumption and exports began to move slowly upward. There was a long haul yet before a return to anything like the halcyon days of the late 1920s, but there was at least the feeling that the back of the depression had been broken.

The Board of Trade was squeezed like every other business operation in these difficult times. Between 1929 and 1934 it suffered the loss of more than one-third of its membership, and for an organization wholly depen- dent for maintenance upon the voluntary payment of annual fees this produced a critical situation. Every inducement was offered to hold pres- ent members and bring in new ones; the entrance fee of $25 was suspended, and if a present member could not pay his account for the annual dues of $25 when rendered he had only to get in touch with the Secretary to arrange for payment by instalments. A by-law was passed enabling the Council to extend the privileges of membership to those whose dues were outstanding or were paid only in part. A form of corporate membership was inaugurated whereby firms might subscribe as an annual fee an amount as agreed between themselves and the Council representing their valuation place upon the Board's work, the total of monies so subscribed to constitute a sustaining fund to assist in meeting outstanding obligations.

In spite of these measures and the exercise of the utmost economy, it became increasingly and painfully evident that the Board would be unable to maintain its existing scale of operations. Its occupancy of two whole floors of the Royal Bank Building, much of the space taken up by club- rooms, kitchens and dining rooms in which only lunch could be served, created in the straitened conditions that prevailed an impossible burden of overhead. Not only had the income from fees declined, but revenues from the dining facilities fell off even more sharply as members evinced an increasing reluctance or inability to pay the modest price of sixty cents for a full luncheon in the Board's rooms.

New accommodation was accordingly sought and by good fortune found in the King Edward Hotel. A lease was arranged giving exclusive occupancy of the mezzanine floor in the new section of the hotel, providing all the space needed for offices, meeting rooms and a commodious lounge for the use of members. The contract with the hotel's management included a particularly favourable provision from the Board's point of view – luncheon privileges for members in a private dining room at special prices. The continuation of this club service was highly desirable, while the assumption of responsibility for serving meals by the hotel as a mere extension of its normal food operations relieved the Board of both overhead and worry. The move into the new quarters was effected at the end of August 1934.

A proposal to amend and consolidate the federal legislation applicable to the Board's operations in order to bring it into conformity with present needs and practices was approved by the membership in January 1933. Originally incorporated by 'an Act of the late Province of Canada in the eighth year of the reign of Her Majesty Queen Victoria, chapter twenty-four of the statutes of 1845,' there had been a good deal of subsequent amending legislation and it was desirable both to consolidate this material and introduce further changes. Under a new Act passed by the House of Commons and the Senate and given Royal Assent on 12 April 1933, all previous Acts were repealed and the new statute, embodying all the desired conditions, was substituted. Although this was largely a tidying-up operation, some significant changes were made, among them an extension of the powers of the Boards of Arbitration to permit consideration of cases involving all provinces, rather than only those within Ontario, as formerly. The scope of the Board's arbitration procedures were further broadened a few years later when, after consultation with the Federation of British Industries, methods were developed for the arbitration by the Board of disputes between members of the Federation and their Canadian customers. This was regarded as a substantial contribution to improved British-Canadian trade relations.

The annual dinners of the Board were resumed in 1933 after a lapse of some years. Nearly a thousand attended the event that year to hear Prime Minister R.B. Bennett deliver a 'state of the nation' address. Mr Bennett spoke again at the two succeeding annual occasions; the Board's Council was presumably convinced of the importance of businessmen receiving a report on conditions and the government's attitude toward them from the head of that government. Mr Bennett seemed happy to comply and on all three occasions his speeches were frank, comprehensive and forthright. Indeed, in one of them he castigated businessmen in general and the Board of Trade in particular for positions taken on some current problems, which he considered were based upon an inadequate appreciation of all the operative factors. The railways especially were the source of much dismay and Bennett himself characterized them as 'the problem beyond all others which threatens the integrity of our national existence and the maintenance of our credit.'

The railways had been suffering enormous losses – the CNR as early as 1929 had recorded a net loss of almost $41 million – and it was the opinion of many businessmen that they were over-extended and that their operations should be drastically curtailed to lessen the drain on the taxpayers, who ended up paying for their deficits. This the government declined to do but it appointed a Royal Commission in 1931 to investigate conditions and upon its recommendation established a board of trustees to oversee total operations and ensure the highest degree of co-ordination between the services supplied by the Canadian National and Canadian Pacific Railways.

Largely because of the extreme economic stringency prevalent throughout the nation in this period the Board and other organizations like it pressed hard for greater economy in public finance. The increasing cost of government was leading to added burdens of taxation and causing grave apprehension among businessmen already suffering acutely from depressed conditions. They were resentful of Ottawa's unwillingness to institute reforms. As a result of recommendations made by the Toronto Board the Canadian Chamber of Commerce in 1932 appointed a National Committee on Economy in Public Finance to consider all of the government's fiscal policies and practices. The work of the national body was to be supplemented by separate studies in each of the provinces by committees set up by the Boards of Trade in their capital cities. The Toronto Board immediately established an Ontario Committee with Dr H.L. Brittain as director of research and for good measure also created its own committee under J.M. Macdonnell to look into the local municipal situation. The intention was to produce recommendations prior to the preparation of budgets for 1933. As a result of its own work the Canadian Chamber submitted extensive representations to the federal government, recommending among other things varous measures for the elimination of redundant services, a reduction in the number of cabinet ministers, members of the Senate, members of the House of Commons and the provincial legislatures, and a thorough realignment of the government's departmental operations at all levels to minimize overhead.

The Toronto Board, after one of the largest membership meetings in its history held on 20 April 1933, submitted its own views to Ottawa, expressing disappointment that the recent federal Budget had so signally failed to reflect the thinking of the country. What was needed, it said, was prompt and drastic action to meet what it considered to be an emergency situation. A copy of the brief was sent to every member of the House of Commons and resulted in an exchange of correspondence with H.H. Stevens, Minister of Trade and Commerce, who insisted that large elements in the federal Budget were uncontrollable. The Board simply disagreed and throughout this entire period worked unceasingly to induce the government to give this problem the attention it felt it deserved. The Board's Council and businessmen throughout the country were genuinely angry that under conditions which were forcing them to introduce extraordinary economies in the conduct of their own affairs the government at Ottawa should so haughtily decline to pare its own costs.

The provincial government appeared somewhat more co-operative, collaborating with the Ontario Committee on Economy in Public Finance and organizing its own study of provincial and municipal taxation. The latter move was wholly in accord with the Board's belief that changes in its revenue-producing methods proposed from time to time by the city of Toronto should be introduced only as a result of a full enquiry into the question of municipal financing by the province. In the absence of data based on such an enquiry the Board successfully opposed a move by the city in 1933 seeking provincial authority to impose a special tax on taxable incomes exceeding $10,000 and to amend the Assessment Act. There was some satisfaction in the city's lowering of its tax rate from 33.9 mills in 1932 to 33.4 mills in 1933, but it faded when the Board discovered that the small change had been made possible only by capitalizing expenditures for unemployment relief and thus merely postponing the day of reckoning. By the end of 1933 tax arrears in Toronto had grown to $12 million, or 34.4 per cent of total taxation for the year. A statement of city financing was produced by the Board for public information at this time which showed that while the city's population had grown by 33 per cent since 1914 taxes had increased by 247 per cent. Possible means of saving money were outlined and a plea was made for the utmost restraint in the undertaking of public works.

Governments, of course, were caught in a serious dilemma. Unless public works were undertaken the costs of unemployment relief rose; in either case high expenditures were entailed and taxes were the principal source of the needed revenues. But tax revenues declined as the business depression continued and worsened, and, in any event, high levels of taxation tended only to accelerate economic decline. There was no perfect solution and the situation could be met only by a delicate process of compromise and adjustment. When the city's tax rate went up again to 35 mills in 1935 the Board reacted with the statement that businesses had reached their taxation limit. It suggested that instead of rate increases the city should broaden its tax base by the removal of unjustifiable exemptions, and if revenues still fell short of requirement methods should be devised for raising money other than by the direct taxation of property. It continued to insist, moreover, that problems of municipal finance could be solved only as a consequence of a complete and independent survey of public financing as it operated at and between the various levels of government, and in 1937 applauded the appointment of a federal Royal Commission on Dominion-Provincial Relations whose studies were to be concerned, among much else, with 'the whole system of taxation in Canada.' A preliminary brief was prepared for submission to the Commission dealing extensively with duplication in sales, income and corporation taxes and succession duties.

A proposal to reduce the representation on the city council from three to two aldermen for each city ward received the Board's hearty endorsement and it further recommended that the term of office of the elected representatives be extended from one to two years. The question of reducing aldermanic representation was put to the voters at the January 1933 civic elections and was approved. As an experiment the 1936 elections of the following year's council were held on 7 December, a departure from the traditional New Year's Day, and the Board, which had always favoured the January date, lost no time in pointing out that the vote registered, at 36 per cent, was the lowest of the past five years.

On 6 March 1934 the city of Toronto celebrated the one-hundredth anniversary of its incorporation. Its population had grown to nearly 630,000 and was in fact almost at its maximum. The suburbs, however, had nearly 150,000 residents and were growing rapidly; the future size and shape of the area was becoming a matter of some concern. The city's long series of territorial annexations had ended in 1914, and it was a question of whether integration in a new form should be contemplated. A Special Committee of the Ontario Government on Metropolitan Area was established in 1934 to conduct studies leading to a plan for a metropolitan area to include Toronto and district, to which the Board of Trade made some contribution, but the effort was premature and the outcome negligible. The Board's initial concern in this matter was to devise a workable relationship among the municipalities that would comprise a Greater Toronto Area.

The Board had itself instigated the formation of a Citizens' Committee for a Greater Toronto some years before and had been criticized by the press for its efforts; it regularly pressed for comprehensive city planning, offering its services and being assured from time to time of the city's intention to prepare a city-wide plan. By 1931 there were 100,000 private automobiles in Toronto and traffic problems were mounting. Parking regulations were imposed, and the Board again advocated the establishment of building lines to permit street widenings as vehicular needs increased.

Housing, too, received attention, largely in terms of the elimination of slums and the rehabilitation of aging structures. The Board was represented on a provincial government committee appointed in 1934 to examine and report on housing conditions and subsequently on an advisory committee formed to consider the establishment of a city Housing Commission. Nevertheless, when the city asked the citizens at the 1937 civic elections to authorize the issue of debentures in the amount of $2 million for slum clearance and the construction of low-cost housing the Board declined its support; it favoured the principle but considered the approach inadequately planned. The voters agreed with the Board and the by-law was defeated. The National Housing Act was brought into effect in August 1938, and in four months Toronto led all other cities in availing itself of its provisions with 6,544 loans totalling almost $2.5 million.

Toronto was rated as one of North America's smokiest cities and the Board made some effort in 1933 to bring about the enactment of better control legislation, although it acknowledged this was a relatively minor problem compared to the more serious economic hazards of the day. The first evidence that noise was regarded as a civic nuisance deserving attention appeared in 1934, and over the next ten years the subject came up on a number of occasions. Support was given to the city's application to the provincial government for legislation validating a proposed revised noise control by-law, and efforts were made editorially to convince the citizens that the sounds of the city were becoming objectionable and that they could be checked.

When the city in 1934 approved plans for a new sewage disposal plant at Highland Creek to cost an estimated $25 million, the board, on the advice of its Engineering Branch, sought and secured a review of the proposal that resulted in a new report recommending Ashbridge's Bay as the plant location at a saving of over $5 million. Meanwhile information had been obtained about new treatment processes employed in the United States, and again the Board recommended delay in the interests of further possible savings. Nothing happened for several years, in spite of increasing need. A Review Board in 1939 recommended the construction of a complete treatment plant, but by this time the city and the Board of Trade had come to the conclusion that the best practical procedure was to build a partial treatment plant now and improve and expand it as circumstances warranted. The matter was still at the argument stage in 1944.

Apart from the temporary measures adopted by the Harbour Commissioners, nothing had yet been done about furnishing Toronto with an airport, in spite of a steadily increasing use of air services: in 1926 there were 6,436 passengers in Canada and three years later more than 75,000. A delegation representing the Board of Trade and other interests again brought the matter forcefully to the attention of the Mayor and Board of Control in March 1931. An advisory committee was appointed, headed by the Board's delegate, A.E. Kirkpatrick. It became obvious, however, that the city was not prepared to proceed, and the Board took the initiative of seeking, again with the support of other organizations, the private establishment of facilities with financial assistance from the federal and municipal governments. In 1934, on the Board's recommendation, the federal government designated the Toronto Flying Club field as an air harbour; by this time, also, other private fields were being expanded and improved, and the seaplane base on the waterfront was in active use. The Harbour Commissioners in fact planned to build a combined airport and air harbour on Toronto Island immediately south of the western entrance to the harbour and had received support for the venture from the federal government in the form of a promise to build a tunnel under the western channel to give access to the airfield. The project received the Board of Trade's support. Then in 1935 the Minister of Public Works, presumably for reasons of economy, decided not to proceed with the tunnel, on which work had actually begun. An annoyed delegation from the city, the Harbour Commission and the Board of Trade travelled to Ottawa in an unsuccessful effort to induce the Minister to change his mind, but the work was stopped and the tunnel was never completed.

The Board of Trade renewed its campaign for a permanent solution of the airport problem. Toronto was one of the few major cities that still had no place on the growing airmap, a particularly grave situation in the light of work undertaken by Imperial Airways in Britain which was expected to establish trans-Atlantic air services by the spring of 1938. A writer in the London *Times* pointed out that 'what happened in the early days of the railways is in process of happening in the air routes. Once an air route is established it is a matter of inconvenience and expense to divert it. The great city which misses its chance today to place itself on a great air route may have the utmost difficulty ten years hence in recovering a lost opportunity.' Finally, on 9 July 1937, Toronto's city council made two decisions: to build the airport and air harbour on Toronto Island advocated by the Harbour Commissioners and to establish an auxiliary airport at Malton. It was the beginning of the end of a long argument and a successful conclusion to the Board's efforts extending over a period of more than ten years. In the same year as the city's decision was made the Imperial Airways flying boat *Cambria* arrived in Toronto after a test flight across the Atlantic, and the Board tendered a luncheon to its crew to mark this significant step in the development of transportation by air.

A part from an element of simple civic pride, the Board's airport concern was the old one of ensuring a place for Toronto on the world's main trade routes and hence preserving its commercial health. To be the hub of a system of railways, steamships, roads and air routes was absolutely essential if the city was to hold its place as a major North American production and distribution centre and forge a prosperous future. The city's roots were in trade and commerce and it had long been recognized that the nourishment of those roots would come from effective spadework by the private sector; those in public office, the Board felt, often seemed to be unreliably motivated. A new worry arose in 1937 when it was rumoured that Trans-Canada Airline's main line would follow a route from Montreal to Ottawa to Emsdale and thence to the Pacific coast, Toronto being served only by a shuttle from Emsdale. This was obviously the shortest and most economical line connecting Halifax, Montreal and Vancouver, but an aroused Board of Trade delegation lost no time in pointing out to TCA President S.J. Hungerford and the Minister of Transport, C.D. Howe, that Toronto was a mainline city and anything short of mainline treatment was intolerable. Mr Howe appears to have readily agreed and the plans were altered. Later representations to the Minister and to Imperial Airways to have Toronto designated a terminus for trans-Atlantic services were less successful. The Board was simply informed that 'Toronto cannot be designated as a port of call.'

The Imperial Economic Conference held in Ottawa in July and August 1932 marked an important turning point in the course of the British Commonwealth and Empire. British Prime Minister Ramsay MacDonald approached it with the attitude that 'at Ottawa ... we can create freer trade conditions over a vast area of the world,' and Canada's Prime Minister

Bennett had said: 'We want Canadians to think of this Conference as the greatest operating partnership the world has ever seen, an effort to so arrange our trade and dealings that it will be for the perpetual advantage of us all.' The Toronto Board encouraged the Canadian Chamber of Commerce to prepare material for the Conference reflecting the position and attitudes of Canadian business, and through its own Foreign and Domestic Trade Committee assembled data respecting such issues as Empire and Colonial preferences, trade agreements, marketing procedures and Empire content, all of which were placed before the Conference's Tariff Preparatory Committee. The outcome of the Conference was in the main gratifying to the Board and vindicated its long effort to achieve greater Empire trade unity. It was not, however, insensitive to the realities of its continental trading position and welcomed a new trade agreement with the United States brought into effect in 1936 which reduced each country's duties on a wide range of products, extended most-favoured-foreign-nation treatment unconditionally with respect to customs duties and virtually eliminating non-tariff barriers. The arrangement nevertheless raised the question of the need to adjust the Brisith preferential tariff structure so as to ensure the maintenance of an adequate differential.

Critical of the extensive powers originally proposed for the Canadian Wheat Board, the Board was relieved that its function finally resolved itself chiefly into responsibility for accumulated wheat surpluses, although it still had some reservations about its authority to fix the price paid to the producers on the grounds that it seemed contrary to the principle of freedom to negotiate.

Much important legislation came under review during this period. Uniform regulations to prevent malpractice in the sale of securities was under consideration by an inter-provincial committee soon after the stock-market crash of 1929; proposed amendments to the Ontario Corporations' Tax Act came under criticism; a revision of the Bankruptcy Act in 1932 led to extensive studies and commentary; an Ontario Bill to repeal the Bulk Sales Act was opposed on the grounds that the legislation was beneficial to the commercial community and needed changes could be better achieved by simple amendment; the Ontario government's proposal to establish a minimum wage for males was scrutinized and efforts were made to ensure that such action did not lead employers merely to replace male by female labour at lower rates. Upon introduction of the Employment and Social Insurance Act in 1935 the government was requested to remove the control of relief administration from the field of local influence and establish standards for such administration in each of the provinces, and also to co-ordinate unemployment relief with unemployment insurance and the federal employment service; with the establishment of a Labour and Industry Board in 1937 to administer the Minimum Wage and Industrial Standards Act efforts were made to ensure impartial terms as they affected employers and employees and also to avoid conflict with existing policies and practices of the Department of Labour.

Because of its long association with the Board of Railway Commissioners for Canada, the Board took special interest in a Senate Bill introduced in 1936 to establish a Board of Transport Commissioners which would exercise authority over transport not only by rail but also by ships, aircraft and motor vehicles. While the move was favoured in principle since it conformed with the Board's views expressed years ago regarding the need for an independent control body, there was some doubt about the terms of the proposed legislation, mainly on the question of possible conflict between federal and provincial authorities respecting highway transport, and on the need for controls over ships of all registry using Canadian waters, not merely those registered in Canada.

The Board participated throughout the depression years, as it had during the war, in works designed to relieve widespread and acute social distress. During the worst days one-quarter of Canada's entire labour force was jobless and 12 per cent of the population was dependent on emergency relief. The Board's President acted on a Civic Welfare Survey Commission appointed to report on the efficacy of unemployment relief, and the Board took an active part in the work of an Emergency Loan Committee set up in 1930 to administer rental and other forms of relief for the city, disbursing some $1.5 million in the four years of its operation. Members were active in the Citizens' Friendship League, formed to aid destitute families. Some 1,800 citizens were engaged in the work of the League, which by 1934 had given assistance in one form or another to more than 20,000 families. Support was also given to a Community Gardens Movement which, by organizing the cultivation of unused land and providing seeds, both contributed to the food supply and gave occupation to well over a thousand unemployed men. The Board was nevertheless dissatisfied with the general structure of unemployment relief administration, which fell heavily upon the municipality; it advocated a greater assumption of responsibility by the federal government and the development of greater uniformity in the application of relief measures necessitated by emergency economic conditions applying on a national scale. It further strongly advocated action by the government to establish a nation-wide training program for unemployed young men, who were becoming deeply discouraged by lack of work and hence ready material for radical political indoctrination, and who would moreover be ill-fitted for skilled occupation in modern business and industry when employment opportunities again became available. Proposals made by the National Employment Commission in 1939 to develop new employment sources were supported, and representatives were appointed to a civic committee dealing with local unemployment problems, one of whose aims was to assist jobless young men to avail themselves of work opportunities in northern Ontario.

In spite of ample evidence of continued business lassitude, there was during the early 1930s a common feeling that such economic ills could not possibly last and that 'prosperity was just around the corner.' Indeed, there were always a few encouraging signs, and by 1935 stock prices began to rise, doubling over the next two years. Then in October and November 1937 a new slump occurred as the result of a sharp recession in the United States and a disturbed international situation which climaxed in the Munich Pact September 1938; 80 per cent of the two-year gain disappeared, to be followed by another slow recovery. Although new and more stable levels were slowly establishing themselves, the dislocations caused by the world-wide depression of the 1930s were not cured until the whole situation was suddenly and radically changed by war.

# 10
# World War II

The outbreak of war with Germany in September 1939 altered the entire pattern of Canadian activities, although for a time it was not clear what Canada's role would be. At first industries in Toronto received few contracts for war materials and there was little plant reorganization; some expectation remained that Britain might still negotiate treaties which would make Canadian supplies unnecessary. Moreover, it was considered a strong possibility that this time Canada would not be regarded as a supplier of general war materials but might play a more specialized role when the situation had been fully assessed.

The War Measures Act was proclaimed and regulations under it were quickly promulgated; new legislation was passed and new tax measures were brought into effect. Prominent functions of the Board of Trade, fulfilled throughout the war, were to keep the burgeoning flow of regulations and directives from Ottawa under review, to see that its members were informed of new conditions affecting their operations and to assist them in adapting to such conditions. Following the declaration of war the Board, in a telegram to the Prime Minister, urged the Government to 'unrelentingly continue the acceleration and prosecution of Canada's war effort,' and offered its services to the federal and provincial governments in any fields where they might be useful. The Board also offered its facilities to aid appeals for funds made to the public by patriotic, charitable and social agencies. Members of the Board who immediately enlisted for overseas service included A.E. Nash, W.W. Southam, O.H. Barrett and J.S.P. Armstrong; by January 1943 there were fifty-five members on active service and the number was still growing. As happened during the previous war the affiliations with the Board of such members were maintained without fee. The Board's First Vice-President, James S. Duncan, was granted leave of absence to serve as Deputy Minister for Air.

By 1940 business was reported as 'good and improving.' Retail sales were high, business failures were 27 per cent fewer than in the previous year and the holding of price levels by the Price Control Board prevented the unwise speculation in commodities which had had such ill effects during the last war. Foreign trade was being regulated by the Foreign Exchange Control Board, one of whose main objects was to ensure the preferential entry of British goods into the Canadian market. The new situation was affording relief from unemployment costs and railway deficits, long the two most serious drains upon public finance.

There were, however, genuine reasons for concern. Labour shortages were beginning to appear and were expected to become general; taxation was steadily increasing; wartime controls were beginning to interfere with regular marketing processes, sometimes, it was thought, unnecessarily; and there was real fear of rampant inflation. In his report to the members in 1940 the Board's President, R.C. Berkinshaw, observed that 'Our country is one of the chief sources of supply for the allied countries. This will undoubtedly cause one of the greatest periods of business activity we have ever known. The problem from now on is not to stimulate business activity but rather to guide it along sound lines properly related to our economy.' While control of the economy was accepted as inevitable, it was not long before the regulations emanating from Ottawa came under fire as being either unduly repressive or ill-adapted to the realities of business. The almost limitless authority assumed by the federal government and its innumerable regulatory bodies, often felt to exceed that required for the discharge of direct responsibilities, caused apprehension not only in its immediate effect but more particularly in the possibility of post-war perpetuation. Addressing the Empire Club, former Board President J.M. Macdonnell remarked: '... men's minds will easily incline to the thought that the solution of all our problems, of peace as well as war, can come through, not a decrease, but an extension of government activity ... Will problems be solved by our system of courage, imagination and initiative, or be left to be solved by government agency, which will inevitably be a regimentation which we all detest?'

By 1941 control was in effect over prices, wages and salaries, installment selling was restricted, supplies of many materials were governed by a strict allocation system and labour was conscripted to meet shortages in essential operations. The following year a number of consumer commodities were rationed and taxes were substantially reducing disposable incomes. The total effect was to deflect the threatened inflation and improve the efficiency of national economic management at the inevitable expense of profits and the general standard of living. In the fourth year of the war Canada's war production amounted to $2.5 billion, while natural and primary products worth another $800 million were being supplied to the allied nations. More then 900,000 Canadians were engaged directly or indirectly in war production and half a million were in the armed services.

The Board of Trade's operations were adjusted to meet the prevailing conditions. In addition to a summary of all new legislation in its *Journal*, a bi-monthly bulletin service was organized to inform members of the essentials of new regulations, orders and directives. Although it realized that most controls were necessary, the Board did not hesitate to point out what it felt to be ill-considered measures whose long-term effects were likely to be the reverse of those desired, and it insisted that artificial controls be lifted as soon as conditions allowed to give business an opportunity to recover and reorganize. In consultation with its Trade Branches and with other organizations it studied the policies and practices of the Wartime Prices and Trade Board and submitted a number of comments, among them a condemnation of cost-plus contracts; it also recommended the appointment of advisory committees of businessmen in all major trade categories to advise the government on the implementation of its policies, a survey of all government departments to ensure the retention of only essential employees and the co-ordination of transportation, shipping and delivery services.

As early as 1943 the Board was concerning itself with the problems of post-war reconstruction and the measures that would need to be adopted to facilitate the passage of the economy from a war footing to one that would provide the best conditions for the resumption of normal business processes. It worried especially about the disposal of war surpluses, which could seriously disrupt orderly marketing if not handled with extreme care. The Board's British Empire Overseas Branch undertook a long and careful study of the factors considered relevant to the post-war development of Commonwealth trade. Out of this work a booklet was developed that received wide circulation in Britain, dealing with the circumstances which had prevented the fullest development of British–Canadian trade in the past and the methods by which a better trading relationship could be developed when the war was over.

Acting on a recommendation also arising from the British Branch's studies, the Board's Council in 1944 directed representations to Prime Minister Mackenzie King advocating the establishment of a Canadian nationality and the right of citizens to be known as Canadian subjects. It was gratified to hear in the Speech from the Throne the following year that 'the government also considers that it is advisable to revise and clarify the definition of Canadian citizenship, and to bring the legislation regarding national status, naturalization and immigration into conformity with the definition of citizenship.' The Board's interest in this question led to an invitation in 1945 to sponsor ceremonies welcoming into Canadian citzenship those who had recently been granted naturalization. The invitation was not accepted, but it gave rise to a new study of the existing regulations governing the admission of immigrants and the qualifications considered necessary for the granting of citizenship. The conclusion reached was that there was need for co-ordination and improvement, and that much more attention should be given to ensuring that new arrivals from foreign parts were given a proper appreciation of Canadian ideals and institutions and a better start on their way to good citzenship. Once these reforms had been instituted the Board would enthusiastically support the idea of organizing suitable and duly impressive welcoming ceremonies.

It was natural that throughout this period the Board should give particular attention to the new fiscal policies adopted by governments at all levels, especially as reflected in taxes. When the Excess Profits Tax Act and the Income War Tax Act were enforced in 1939 it was quick to point out certain inequities and most of them were rectified. As the burden of taxation mounted fears were expressed that the operations of some businesses would be permanently impaired; commentary and criticism were regularly directed to Ottawa in an effort to preserve the greatest measure of commercial stability possible in the circumstances, and these efforts had some success. After lengthy studies by its Taxation Committee the Board in 1945 presented a brief to the Ministers of Finance and Reconstruction, J.L. Ilsley and C.D. Howe, setting forth in some detail recommendations for post-war tax policies incorporating features designed to ameliorate the adverse effects of high rates and attempting to find an acceptable mean between the levels of 1938 and the wartime peaks.

At the provincial level the Board led opposition to proposed amendments of the Ontario Corporations Tax Act substantially increasing rates and introducing certain retroactive features considered highly objectionable. The latter were modified as a result, but the Board remained dissatisfied with the province's attitude, believing that its place in the tax field should be a modest one in view of the dominant role played by the federal government in the wartime economy. When the province showed a surplus in its accounts in 1941 an appeal was made to lower its tax on corporations; the Board supported the idea that such taxation should be placed permanently within the federal government's jurisdiction.

Meanwhile the progress of the Royal Commission on Dominion–Provincial Relations was being closely observed, and the Board's preliminary brief to the Commission was followed by detailed representations during its hearing in Toronto. Support was recorded for Plan I in the Commission's eventual report which, among other things, called for federal jurisdiction over the administration of unemployment relief, compulsory contributions to old age annuities, if established, the exclusive jurisdiction of the Dominion over personal income tax, corporation taxes and succession duties, and national adjustment grants to certain provinces to permit, under specified conditions, the balancing of provincial budgets. The Board's delegation also made the main submission at the Toronto hearing of a Royal Commission on Co-operatives in 1945, taking the position that 'co-operative organizations should be taxed in the same way as other businesses trading in similar circumstances and under similar conditions.'

The battle against tax inroads into corporate incomes had to be fought at the municipal level as well. A proposal of Toronto's city council to introduce such a tax in 1938 had been bitterly and successfully opposed; the Board made it clear that Toronto businessmen were unwilling to make any greater contribution to civic revenues until the long-sought independent survey of municipal financing had been undertaken. At last, in May 1940, Mayor R.C. Day asked the Board to recommend a committee which would act in an advisory capacity respecting the city's proposed assessment and tax accounting plan. The Board's nominees were H.D. Lockhart Gordon, as chairman, H.M. Turner, James Turner and R. Wilkinson; they were duly appointed and after considerable work submitted a report with numerous proposals for improvement of the city's assessment and tax accounting methods, many of which were implemented.

As a means of improving its revenues the city attempted to reduce the number of tax-exempt properties, and this time found in the Board of Trade a staunch ally. In the Board's view all federal and provincial properties in the city should be subject to normal tax, and churches should be exempt only if they were used exclusively for religious purposes. It further recommended that the properties of the Toronto Hydro-Electric System not be exempt from payment of the $75,000 annual tax that would apply if the System were privately owned and operated, and generally upheld the policy of taxing the properties of publicly owned or operated enterprises in the same manner as those in private hands. Unexpectedly, the Toronto Transportation Commission, admitting that it had been influenced by the Board's arguments, voluntarily agreed to assume normal tax obligations on its properties and contribute to other civic costs associated with its operations.

In 1938 some 4,000 delivery horses were still plodding Toronto's streets, although they were being displaced by motor vehicles at the rate of a thousand a year and hence were expected to disappear completely by 1942. Among the problems created by the thickening motor traffic was that of parking: there was curb parking space in the downtown area for about 4,000 cars, or 5 per cent of the total vehicular traffic, and little provision for the remainder. The Board successfully opposed the installation of parking meters and objected to a reduction by half of the existing one-hour parking limit on the grounds that both measures would be detrimental to the transaction of business. It had seen no merit, moreover, in an amendment of the Municipal Act proposed in 1939 which would have authorized municipalities to require the owners of certain types of buildings to provide off-street parking, and its opposition undoubtedly contributed to the defeat of the measure. To clear the streets for traffic movement in winter, however, the Board urged the city to acquire adequate snow-removal equipment. Back in 1891 Toronto had been proud of its spanking new snow-sweeper, drawn by twelve horses, but for a long time since then clearance had been largely a hand operation and in severe winters the streets remained clogged and hazardous for weeks at a time. The Board thought the time had come for the employment of modern mechanical processes.

On one aspect of city management the Board took a firm and consistent stand: it wanted the appointment of a permanent body responsible for overall planning, including the designation of zones of permitted land uses. Zoning was permissible under the Municipal Act, and in 1917 municipalities had been given the authority to appoint town planning commissioners, but so far Toronto had taken no effective action in either area; the Board considered the establishment of a non-partisan commission to advise the city council on all issues affecting planning policies long overdue.

The city began studies of a proposed zoning by-law in 1939, and the Board, in addition to participating in the investigations, set up its own committee to look into the broader issues. The city decided to defer action pending a report from the Board, which was submitted in October, 1941. It recommended the appointment at the earliest possible date of a planning body to be known as the City Planning Board, which would act in an advisory capacity to the city on any and all matters connected with the use and development of lands in and adjacent to the city, deal with all relevant concerns and prepare proposals and plans for suggested development works. The Planning Board would be composed of seven property-owning citizens who would carry public support, serving three-year terms without remuneration. In addition the Ontario government would be requested to appoint two of its officials to the Board to furnish a liaison with the province.

These proposals of the Board of Trade received support from the press and other interested organizations, and when they came before the city council were unanimously adopted. A City Planning Board as recommended was appointed in 1942, with A.C. Partridge as chairman; the Board of Trade was represented by its General Manager, F.D. Tolchard. By 1944 the Planning Board had produced a Master Plan for 'the use of land, buildings, structures and improvements in order to improve living conditions, create conditions favourable to the development of industry, and provide the maximum employment for the inhabitants of Toronto.' It was designed for implementation as a part of the National Post-War Construction Program with financial assistance from the federal and provincial governments. The Plan encompassed an area of one hundred square miles – forty-five more than the existing city – and was designed for a thirty-year period of growth, when it was foreseen that the area would contain between 1,250,000 and 1,500,000 inhabitants. The Board of Trade gave much attention to the Plan, advocated its adoption, subject to some modification, and noted that it made more than ever necessary the enactment of proper zoning legislation. The urgency of remedial works in the city was emphasized by the fact that by 1944, of a total area population of about 900,000, almost one-third were domiciled outside the city proper. The exodus to the suburbs to find acceptable living conditions was well under way and was likely to accelerate, leading inevitably to central decay unless a project on the scale of the Master Plan was undertaken. Unaccountably, the City Planning Board terminated its activities in April 1945 and its work was taken over by the permanent civic departments. Perhaps the Planning Board considered its mission accomplished with the preparation of its Master Plan, although it is nowhere evident that either the city or the Board of Trade initially considered the Planning Board to have had a limited mandate.

Efforts were renewed in 1943 to overcome citizen lethargy in the matter of voting. Previous efforts had met with some success, and the Board in 1943 decided on a new course by setting up a Voters' Information Bureau, a non-partisan, non-political service designed to encourage interest in the elections and furnish information requested by voters about polling places, hours of voting and the like. The Bureau, which gained the support of other organizations, also operated prior to the provincial and federal elections of 1945, providing even more extensive services; a material increase in the number of voters in both cases was attributed at least in some measure to its work.

The Board objected to a program of public works proposed by the city in 1940 on the grounds that it was untimely and ill-considered. The Board took the position that any major enterprises should be undertaken only in terms of a scale of priorities and in strict conformity with the city's financial competence. Through its representation on the city's Advisory Committee on Housing, however, the Board two years later advocated the erection of needed temporary wartime housing and some new permanent housing under the terms of the National Housing Act and the Home Extension Plan. Application would be made for the granting of the necessary priorities on building materials, although again it insisted that any such work be undertaken in conformity with a fully-developed plan. It dissented from a recommendation of the Advisory Committee, to the extent of issuing a minority report, that the city enter into negotiations with Wartime Housing Ltd for the construction of two thousand low-cost dwelling units in Greater Toronto, again because it considered the scheme too hazy and also because it feared that its execution would conflict with the normal operation of the building industry, with possible long-term effects. Moreover, it did not agree that such an undertaking was proper for Wartime Housing Ltd. The city was likewise strongly criticized when in 1943 it proposed to enter the fuel business in order to facilitate and regularize coal deliveries. This was a conspicuous contravention of the rights of private businesses and the Board, acting for the city's fuel dealers as well as on principle, first requested time to consider the proposal, then submitted arguments sufficiently cogent that the intention was abandoned.

About this time the city had some pangs of conscience in the matter of the domiciliation of certain of its debentures. These had been placed in the United States and the question was whether there was any obligation to retire them in American funds, which at the prevailing rate of exchange would have represented a considerably higher cost. The Board of Trade first took the position that the matter had to be settled by legal interpretation, but when legal opinions differed, it came down strongly for discharging what it saw as in fact a moral obligation and advised the city to pay up in spite of any technical excuses it might find for avoiding the extra cost, and this advice was eventually acted upon.

The multiplicity of separate appeals for charitable funds had long been a bugbear of the commercial community, and the Board, with other organizations, had for years urged their co-ordination as a means of reducing the overall number, effecting administrative economies and defining with more clarity the actual fields of social activity in which the numerous agencies were operating. A conference of representatives from many of the interests concerned was convoked under the Board's auspices, leading to some agreement that there would be genuine benefits for everyone in a joint campaign rather than separate ones for each organization, but in spite of continued pressure by the Board on behalf of the business community it was 1943 before a United Appeal could be organized. The campaign of that year, in which members of the Board took an active part, proved wholly satisfactory and provided reason to hope that still greater unification and efficiency might be accomplished in the future. As a further means of streamlining fund-raising in the city, the Board helped establish the Canadian Employee Chest, which provided a means of ensuring systematic support out of earnings for both home-front and vital war services. The Board also played a major role in work undertaken in 1944 to bring about the organization of a central body to co-ordinate juvenile delinquency rehabilitation programs and youth services in the Greater Toronto area, work which culminated in the creation of a Youth Services Department of the United Welfare Chest.

The statutory regulation of the relationship between employers and their employees assumed increased importance during the war. When the Ontario government in 1942 proposed the enactment of compulsory collective bargaining legislation, the Board canvassed its membership to secure an expression of the employers' viewpoint and, based on their response, raised a number of questions with the government: Was the time opportune for the introduction of such legislation, particularly in view of the extensive controls already being exercised by the federal government? Would not Ontario employers be placed at a disadvantage by controls applicable only in that province? Should not equivalent responsibilities be assigned to employers and employees? It was the Board's view that the times demanded the utmost care in preserving good relations between workers and management, and it felt that the province's proposals needed careful review on these grounds as well as clarification respecting a possible conflict of jurisdictions. As a result of these representations the Minister of Labour invited the Board's representatives to confer with him; this provided the opportunity for an elaboration of these points and an expression of general opinion on labour relations matters, and led to the appointment of a Committee of the Legislature for a re-examination of the whole subject. The Board appeared before the Committee, this time represented by legal counsel, and its views were well received; when a government Bill was finally introduced, however, although it incorporated some of the Board's suggestions, it still contained undesirable features and again the Board made itself heard. But the legislation passed substantially unchanged, leaving the Board with only the minor satisfaction of having been instrumental in modifying some of its more objectionable features. When there were indications that the Workmen's Compensation Act would be expanded to provide benefits considered to be in the realm of social service rather than compensation, the Board registered with the Minister of Labour its disapproval of any deviation from the original principles of the legislation or changes in administrative procedures without fullest examination of the consequences, and its efforts proved successful.

At the federal level, an enquiry launched by the National War Labour Board into labour relations and wage conditions in Canada elicited a response from the Board of Trade in the form of an extensive commentary on labour conditions and the effects of the government's policies in the Toronto area. This was followed by representations to the Minister of Labour dealing with suggested changes in the Wartime Labour Relations Regulations. In the main the Board's argument was that compulsory bargaining should be limited to questions of wages, hours and related terms of employment and not be concerned with matters of union security, and that there should be provision for the use of conciliation machinery where no union was certified. Emphasis was placed on recognition of the right to strike only after all existing procedures for amicable adjustment had been exhausted.

Renewed concern with labour affairs was evinced after the war in representations made in connection with the Industrial Relations and Disputes Investigation Act. The Board's aim in this case was to ensure the observance of principles which would provide an equitable basis in law for the administration of labour affairs. When the Act was passed in 1948 the views of the larger employers in the Board's membership on its effects were sought and conveyed to the Minister of Labour, with particular reference to the inter-relationship of federal and provincial labour law. Since it had anticipated a return to provincial jurisdiction of much of the authority exercised federally during the war, and hence new provincial labour legislation, the Board in the previous year had presented to the Ontario Minister of Labour a consolidation of the views and comments which had been transmitted over the past several years to the federal minister.

At its annual dinner held at the Royal York Hotel on 24 January 1944 the Toronto Board of Trade marked the one-hundredth anniversary of its formation. The guest of honour and speaker on this occasion was His Excellency the Rt Hon. the Viscount Halifax, United Kingdom Ambassador to the United States; the Board's President, Luther Winchell, chaired a gathering of some eleven hundred guests that included distinguished representation from both the public and private sectors and managed a considerable glitter in spite of wartime restraints. Lord Halifax's address was concerned in the main with the state of the British Commonwealth and Empire and its part in the shaping of future world affairs. He was frank enough to voice some opinions about the inevitable development of greater independence in the larger Dominions and his remarks were the subject of a good deal of press comment the following day in both Canada and Great Britain, not all of it favourable. He saw the decline of Britain as a world power, but felt that its former influence should be perpetuated as a Commonwealth force. 'If we are to play our rightful part in the preservation of peace,' he said, 'we can only play it as a Commonwealth, united, vital and coherent.' With respect to the Commonwealth's constituent parts he pointed out that '... between the Durham Report and the Statute of Westminster the whole trend of development in the Dominions was toward equality of status. But there was hardly an equivalent effort toward securing what I would call equality of function ... while the Statute of Westminster assured to each and every Dominion complete self-government, it perforce left unsolved the more obstinate problems arising in the fields of foreign policy and defence.' An appreciation of Lord Halifax's participation in the program was conveyed by the Premier of Ontario, the Hon. George A. Drew.

The Board looked back with some pride upon the accomplishments of its first hundred years. It had grown from a body comprising a handful of local merchants, possessing little status or power even in its immediate jurisdiction, to an organization whose views were not only heard with respect but were often sought by the governments of the city, the province and the nation and by groups representing various commercial interests. It had experienced many vicissitudes and some serious setbacks, but on balance successes had outnumbered failures, and some of its victories had been notable ones. One of its most significant achievements, and one which accounted probably more than any other for its sustained vigour, had been its ability to attract to its service so many capable and dedicated men, men who were prepared to devote voluntarily their time and abilities to the wider concerns of their community.

During the war membership strength lost through the depression was recovered and surpassed; by April 1945 there were 3,462 members, a greater number than at any previous time in the Board's history. The influx was due in some measure to the simple fact that business activity reached a high level and the payment of fees was no longer a problem, but a more important reason was that during a time of extraordinary regulation of business by government there was a genuine need for an organization like the Board as an intermediary to interpret rulings, assist in the solution of unusual problems created by wartime regulations and, most important, act as a vehicle for the transmission of the ordinary businessman's views and concerns to the officials of government. The Trade Branches were especially active throughout the war and proved an invaluable means of dealing in a concerted way with difficult times. Ottawa had itself indicated a desire to work with various categories of businesses as groups or associations, rather than with individual enterprises, in negotiating methods for maintaining optimum civilian operations in the face of a severe shortage of manpower and materials of every description.

Much attention had been given in both the public and private sectors to the problems of post-war reconstruction long before hostilities came to an end in mid-1945, and by the close of that year less than 10 per cent remained of the controls over the supplies of goods that had existed at the peak of war activity. Of those that remained many were considered necessary to avoid the effects of inflation which threatened as the result of a suddenly released demand and a continuing inadequate supply of most goods, aggravated by widespread labour unrest. In spite of a desire to be rid of controls as quickly as possible, most businessmen were aware of a continuing need for them during an adjustment period if general conditions were to be maintained which would be favourable to the solid re-establishment of their enterprises. A federal Bill in 1945 to extend the government's emergency powers was, for example, not opposed; the Board of Trade merely urged that any delegation of the powers of Parliament to the Governor General in Council be accompanied by the prompt registration with a central authority of all orders and regulations to ensure that an official record was available.

The conversion back to peacetime operations was in fact accomplished with relative ease. There were indeed many new problems arising out of a return to free marketing amid conditions of considerable complexity at both the domestic and international levels, but a high degree of business activity was sustained and by 1948 both Gross National Product and national income greatly exceeded any previous record. At the middle of that year unemployment stood at 1.6 per cent of the total labour force. Such economic prosperity was not achieved without cost however: the cost of living steadily advanced and by 1948 reached a point 58 per cent higher than 1939 levels.

In trade, the development of enormous export activities during the war had placed Canada in a position of greater dependence than before on world markets, and to maintain her position not only great ingenuity and aggressiveness on the part of commerce and industry but a fuller measure than ever before of understanding and co-operation among governments, management and labour were required. A strong Canadian delegation attended an Empire Trade Conference convened in London in October 1945 under the auspices of the Federation of Chambers of Commerce of the British Empire to consider the resumption of Imperial commercial relations on a peacetime basis, and the report of the Conference, covering a wide range of relevant issues, was deemed to represent an important contribution to the restoration of sound and desirable procedures. It was agreed that the conclusions reached at the Conference should be placed before the appropriate authorities in each of the Empire countries, and the Toronto Board of Trade, after reviewing the material, directed it to the attention of the Canadian Government.

In the emerging pattern of conditions affecting business after the war, no element more consistently engaged the Board's attention than taxation. It had always struggled to keep rates of taxation at levels which would provide necessary revenues without unduly impeding productive enterprise, and with the war's end its efforts were directed towards an alleviation of the heavy but unavoidable burden of special imposts. A brief recommending revision of the provisions and administration of the Income War Tax Act and the Excess Profits Tax Act was presented to a Special Committee of the Senate in 1946, and many of its recommendations were implemented in the subsequent federal Budget. The following year a recapitulation of all the Board's major tax reform proposals was directed to the Minister of Finance, advocating numerous changes in income tax law and a reduction in the tax rates on both business and personal incomes consistent with the Dominion's financial requirements. A federal Bill providing for the disclosure of income tax information was opposed, and a previous suggestion that co-operatives be taxed no differently from other private enterprises was reaffirmed. With the introduction of a new Income Tax Act by the government in 1947, representing an important revision and consolidation of income tax law, new studies were begun and further extensive representations on the draft legislation were made to the Minister of Finance. The Act passed in 1948 seemed to reflect at least in part the businessmen's thinking, although not unnaturally it contained elements they found objectionable.

A report of the Department of National Revenue issued the previous year showed that 2,366,456 taxpayers paid $622.3 million in taxes on a total net taxable income of $5,581 million. More than 63 per cent of taxpayers received incomes of under $3,000 a year, while less than 10 per cent were in the over-$10,000 category.

After the restoration of the Ontario Corporations Tax Act following its wartime suspension, the Board was concerned that certain principles be observed in its application to avoid difficulties which had been previously encountered arising chiefly from the joint incidence of federal and provincial taxes on corporations. With regard to the respective jurisdictions of the federal and provincial governments in the tax field, strong objection was registered by the Board in 1951 to a proposal to amend the British North America Act to confer on the provinces the right to levy an indirect tax on retail sales, and the next year representations were made on several occasions in an attempt to correct what were seen as inequities and anomalies in the Dominion–Ontario Tax Agreement.

Year after year the Board's tax commentaries and criticism arrived in Ottawa, usually just before budget-time. They were prepared by a Taxation Committee composed of knowledgeable men from varied business categories, many of them highly qualified in the field of corporate finance, and they were submitted only if they expressed a policy deemed justifiable in terms of both the public and private interest. As time went on and the principles of tax policy were established and clarified, the Board's concern was more and more with the technical details of tax incidence and administration. The officials of government undoubtedly knew what to expect from Boards of Trade and similar organizations, but there is evidence that well-considered views were welcomed: a surprisingly high percentage of the specific recommendations advanced by the Toronto Board became incorporated in legislation over the years and in the federal Budget of 1955 the Board at last saw a measure of relief afforded to individual taxpayers and a reduction in the rate of tax applicable to corporate profits, together with some amelioration in the area of special excise taxes.

Inherent in the Board's attitude toward fiscal measures was of course the question of how extensive should be the powers accorded to governments to supervise the welfare of Canadians. While the vast regulatory responsibilities vested in the federal government during the war had, on the whole, worked well in an emergency situation, the Board and others were not slow to point out that this had been due not only to the extraordinary conditions then prevailing but also in considerable measure to the fact that much of the administration of wartime controls had been in the hands of men recruited from business and applying business methods. It would be very different, it was argued, if permanent peacetime regulations were applied by civil servants. These considerations assumed new force as ideas of social reform spread throughout the world and signs of 'welfare statism' became more and more prevalent in Canada. To old-guard businessmen the administration of welfare schemes by government beyond a scale necessitated by strictly emergency conditions was unnecessary, undesirable and contrary to the competitive free-enterprise concept of economic development. There was, however, an increasing number who realized that change was in the air and whose attitude veered away from being merely obstructionist to one which would adapt to new conditions but retain substantial initiative within the private sector. In an address delivered in January 1950 the Board's President, E.G. Burton, characterized the times as presenting a great challenge to business. Those in positions of responsibility had to decide whether to accept socialist thinking or meet it with adequate alternatives such as the stabilization of employment, the underwriting of retirement security, opportunities for profit sharing and the conduct of operations in a way that would permit individual employees to identify their own fortunes more closely with the success of the business that employed them. 'Welfare,' he said, 'should not be approached grudgingly or as a charity with no return, but positively as a good investment ... The more we ask from government, the more powers we must give to government. It is the pathway to rule by compulsion. It is a sure way of getting not more, but less democracy, not a higher but almost certainly a lower standard of living for all.'

The Board itself had little love for government-initiated welfare plans. It remained suspicious of Workmen's Compensation and opposed an extension of benefits to new categories of workers, proposed in 1949, without a full investigation of the effect upon rates; it considered the appointment of a Royal Commissioner in that year to investigate the soundness of the governing legislation long overdue. When the government in 1952 proposed to introduce a plan of National Health Insurance, the Canadian Chamber of Commerce was urged to investigate needs and costs and make some assessment of the country's ability to meet those costs, and to consider how any such scheme might be effectively integrated into the private enterprise system. Later, after further information about the suggested Health Insurance scheme had been presented to the Ontario legislature, attention was again given to the issue and the Board recorded that it was not in favour of any state system. A survey had shown that a relatively high proportion of workers already possessed protection against health hazards through private plans offered by their employers; it was believed that the most effective and least costly improvement of the existing situation would be an upgrading of the coverage offered by private agencies accompanied by government contributions of an indirect nature to the costs of health services.

From the Board's point of view most welfare questions related to the contractual terms in effect between employers and their employees. An improved service was organized to provide advisory assistance to members dealing with labour relations problems; a legal department had been set up some years previously under A.C. Crysler to serve the Board's committees and its members, and activities became increasingly directed toward tax and labour concerns. Action was taken to ensure adequate and continuing employer representation on the Ontario Labour Relations Board; a delegate of the Board was appointed to the newly-formed Ontario Employers' Labour Relations Committee and steps were taken to establish a legal panel to advise that Committee. Beginning in 1950 and for a number of years afterwards efforts were made to prevent the threatened withdrawal of judges' services from arbitration and conciliation boards dealing with labour matters.

The Ontario Labour Relations Act of 1950 was the subject of a commentary directed to the Minister of Labour pointing out what were considered inherent defects in the legislation and urging that, in the interests of equity, trade unions be charged with responsibilities commensurate with the privileges they were accorded in collective bargaining. Later an attempt was made to induce the Ontario government to enact legislation permiting the settlement of labour disputes by Order-in-Council when normal conciliation procedures had failed, particularly when work stoppages affected public services in such a way as to cause emergencies endangering public health and safety. Support was also given to a proposal that the government make provincial police action available in cases of illegal picketing, and that the Crown rather than the private interests concerned launch prosecutions in cases of illegal strikes. A campaign organized by the Ontario Federation of Labour designed to influence the Ontario government to introduce legislation incorporating in the Labour Relations Act provision for the check-off of union dues was opposed on the grounds that such considerations belonged, and should remain, subject to collective bargaining.

Although labour affairs and taxation were among the prime concerns of the day, there was limitless opportunity for debate in other fields. The pattern of the Board's operations was well established: its committees met regularly to review and consider the issues within their terms of reference, with special attention given to current legislation at all levels of government; the Board's Council then relied heavily on their advice and recommendations in determining a policy position for the Board as a whole and possible action. While the membership at large was rarely consulted in this process, it was kept fully informed of decisions and actions through reports in the monthly Journal and there are virtually no instances of substantial objection being taken to the policies established by the Council on behalf of its constituents, who were in effect the Toronto business community. Not only were the Council and committee members themselves representative of a broad cross-section of that community, but it was always basic policy that any public expression by the Board should be in matters of principle and not make distinctions among the various categories of business enterprise.

The decade immediately following the war was characterized by a generally vigorous and expansive business tempo. Industrial production reached a new peak by the early 1950s and both export and import volumes attained record heights. The outbreak of war in Korea in 1950, however, soon led to the re-imposition of some commodity controls and growing outlays for defence, and these, together with the new responsibilities for social services and national contributions to world recovery, were imposing considerable buying restraint and inducing stress evident in the perplexed attitudes of trade and industry. Retail sales in 1951 declined from a volume 12 per cent higher than the previous year in January to 10 per cent lower in September. World tension and economic disorder were breeding fears of another downward turn in the indicators of the country's own economic health.

While these conditions were reflected in the Board of Trade's concerns, its attention was for the most part directed to new aspects of old problems. After intensive study of a Senate Bill to amend and consolidate bankruptcy legislation, detailed representations were directed to the Banking and Commerce Committee of the Senate to ensure the preservation of equity and counter misrepresentation and abuse. Some adjustment was secured to accomplish these ends and the eventual Act was thought to establish acceptable conditions, although further effort was required to bring about changes in many of the regulations subsequently established under the Act. Attempts to bring about a revision and unification of the Provincial Companies Acts and Insurance Acts were supported, and when the draft of a proposed new Ontario Corporations Act appeared in 1953 strenuous objection was taken to many of its provisions as inimical to the interests of provincially incorporated companies. The legislation was passed in substantially revised form, but because of the Board's intervention its effective date was deferred to permit a re-examination of certain features; the Board finally withdrew its objections, but left the clear impression that it remained dissatisfied.

When the government in 1951 announced its intention of introducing legislation to withdraw the right of suppliers to maintain the resale prices of their goods, in conformity with a recommendation in an Interim Report by a committee appointed to examine the operation of the Combines Investigation Act, the Board surveyed its membership in an effort to determine a consensus which would provide a basis for its own position. Such a diversity of opinion was elicited that it contented itself with a brief on the subject confined largely to a recapitulation of the views obtained, with a plea that if legislation were enacted provisions be incorporated to safeguard normal transactions between suppliers and their resale outlets. Strong representations were made to Ottawa the following year, however, seeking a revision of proposed amendments designed to extend the powers accorded under the Combines Investigation Act, which were considered inconsistent with prevailing legal business procedures. The wide powers granted the Crown in combines prosecutions were in fact regarded as violating the principles of British justice. The Board remained uneasy about the administration of combines legislation, and some years later arranged for the Director of Investigation and Research of the Department of Justice to appear at a session attended by a wide representation of Toronto businessmen to clarify some of the issues. The event produced nothing new, but it at least threw some light into an area that had proved troublesome by virtue of its obscurity.

In a related field, changes were proposed in the Unfair Competition Act and the Secretary of State appointed a Trade Mark Law Revision Committee to look into them. The Board undertook its own examination and put forward a general commentary on matters connected with the law of trade marks in order to ensure effective procedures and adequate safeguards, and its views were apparently fully taken into account. When the government in 1954 announced the appointment of a Royal Commission under J.L. Ilsley to examine the workings of the law governing patents, trade marks, industrial designs and copyrights the Board first conveyed to the Secretary of State its views concerning the desirable scope of the enquiry and subsequently appeared before the Royal Commission with an extensive brief on questions relating to patents and industrial designs. Two of the Board's Trade Branches – the Book Publishers' Association and the Canadian Music Publishers' Association – made separate representations to the Royal Commission seeking what was felt to be much-needed reform and up-dating of the Copyright Act. The eventual report of the Commission appeared to satisfy nobody and was, in effect, shelved indefinitely.

Transportation and communications also remained subjects of constant attention. Every adjustment affecting the interests of shippers was scrutinized and taken up with the appropriate authority if it was felt that any discrimination or special hardship was involved. Efforts were made to bring about the improvement of railway terminal facilities in Toronto; a long campaign was fought to secure the adoption of a straight simplified bill of lading; and the so-called 'freight-rate equalization case' was debated in great detail. A staunch advocate for many years of the St Lawrence Seaway and power development project, the Board in 1947 brought to the notice of the federal and Ontario governments an interesting idea, largely the brain-child of J.G.G. Kerry, a member of the Engineering Section, for keeping the St Lawrence passage open to shipping for twelve months of the year. It was based on the theoretical feasibility of controlling the outflow of water from Lake Ontario, which was always a few degrees above freezing point, through channels in the river in such a way as to prevent ice formation and thus permit year-round use of the waterway. The Board thought that the concept at least deserved investigation on the basis of more extensive data than were then readily available but most engineers were incredulous and nothing was ever done.

To mark the inauguration of a direct shipping service between the ports of Manchester and Toronto the Board in April 1952 received from the Manchester Chamber of Commerce a suitably inscribed ship's bell, mounted to stand at the chairman's place in the Council Chamber, where indeed it has stood ever since, its voice ringing a call to order either commanding or apologetic according to the mood or temperament of the presiding officer. At the close of that season a reciprocal presentation was made to the Manchester Chamber of a desk set mounted on a block of polished Ontario silver ore. The importance of low-cost water transportation had always been stressed and had been the motivation of many of the Board's undertakings over the years, leading to the maintenance of Toronto's position as a major lake port and its development, to a limited extent, into a port for international shipping. When a Royal Commission on the Coasting Trade was appointed in 1955 the Board was concerned that there be no revision of existing regulations which would limit the free flow of goods in direct routes between Canada and overseas ports.

In the matter of communications, a 1951 increase in postal rates was resented because it had no apparent justification and was introduced without reasonable notice; moreover, there was considerable dissatisfaction with a deteriorating postal service and little patience with explanations that admitted shortcomings were largely due to handling facilities that simply could not cope with volumes of mail that had increased enormously since the war. A representative of the Board attended the hearings before the Board of Transport Commissioners on an application for rate increases made by the Bell Telephone Company in 1950. Again, the concern was not so much with the requested increase as such as to ensure that all aspects of the case received due attention, and to protect business operations against an assessment of more than their fair share of any overall increment. The Board was prepared to battle strongly once more against any proposal to introduce a metered system of charges. The same position was taken at a further hearing the following year, but this time the Board indulged in a little lecturing of the Bell Telephone Company, advocating internal economies and a review of its whole basis of financing.

By 1950 a small but growing number of Canadians owned television receivers, but they were wholly dependent on broadcasts originating in the United States since there were as yet no Canadian stations originating or transmitting television programs. The great social impact this medium would possess was not – indeed, could not have been – foreseen. The Board of Trade, which had shown some concern about the regulation of radio broadcasting years before, gave television not even a glance.

No matter how far, or how justifiably, the Board ranged into provincial and federal affairs, it never lost sight of the fact that the main and proper focus for its attention was the city of Toronto. The physical development of the city and its administration were constantly under scrutiny; comment and suggestions were frequently offered in important matters affecting the community's well-being. Civic revenues, expenditures and tax policies were regularly reviewed and summaries of the city's fiscal condition were supplied for the information of businessmen in the pages of the *Journal*. Methods of civic financing had never met with the Board's wholehearted approval and from time to time proposals were advanced for the adoption of procedures considered to be based upon sounder principles. Such efforts were in the main directed toward an amelioration of the tax burden on industrial and commercial operations in the firmly held belief that prosperity in the broadest sense depended on the creation and preservation of conditions favouring business enterprise. This outlook, the Board felt, had moulded Toronto from the beginning.

So concerned had the Board become in 1951 with the city's shortcomings in the matter of determining a practical approach to the problem of ensuring adequate revenues without imposing a crippling burden of property taxes that it recommended to the Premier of Ontario the appointment of a Royal Commission to enquire into the whole question of provincial–municipal financial relations and, at the same time, placed before the city council a series of recommendations for instituting economies and improving administrative procedures.

# 11
# The New City

The question of municipal administration had been thrown into a state of flux by a request of the city of Toronto in 1949 for the amalgamation of the city and its suburbs into a single city. The idea was not a new one; it had been informally debated by the Board of Trade and others for a number of years, but in the absence of clear necessity or a detailed formula by which integration could be achieved the debate had remained academic. Increasing internal strains were bringing the issue into sharper focus.

Between 1883 and 1914 the city of Toronto had been expanding its borders by land annexations every two or three years. The last major one was the township of North York in 1912, after which deliberate policy halted the process. But the population of the region continued to increase – by 200,000 in the period 1941 to 1951 – and Toronto found itself surrounded by a tight ring consisting of five townships, four towns and three villages, all independent and some of them beginning to assume an urban character. As the vendor of a number of services to its neighbours Toronto found the situation not wholly unsatisfactory, but by the late 1940s and early 1950s some of the suburban municipalities were beginning to experience difficulties in providing the services demanded by their burgeoning populace; agreements governing the supply of services broke down and it became clear that some at least of the suburban municipalities were headed for financial disaster. It was at this point that the city requested amalgamation of itself with nine of the suburbs in their entirety and with the urbanized parts of the remaining three (North York, Scarborough and Etobicoke). The Ontario Municipal Board prevailed upon the city to alter its application to include all twelve suburban municipalities in their entirety. The town of Mimico supported the city's application, with a rider that in the event of its refusal a Board of Management should be established to administer all basic services throughout the area of the thirteen municipalities, each of the latter, however, to retain its separate identity. Both proposals were opposed by the other eleven.

Hearings of the applications took place before the Ontario Municipal Board under the chairmanship of Lorne R. Cumming from June 1950 until June 1951. The decision of the Ontario Municipal Board which gained some fame as the 'Cumming Report,' was handed down on 20 January 1953. It recommended the establishment of two levels of government within a federation: each of the thirteen municipalities would maintain its identity and continue to be responsible for local administration, and a senior level of government would be established with jurisdiction over those affairs defined by the report as of common concern to the federation as a whole.

The provincial government acted quickly and decisively. Bill 80, an Act to provide for the Federation of the Municipalities in the Toronto Metropolitan Area, was enacted, implementing in substance the recommendations contained in the Cumming Report and creating the municipality of Metropolitan Toronto. Under the legislation the individual municipalities continued to discharge their own local functions, and a central body, the metropolitan council, comprising twelve representatives from the city and one from each of the suburban municipalities, was vested with the authority to administer water supplies, sewage treatment, major sewers, basic standard education, all public transport, major arterial roads, regional planning, the lower courts of justice, some public housing and regional parks. The first meeting of the Metropolitan Council was held on 15 April 1953.

A master stroke of the provincial government was the appointment of Frederick G. Gardiner as the first Chairman of the metropolitan council for the years 1953–4, after which the council was to appoint its own chairman. Mr Gardiner, a lawyer, had been Reeve of the Village of Forest Hill and was thoroughly experienced in the politics and problems of the Toronto area. He was reappointed to the metropolitan council chairmanship each year until his retirement in 1962 and his special qualities of good sense, persuasion and occasional bullying were undoubtedly responsible in great measure for giving form, life and effectiveness to a novel and wholly untried concept. His capabilities were recognized in a tribute paid to him by the metropolitan council upon his retirement: 'Under the dynamic leadership of Mr Gardiner, the Metropolitan Corporation in its relatively short span of eight years has accomplished what was considered by many to be the impossible.' Also on his retirement, and as a mark of the business community's appreciation of Mr Gardiner's yeoman work, the Board of Trade organized a testimonial dinner for him at the Royal York Hotel on 23 November 1961. The 1,400 businessmen attending subscribed a sum of money to create two scholarships in political science at the University of Toronto bearing Mr Gardiner's name and to be awarded annually to outstanding students.

There were deficiencies in the new system and enormous problems to overcome in the early stages, but gradually the machinery began to work and for the most part it worked well. The co-ordination of functions was continued with the amalgamation of the various police forces in 1957 and the assumption by Metropolitan Toronto of responsibility for municipal licensing and air pollution control. There was legitimate reason to doubt whether a metropolitan federation was the final answer, but for many years there was also great hesitation in tampering with a workable formula. The Board of Trade followed the whole course of events leading to the birth of the metropolitan community with great attention, but it took no direct part in the arguments, since it believed that the case was receiving a fair and adequate airing before the Municipal Board and that it was probably not in a position to make a significant contribution. When Bill 80 had been drafted it indicated qualified support to the extent that some form of unification was inevitable and the proposed federation was a constructive step in the right direction. It advocated continuing studies to work out solutions to the formidable problem of bringing about full co-operation among the participating municipalities, and was particularly worried about the redistribution of financial responsibilities and the probable net result of an increased tax burden. A one-year term for members of the metropolitan council and the School Board was considered too short, and a variety of comments was offered on such matters as educational arrangements, the responsibility for roads, planning jurisdiction and the continuing difficulties the local municipalities would face in the field of health and welfare services.

The physical growth of the city of Toronto proper and the undertaking of necessary works to guide and control that growth became increasingly important. The Board's objective was the creation of an overall long-term plan into which agreed projects could be fitted as they were required in accordance with financial capabilities and which would retain sufficient built-in flexibility to permit adaptation to new needs, ideas and processes as they appeared. An Advisory Planning Committee made up of members with special qualifications had been appointed in 1947 to assist the Board's

Council in its consideration of current and proposed projects, and later it amalgamated with the old Engineering Committee since the interests of the two were closely related. Through this new body various ideas and suggestions were funnelled to the City Planning Board. There was, for example, a strongly supported plan to develop University Avenue as Toronto's 'show street,' with suitable decorative treatment and control over the size and, to some extent, the character of structures on its borders – an undertaking that was not fully carried out until after the completion of subway construction on this alignment in 1963. A draft zoning by-law prepared in 1951 to establish permissible land uses throughout the city and complement the Master Plan was endorsed with some reservations as to the maximum floor areas it would allow and its requirement for off-street parking facilities to be provided in conjunction with new buildings. On both of these issues it recommended further study and adjustment and pursued its arguments to the hearings on the by-law before the Ontario Municipal Board whose eventual ruling substantially upheld the Board's contentions. Zoning controls were regarded as essential, but the Board was concerned that they should not be unduly restrictive and inhibit new construction, thus working against the city's growth potential. A few years later it was observed that the by-law was not properly fulfilling its purpose owing to the practice of 'spot-zoning,' whereby zoning principles were abrogated by administrative relaxations to accommodate specific construction projects. The whole question of zoning as a method of establishing a substantial framework of land use control continued to receive close attention.

Related to the designation of permitted land uses was the regulation of building structures. The city was urged to establish the means for a continuing review of its Building by-law to ensure that it kept abreast of modern construction methods, and an arrangement was made whereby the rulings of the Department of Buildings regarding the use of new materials and methods should all be directed to the Board of Trade for circulation among architects and other interested persons. Formerly there had been no way of knowing about even the existence of such rulings. With the formation of the metropolitan municipality it became obvious, too, that something had to be done to unify the different building by-laws of the thirteen federated communities, and the Board led in the establishment of a committee to undertake the tedious task of conciliating all diverse components into one Toronto Area Building Code which would, at least in its principal elements, conform with the National Building Code. After ten years of work such a code was produced and generally adopted. The creation of shopping centres was noted in the early 1950s as the beginning of a new trend in retailing to meet the needs of the booming suburban population. Among the first was the Sunnybrook Shopping Centre; other larger ones were being planned and it was recognized that this dispersion of services would likely have a profound effect on traditional marketing patterns and hence all other aspects of urban organization.

A long-term plan for the development of Toronto Island prepared jointly by the Toronto Planning Board and the Harbour Commissioners in 1951 received the Board's endorsement. It was designed to improve accessibility and expand the park and recreational areas, and it also provided for limited residential uses in apartment buildings and even for certain commercial facilities. The plan, however, aroused little public enthusiasm and was later supplanted by one which envisaged retaining the Island exclusively for recreational purposes.

The Island had figured earlier in renewed studies of the city's airport needs. At the close of the war a civic committee, including representatives from the Board of Trade, delegates from other organizations and officials of both the federal and provincial governments, had been appointed to study airport requirements for the whole Toronto region, and in particular to assess the adequacy of the existing facilities on the Island and at Malton in terms of anticipated future needs. The Board had been urging for some time that such an investigation be undertaken as a result of recommendations emanating from its Aviation Branch formed in 1943 to concern itself with the whole question of air services, and in particular with the provision of necessary airfields and the promotion of feeder-line operations. The original Island Airport had been greatly enlarged, but it was 1956 before any significant plans appeared for the development of facilities to replace the somewhat haphazard arrangement of terminal buildings and runways at Malton. The following year representatives of the Board conferred with officers of the Department of Transport on the latter's proposals for Malton, designed to meet the needs of the region until 1971, and arrangements were made for a continuing liaison to ensure full integration of all elements of the proposed development program. When actual plans were produced the Board found them commendable, but it agitated strongly for improved attention to the question of highway access, since it foresaw serious traffic congestion resulting from an inadequate road system and the inevitable build-up of airport use. The fine new terminal buildings were opened in 1964, but a few years later the Board found itself in outraged opposition to a proposal of the Department of Transport to name it Malton International Airport, thus eliminating its Toronto identity. Largely as a result of the Board's intervention, the proposal was quickly abandoned and it remained in name and substance Toronto's airport. By this time a new problem, the noise of jet aircraft in the vicinity of the airport, was creating a need for more stringent land use controls.

The advent of commercial air travel with its special needs and problems in no way detracted from the less spectacular but equally pressing problem of accommodating ordinary vehicular traffic at ground level. The city had been forced to impose more stringent parking and delivery controls in the downtown area at the beginning of 1947; the Board saw these as necessary, although it remained concerned that undue restraint might harm business operations. What it wanted and urged in a brief to the city council was relief of the serious parking situation by the adoption of a long-term plan and the exercise of adequate municipal controls, all based on the results of a proper survey of needs and capacities. Its persistent advocacy resulted in the city's appointment in 1952 of a Parking Authority responsible for assessing and, to the extent necessary, meeting off-street parking requirements. A nominee of the Board, J.F. Ellis, was appointed a member of the three-man Authority. The principles, policy and initial program formulated by the Authority were supported as a realistic approach to the problem, along with the recommendation, however, that all possible use be made of existing facilities and that adequate safeguards be instituted to prevent conflicts of interest. The Board thought that the operation of parking facilities should be left in the hands of private operators whenever possible, with some control over rates, and it foresaw the need to protect properties acquired for parking purposes from reverting to other uses.

The most striking contribution made by the Board in this period with regard to civic design and the accommodation of motor traffic had to do with a proposal to build a Lakeshore Expressway. The Metropolitan Council had authorized engineering studies, and when functional plans had been prepared by consultants and were publicly announced in 1954, they were immediately directed by the Board to its Advisory Engineering and Planning Committee for an assessment of their general feasibility, the impact of the new roadway on existing traffic patterns and its effectiveness in serving the business community. The Committee was horrified. The alignment chosen for the Expressway was probably the most direct and economical from a strictly engineering point of view, but by closely following the shoreline from the Humber River to a point well east of the harbour area it would have ruined the parks and beaches in the western sector, created at great cost and with such pride years ago, and blocked for all time any possibility of further lakefront development for public use and enjoyment.

The Board signalled its dislike of the plan to the metropolitan council and was promptly accused of being ill-informed and obstructionist. But it was a question of preserving the Board's long-loved waterfront and it was not to be deterred. With assistance from Norman Wilson, one of Toronto's best-known traffic experts and a member of the Board's Engineering Committee, an alternative plan was developed which showed that the Expressway could be built along the Hydro right-of-way, paralleling the railway tracks and fulfilling all desired requirements without in the least impinging upon lakefront lands. This meant burying the Hydro's high-tension lines, an acknowledged but not insurmountable problem. Somewhat grudgingly the Board was invited to work out its ideas with the project's co-ordinating and technical committees, and pending this re-study all further development work was halted. The Harbour Commissioners wholly supported the Board's position, producing their own studies which indicated the feasibility of the alternative alignment, and after innumerable conferences and arguments at all levels the Metropolitan Council at last gave in and ordered its consultants to prepare a new design. This was done and a new plan was submitted with the Expressway re-located almost precisely as the Board had advocated on the northerly alignment of the Hydro right-of-way. The Board found it acceptable, although it recommended staged construction to permit a reassessment of some still controversial elevated sections through the central city. The new plan and a procedure for construction were approved by the metropolitan council in November, and the first stage of construction was scheduled to begin in the spring of 1955. Irreparable damage to the lakefront lands was prevented by the Board's action without any reduction in the effectiveness of the new Expressway, which was later named in honour of its chief instigator, Frederick G. Gardiner, who had at first been much irked by the Board's intervention, but years later was gracious enough to acknowledge publicly that the Board had been right and he had been wrong.

The increasing difficulty of accommodating motor traffic had inevitably drawn attention to the need for improved means of public transportation, and the Transportation Commission had long ago foreseen that this entailed the building of an underground system. A rapid transit plan for the city involving the immediate construction of the first link of a subway network following the Yonge Street alignment from Union Station to Eglinton Avenue was produced by the Commission in 1946, receiving public commendation and the Board of Trade's endorsement. Fore-sighted budgeting by the Commission facilitated the financing of this initial stage of the plan and subway construction began in March 1950. Unfortunately, mainly for reasons of economy, the 'cut and cover' method of construction had been adopted and chaos resulted from the digging of an immense open trench right up the middle of Yonge Street, the city's main thoroughfare. Those whose places of business abutted the street showed remarkable forbearance, but they became increasingly frustrated and irritated as the work, and particularly the interminable removal, repair and replacement of the various utilities affected, dragged on. Toronto's – and Canada's – first subway, 4.54 miles long, was opened to public use with due fanfare on 30 March 1954.

A second element of the underground system, paralleling the Yonge Street line on the University Avenue alignment from Union Station to Bloor Street, was built between 1959 and 1963; as early as 1957 consideration was being given to an east-west line along the Bloor Street alignment. At this point the Board of Trade offered a number of comments to the metropolitan council on subway financing as it would affect the undertaking of other necessary capital works, on the adoption of a better co-ordinated work program to avoid undue disruption and on the need for a full-scale transportation plan so that the merits and priorities of the various alternative ways to move goods and people could be properly assessed. Moreover, as subways inevitably raised important questions about the use of contiguous lands, the Board felt that means should be established to ensure that they were effectively dealt with, probably through a body representing various interests which would act in an advisory capacity to the metropolitan council. Considerable controversy arose over the question of the alignment to be adopted for the east-west subway and the opposing views of those concerned with its design for a time seemed irreconcilable. The Board of Trade declined to take sides in this issue, contenting itself with advocacy that the basic decisions be worked out as quickly as possible by the competent authorities so that important questions still outstanding, such as financing and integration with other transit modes, could be settled.

One way in which the Board thought a significant contribution might be made to a solution of traffic and parking problems was the creation of a railway commuter service for the increasing number of town workers who resided some distance away. A committee was set up, again including Norman Wilson, to look into the matter, and it conducted a very thorough investigation, examining systems in effect in other cities, conferring with railway officials and studying all routes into the city that might be used for such a purpose. Voluminous reports were prepared which, while supporting the idea and suggesting that one or two experimental services might be established, reluctantly concluded that the inadequacy of available rolling stock and of rail and terminal facilities made the outlook for the foreseeable future anything but promising. Decisions in any event depended entirely on the railways themselves and, leaving aside the physical difficulties, they remained unconvinced that under the rate structure set by the Board of Transport Commissioners a commuter service with a dubious usage potential could be made self-supporting. Some years were to pass before increasing traffic pressures, changed railway operations and direct participation by the Ontario government led to a fully operative, but still limited, commuter service for Toronto. It justified itself by near-capacity use from the day of its inauguration.

The question of air pollution control, long disregarded, became an issue again in 1946 when the city requested the Board to submit recommendations for a new smoke abatement by-law; it is significant that at the time smoke was widely regarded as the only important polluter. A study group was brought together and after much work and consultation it produced and submitted a draft of what it considered to be adequate and realistic legislation. The city proceeded by securing authorization to adopt control measures and a by-law incorporating most of the Board's recommendations went into effect on 31 December 1949. At the same time a Smoke Abatement Advisory Committee, to which a representative of the Board was appointed, was formed to supervise the administration of the by-law and to secure to the greatest extent possible the co-operation of plant operators in fulfilling its intentions. Some years later air pollution passed into the jurisdiction of Metropolitan Toronto and the problem was recognized as having much larger dimensions.

One of the very few instances of internal conflict in the Board arose out of a metropolitan council proposal to construct a sewage treatment plant near the mouth of the Humber River which would serve expanding needs and permit the dismantling of some of the existing and unsatisfactory 'package' plants further north. On the grounds that it fulfilled an urgent need the Board's Engineering and Planning Committee supported the project but stipulated, however, that the plant should be built to adequate standards with regard to both design and siting and should always be operated at maximum efficiency. Members in the area affected took strong objection to the proposal; sewage plants were necessary, but nobody wanted them in their territory. A family squabble resulted and attracted some press attention, but the Board's Council, on the basis of favourable engineering reports and in the interests of the common good, affirmed the Board's support of the site proposed. The plant was built, incorporating design features recommended by the Board, and by 1961 its operations seemed to be bearing out the Board's contention that an unpopular operation of this kind could be carried out without harmful effects on the neighbouring community.

The idea of creating a civic square in the central city had been bandied about for fifty years and the Board of Trade had always been an ardent supporter. The concept had received citizen approval in a 1947 plebiscite and most of the property designated for the purpose bounded by Bay, Queen, Chestnut and Hagerman Streets had been acquired by the city. With the formation of the metropolitan government the inadequacies of the administrative accommodation provided in the old City Hall became apparent, and in 1955 a new move was afoot to develop a square which would include municipal buildings sufficient for the purposes of both the city and metropolitan governments. At the next civic elections voters were asked to approve an expenditure of $18 million on the project; the Board urged an affirmative response, but the citizens declined to give their approval, probably because of a widely held misconception that the plan envisaged the destruction of the old City Hall, a Toronto landmark for more than half a century. The question was put to the electors again the following year in clearer terms and this time received their assent. The undertaking was on its way and the Board of Trade appointed a committee to keep in touch with developments; its main concern was to avoid unnecessary delay and in particular to ensure the production of a comprehensive plan for a downtown square effectively co-ordinating municipal buildings and related amenities and best serving the purposes intended.

The city decided on an international competition for the design of a new City Hall while the Board of Trade continued to insist that no commitment on structures be made until agreement had been reached on the other considerations involved and the site had been fully planned. Designs were submitted by 520 architects from forty-four countries: the judges finally selected the plan of a Finnish architect, Viljo Revell, whose concept first startled, then intrigued, the staid citizens of Toronto. Construction was begun in conformity with a plan of development for the entire square, and the building was formally opened by General Georges Vanier, Governor General of Canada, on 13 September 1965. The square itself, 11½ acres in extent, was named after the man who had been mayor of the city at the time of the project's inception, Nathan Phillips. The city's proposal to acquire additional land on the south side of Queen Street facing the square in order to prevent conflicting development was endorsed by the Board of Trade, as

was a design concept subsequently prepared by the Toronto Planning
Board indicating the type of structure considered appropriate on this site.
A major feature of this concept at the time was that, to avoid overshadow-
ing the civic square, building heights should be limited to nine storeys.

Citizens' apathy toward municipal elections continued to irk the Board
both as an indication of insufficient interest in the way the city was managed and because it permitted the election to office of candidates possessing inadequate qualifications. Campaigns to 'get out the vote' were regularly conducted and surveys were made to determine the factors that
influenced voting behaviour. Efforts were made to secure an improvement
of elective procedures, and the adoption of a two-year term of office was
advocated at every opportunity. It was felt, moreover, that there should be
a uniform date for municipal elections throughout Ontario and by this time
the Board had abandoned its preference for 1 January as voting day and
was recommending the first Monday in December to bring the city in line
with other Ontario centres. When three communist candidates offered
themselves for election to office in 1951 the Board stepped up its efforts to
bring out the citizens, in the belief that a sufficient response would defeat
them, and they were in fact all unsuccessful.

To what extent such concern may have been justified is a little uncertain,
but in the early 1950s the Board worried a good deal about what it considered to be the inroads made into Canada's affairs by communists and the
insidious influence exercised by foreign powers working through local
agents and organizations. There were many who shared this concern,
which may have been to some extent a spill-over from the United States
where anti-communist feeling was rampant. In any event the Board for a
number of years kept an eye on groups known to have far-left leanings, and
a program was organized for its junior members to provide them with a little
historical background and, in particular, an understanding of some of the
ramifications of international communism. In conjunction with the Canadian Chamber of Commerce series of radio talks were sponsored for
several years which, while not directly attacking any political theory or
activity, were designed to alert Canadians to the possibilities of subversion
and to give them a pride in Canadian ways and ideals.

In the realm of social services the Board continued to reflect the dissatisfaction of businessmen with the waste and inefficiency evident in the
multitude of appeals still being conducted to raise funds for a variety of
charitable and related purposes. In 1944 leadership had been given to work
resulting in the formation of a Community Chest operation, which it was
hoped would produce a unified and more effective effort, but it had had a

limited success and the number of separate campaigns steadily increased. An effort by the Board in 1951 to have an Appeals Review Board of independent and responsible citizens established in order to examine all appeals before they were launched and determine their validity and relative entitlement to support aroused some interest but could not be implemented, and it was decided that the Board should set up its own Solicitations Advisory Service. Reports were prepared on all organizations in Toronto seeking contributions of funds to support their activities, and these were made available to anyone requesting them, not in any attempt to assess the relative merits of the fund-raisers, but rather to provide factual data on which potential donors could base their own decisions.

A renewed effort to set up a United Fund operation in Toronto was organized in 1955, with strong support from the Board of Trade and a number of individuals representing large business interests. An approach and program were prepared and presented by E.G. Burton at a public meeting held on 10 May 1956 and approved. This led directly to the formation of a Community Chest organization and the conduct of an annual United Appeal which removed most of the previous criticism, consolidated fund-raising efforts and produced results which were for the most part satisfactory to those concerned. The Board used all means at its disposal to secure citizen support for the enterprise and many of its members became deeply involved in this community service.

An opportunity for further participation in direct relief efforts had occurred in 1950 when the Board, by appealing to more than a thousand Toronto firms, raised nearly a million dollars to assist the victims of devastating floods in Manitoba. But its greatest challenge presented itself a few years later on 15 October 1954 when, after a long period of unusually heavy rains, the tail-end of Hurricane Hazel hit viciously at Toronto, flooding all its river valleys, killing seventy-seven people and causing immense property damage throughout the entire region. The Board's President, Courtland Elliott, immediately sent a wire to the metropolitan chairman: 'Board of Trade offers unreserved co-operation in any relief and reconstruction measures for Metropolitan Toronto.' Officers of the Board and of the Canadian Red Cross met on Sunday morning (the hurricane had hit on a Friday night) to devise strategy, and another meeting with representatives of other organizations was convened that afternoon. An offer of the Board of Trade's physical facilities and staff for the administration of relief was accepted and as soon as the necessary steps could be taken an Ontario Hurricane Relief Fund was established as a corporation without share capital with W.E. Phillips as Chairman and President and Neil J. McKinnon, the Board's first Vice-President, as Honorary Treasurer. Headquarters were set up in the Board's premises. A board of directors was constituted of prominent businessmen and an advisory committee of experts in a number of fields was brought together to deal with the innumerable technical problems anticipated.

Financial contributions to the relief fund were slow at first, but as the extent of the disaster and the resultant hardship became known and fund-raising efforts began in earnest, donations poured in. A total of more than $5.25 million was collected; contributions were received not only from all parts of Canada but from the United States and several overseas countries. The Fund was administered with the utmost care to relieve immediate distress, provide for the widows and children of men who had lost their lives and assist in the re-establishment of those whose properties had been wiped out or damaged by the rampaging floods. The Fund was not wound up until April of the following year. The undertaking proved to be much larger than anyone could have foreseen at the beginning and involved complex and delicate negotiations, but it proved outstandingly successful in fulfilling the purposes intended. Satisfaction was taken in the fact that administrative costs had been held to about 1.2 per cent of the moneys administered; this was due in large measure to the extraordinary contribution of voluntary services made by men and women at all levels of community concern. Members of the Board of Trade and its staff were from first to last at the very centre of the operation.

The strength of the Board as measured in terms of membership continued to grow from 3,600 at the end of the war to some 6,000 by 1949. In spite of this solid base the necessary margin between revenue and steadily increasing operating costs continued to narrow and in 1952 the by-laws were amended to increase the annual fee of individual members from $25 to $35 and to establish a new schedule of fees for corporate members, making their contributions wherever possible commensurate with company size and hence with the assumed benefits of affiliation.

Tours organized for members, discontinued during the war, were resumed in 1947 with a trip, accompanied by members of the Ontario cabinet, to the northwestern part of the province to inspect recent power and mining developments. Similar tours conducted in subsequent years followed a pattern of travel by private train over a period of five or six days and visits to industrial and development operations. Sufficient relaxation and social intercourse with local Chambers of Commerce was provided en route to produce a program which most participants found both rewarding and thoroughly enjoyable. In 1956 a large group was organized for a trip to five

American cities – Philadelphia, Washington, Pittsburgh, Cleveland and Detroit – for the principal purpose of seeing something of the scales and kinds of urban development in progress and being thus enabled to form better opinions about Toronto's desired directions. Two years before there had been a sudden realization that many Toronto businessmen had a very limited appreciation of what was happening to their own city, and three hundred of them were taken by bus on a full day's trip around Metropolitan Toronto, under the enthusiastic leadership of F.G. Gardiner and members of the metropolitan council, to gain some appreciation of the community's growth, problems and potential. These tours were repeated at intervals of a few years to keep pace with the unparalleled development taking place.

In 1948, in an effort to impress Ottawa with the importance of the country's second city, the Board had invited the members of Parliament to be its weekend guests in Toronto. One hundred accepted and took part in a program designed to acquaint them with the city and its plans and prospects and at the same time to provide a maximum content of social enjoyment. A federal election produced many new faces in Parliament, and a similar invitation extended three years later resulted in a second visit with an even larger number of participants. The Board considered itself signally honoured when it was invited to act as host to H.R.H. The Duke of Edinburgh in the course of his tour of Canada with Princess Elizabeth in 1951. At a luncheon given under its auspices at the Royal York Hotel on 13 October with 1,700 members in attendance, the Duke delivered the only formal address he made in the course of the tour.

Among the services for members inaugurated in this period were surveys of clerical salaries, business practices and holiday observances, designed to assist businessmen in the organization and conduct of their individual affairs. In the matter of holidays, the Board had for a number of years advocated that Victoria Day (24 May) and Dominion Day (1 July) be observed on the first Monday following 23 May and 30 June, rather than on the actual traditional days, to avoid the disruption of a break in mid-week. Its advocacy was implemented by federal legislation in 1952 with respect to the Victoria Day observance but Parliament steadfastly, and perhaps understandably, declined to make Canada's National Day a movable feast.

A long-held interest in improving the relationship between the business and educational communities was furthered by the Board in a novel way with its inauguration in 1956 of Business-Education Days. The Board of Education and a number of business houses collaborated to provide an exchange of visits whereby secondary school teachers on one day toured an industrial, commercial or service operation and on a subsequent day the schools played host to businessmen. The object of the exercise, to create a better mutual understanding of problems and objectives, was so successfully fulfilled that the program was repeated every year thereafter on an increasing scale, and, in a later undertaking, special arrangements were made for the acquisition of a similar direct understanding of business methods and viewpoints by teachers responsible for giving vocational guidance to pupils in secondary schools.

The rapid growth taking place in the suburbs and the creation of the municipality of Metropolitan Toronto combined to produce a new situation for the Board of Trade. Its jurisdiction was defined in its Act of Incorporation as the City of Toronto, although neither its interests nor its membership had ever been strictly confined within the limits of the city proper. It was becoming evident, however, that some suburban businessmen considered their first concern should be with their own local affairs and that to discharge this responsibility they needed their own local organization. In the Board's view any such disjunction would weaken the business voice and in the long run benefit nobody, so an alternative was suggested: the Board of Trade would establish regional committees to make its own services directly available to members in the outlying districts and to provide a channel through which the special problems originating in those districts could receive attention. It was reasonably contended that the established and well-known Toronto Board could act much more forcefully than any new group speaking for a segment of the community. The idea was accepted with alacrity. As pressures had first arisen in the western area, a Western Metropolitan Committee was first established, on a provisional but fully operative basis, to represent Etobicoke, Swansea, New Toronto, Mimico and Long Branch. It started work immediately on a number of troublesome issues, most of which had to do initially with improving the services available to establishments in the areas beyond the city's western limits. The Committee's activities were carried on successfully for a number of years, eventually becoming redundant as the distinction between suburbs and city gradually disappeared. It had originally been the Board's intention to set up corresponding committees in the north and east, but in the absence of any enthusiastic response from those territories the idea was not pressed.

The considerations leading to the establishment of area representation brought the Board a few years later to the realization that a formal recognition of its expanded jurisdiction was necessary. If it was to be in fact the single organization acting on behalf of the total Toronto business community its name should suitably designate that responsibility. The authority to apply for a change of name was granted by the membership at the Annual Meeting held in May 1958 and steps were taken to secure passage of a federal Bill amending the Act of Incorporation to alter the name from The Board of Trade of the City of Toronto to The Board of Trade of Metropolitan Toronto and to make the other minor changes this would necessitate. The Bill was passed and given effect as of 2 September 1958.

The Board's uninterrupted growth and expanded activities in the years following the war had led to necessary staff increases and administrative reorganization. In addition to transportation and legal departments, new operations were established to deal with the steady flow of trade enquiry and with urban planning affairs. The operations of trade branches and trade associations that had become affiliated with the Board to secure secretarial and related services were gradually built into a separate administrative division. F.D. Tolchard retired as General Manager in 1952 after forty-two years of service but continued to act as special adviser to the Council for the next three years. The post of General Manager was assigned to James W. Wakelin, who had for some time been acting as Mr Tolchard's assistant and had been a staff member since 1930. The general management and secretarial functions had been separated with the appointment of G.H. Stanford as Secretary of the Corporation in 1947.

It became obvious that new premises had to be acquired better adapted to the board's new stature. Those in the King Edward Hotel had become inadequate; moreover, although their continued occupancy had been negotiated year after year, the hotel had long made clear that it wanted the space for its own purposes. Luncheon facilities for members had been withdrawn by the hotel during the war so that the Board's club services and social amenities were restricted to those available in the members' lounge. A special committee appointed by the Council in 1955 began a study of the kind of accommodation that would better serve existing and long-term needs, with particular regard for the desirability of re-instituting full club services and providing better facilities for meetings of its own committees and for private members' groups. There was no dearth of proposals. A score of possibilities was reviewed on the basis of submissions made by the owners of existing buildings or those proposing the erection of new downtown structures. A decision was at length reached to take over the top three floors of a new thirteen-storey office building to be erected at 11 Adelaide Street West, the site once occupied by the Grand Opera House and, many years earlier, by Jesse Ketchum's tannery. As prime tenant with a twenty-year lease the Board was able to specify the special structural requirements on its three floors which would provide extensive dining and lounge accommodation, with their attendant kitchen and service areas; one entire floor would be devoted to offices and meeting rooms. As long as the Board occupied premises there, the official name of the structure would be The Board of Trade Building.

All members were to have full club privileges, and to provide the funds required for the outfitting and maintenance of this very desirable facility and create a dues structure commensurate with the scale of services afforded, the schedule of membership fees was again revised. The individual annual fee went up to $50 and the corporate rates increased correspondingly, but the adjustment brought not a murmur of protest – most members found very attractive the acquisition, at such a modest cost, of downtown club privileges comparable with almost any available. The Board had long believed in the merits of offering such supplementary services as a means of attaching a tangible value to an affiliation usually sustained solely on the basis of supporting a worthwhile community enterprise. Construction of the new building proceeded through 1957 and the new quarters were occupied and opened to the members by the end of November. An opening ceremony was deferred until the following January, when the Hon. John Keiller Mackay, Lieutenant Governor of Ontario, officiated at a dinner in the new dining hall attended by distinguished representatives of business and government. Later on arrangements were made whereby members of the Toronto and Montreal Boards of Trade were accorded reciprocal privileges in one another's club premises, the Montreal Board being the only other such body at the time offering these services. In the next several years, however, other Canadian Boards of Trade and Chambers of Commerce in Winnipeg, London, Ottawa, Hamilton, Oakville, Halifax and Vancouver were influenced to create their own facilities. A reciprocation of privileges was arranged in each case so that membership in the organization acquired a new value for the travelling businessman.

Although the Toronto Board was the largest organization of its kind in Canada and one of the largest in North America, Boards and Chambers in other towns and cities were growing and strengthening too; Chambers of Commerce had become significant intermediaries between business and governments and were playing an increasingly important part in community building. Largely dormant during the war, the Ontario Associated Boards of Trade and Chambers of Commerce resumed its activities in 1945 with assistance, financial and secretarial, from the Toronto Board. By 1951 it had progressed to the point where it was felt it should become a separate entity with permanent staff, supported by and representing all Boards and

Chambers of the province, and an arrangement was made to reconstitute it as the Ontario Chamber of Commerce. Headquartered in Toronto, it was to receive a subvention, guaranteeing the continuance of its operations, from the Canadian Chamber of Commerce, which would also provide assistance in the matters of premises and personnel. Its work was thus more effectively organized and carried out, and the concerns and policies of its constituents were developed at general meetings held annually in the province's principal cities.

At the national level the Canadian Chamber of Commerce, with its head office in Montreal, had built a strong organization and attracted to its service as officers and directors some of the country's most distinguished businessmen. Directing its attention to issues having nation-wide application, it too threshed out major policy at annual conventions held in the main cities of the various provinces, although a considerable program of continuing work was conducted under the direction of its administrative officers and staff.

The Toronto Board participated fully, as one unit among many, in the activities of both the provincial and national bodies. While there was little disagreement on issues, it nevertheless pursued its own way and recorded its views independently whenever it felt called upon to do so at any level of jurisdiction. An example of its efforts to combine a local function with broader concerns was a decision not to submit a formal brief and representations to the Royal Commission on Canada's Economic Prospects during the latter's hearings in Toronto in 1956, but instead to take the members of the Commission on a seventy-mile tour of Metropolitan Toronto, with commentary by the metropolitan chairman, to illustrate in a direct and forceful way the scale of urban development taking place and the entirely new kind of problems in the national economy thereby created. The Chairman of the Commission, W.L. Gordon, remarked afterwards that 'it was the most delightful and convincing brief presented to the Commission to date.'

The complexities of urban management in a city growing as rapidly as Toronto under an untried system of government raised many questions to which there were no ready answers. When a Commission of Inquiry into the Metropolitan Toronto system was appointed in 1957 the Board recorded its approbation of the great strides that had been made but was of the opinion, nevertheless, that under the new municipal federation there remained a number of areas in which wholly satisfactory arrangements had not been achieved. The form of representation on the governing body, for example, left much to be desired; it appeared unlikely that operations could be conducted on as favourable a cost basis as under a unitary form of government; as a result of the split in financial jurisdictions inequalities had been created between the area municipalities; and it seemed unlikely that the best physical planning for the region could be carried out while each component was preoccupied with its own interests and strove for types of assessment which would produce the best tax return. The Board considered metropolitanization to have been a great, albeit not final, step forward; it advocated that the existing and workable form be not unduly disturbed, but that steps be taken when considered timely and feasible to effect a progressive merger of the functions and financial responsibilities of the constituent local governments.

# 12
# Into the Future

Considerations relating to the city's future engaged much of the Board's attention in this period. There was still opportunity to guide its growth so that desirable features would be retained while providing for an expanding population and all the services that would entail, but every year that passed and every decision made reduced the choices open and indicated how easily what seemed like progress might become in fact the creation of a monster. No one, least of all the Board of Trade, wanted to hamper the city's development; there were, however, enough examples of other cities which had lost their desirable qualities in the process of growth to warrant anxiety lest Toronto, by insufficient forethought, destroy itself.

An amendment of the zoning by-law in 1957 proposed regulations governing the height, bulk, location and spacing of buildings, the provision of off-street parking in conjunction with these buildings and criteria for the creation of landscaped open space. The principles embodied in this amendment were supported by the Board as contributing to the maintenance of good design standards, and at the same time the view was expressed that Toronto could well do without a congestion of unduly tall buildings. The Board repeatedly emphasized the need for strict observance of conditions laid down in the zoning by-law, which was designed to define overall objectives but which all too often was being abrogated when tempting proposals for new construction requiring major deviations were put forward. It was strongly argued that every control mechanism should be rigidly and impartially applied unless or until it was formally changed as a result of full enquiry and agreement. Maintenance of the central business district was considered in many respects the key to the preservation of the city's general health, and a proposal of the Board that detailed studies of this area be undertaken as a means of determining a basis for future controlled growth and renewal had two significant consequences. The first was the appointment by the city in 1959, with recommendations from the Board as to personnel, of a Redevelopment Advisory Council made up of business and financial leaders to counsel the city on redevelopment problems and generally to promote an integrated and forward-looking plan of urban renewal. The second was the production of a report by the City Planning Board on the downtown area, assessing the problems and offering a concept of control, renewal and development.

Official plans for the city of Toronto and for Metropolitan Toronto were scrutinized in their draft forms by the Board's Advisory Engineering and Planning Committee and many comments were offered which affected the ultimate plans in a number of important particulars. While the official plan for Metro was not adopted as such, it constituted and was used as a guide in subsequent planning work. In the Board's view an inherent weakness in any planning of the metropolitan area was the inability to exercise effective influence over what happened beyond the official but imaginary line delineating the area's boundary; the most enlightened approach to planning within its territory could be invalidated by permissive attitudes on the part of local authorities in adjoining jurisdictions. Broader concepts were needed, and in 1966 this view was conveyed to the provincial government with a recommendation that a regional plan be produced to co-ordinate and control the basic elements affecting or likely to affect future development. Over the next few years this idea was developed in further commentaries directed to the province. They recommended that a complete study be made of the anticipated pattern and extent of urban settlement in the Toronto region over the next fifteen to twenty years, that an appropriate planning area be designated and that government organizations be devised which would be competent not only to plan but also to provide the works and facilities necessary to sustain the growth expected. A report of the province's Committee on Taxation (the Smith Committee) had proposed in its report issued at this time a pattern of regional governments, but the Board considered these unsuitable and favoured instead an extension of Toronto's federal system to include at least those parts which would inevitably fall within the sphere of urban development in the foreseeable future.

A significant document produced in June 1968 was a Metropolitan Toronto and Region Transportation Study, the work of a committee established by the province to consider possible development within an area comprising some 3,200 square miles centred on Toronto. Its approach was tentative and introduced various concepts which invited evaluation. The Board's commentary was in effect a restatement of its belief that direct participation by the provincial government was necessary to ensure that regional land-use planning, including transportation, was pursued in a manner that would lead to orderly development in the various regions of the province as long as care was taken to relate government programs systematically to regional objectives. It suggested that provincial action was now a matter of some urgency and that any such action must co-ordinate physical planning as such with a restructuring of local government. Moreover, the government itself should integrate the functions of its own numerous departments and agencies responsible for planning, public works and capital budgeting.

Late in 1968 the Ontario government announced its intention of creating new forms of local government throughout the province, but after examining the proposed scheme the Board expressed its opinion that, as applied to the Toronto area, it would be likely to produce not a regional government but rather a group of large and competing municipalities. The need to avoid competitive planning and disruptive rivalries was one of the Board's main concerns, constantly stressed in its representations to the province. The latter's announcement in 1969 that it would review the whole situation was warmly welcomed, and when a 'Design for Development: the Toronto-Centred Region' was produced early in 1970, offering a radical departure from previous thinking and a grand strategy for land use and transportation within a framework of social and economic policy for a region encompassing some 8,600 square miles, it was eagerly debated. On sober assessment, however, the Board had to conclude that although the concept fulfilled its advocacy of regional planning, the report as such left too many questions unanswered and raised too many new questions to permit a proper assessment of its validity.

On a smaller scale there was an effort to preserve adequate open space for recreational purposes in and near the city in the face of an onrush of land acquisitions for new buildings, and a plea for the adoption of a long-range tree-planting policy that would assure replacement of those falling in the path of urbanization. Hurricane Hazel had exposed Toronto's heretofore unexpected vulnerability to floods, and support was given to a ten-year program developed by the Metropolitan Toronto and Region Conservation Authority with the double objective of carrying out various works on rivers and streams as flood-preventive measures and at the same time creating lands to be held in perpetuity for park purposes. The program, vigorously pursued, produced a vast and invaluable addition to the stock of maintained open space in the city's environs. Toronto Island, too, after being designated for a variety of purposes through the years, finally received a master plan of development for recreational use in 1964 which the Board, despite its previous ideas on the subject, heartily endorsed. Discussion of the Island always raised the question of the best means of access. Although it gave some weight to the desirability of a tunnel under the western harbour entrance to serve the Island Airport, the Board opposed any plan that would put motor vehicles on the Island proper and retained an old-fashioned preference for the ferry-boat service.

If the Island's future seemed to be fairly well defined, that of the mainland waterfront became the subject of renewed debate when a number of proposals for various kinds of treatment were introduced. The first of these, generally supported by the Board in 1962, was a plan prepared by the City Planning Board to provide the central waterfront with the various facilities proper to the harbour area by linking it to the downtown business district through an imaginative series of high-level plazas. There followed a project proposed by a private developer which would create in the heart of the area a conglomerate of high-rise commercial and residential structures, and about this the Board had serious misgivings; it raised again the old bugbear of a barrier between the city and the lake and in any event there was little evidence that adequate transportation linkages could be provided. The Harbour Commissioners then proposed extensive new uses for their lands and the creation of new lands by dredging. This idea was followed by the even grander Metro Centre project sponsored jointly by the Canadian National and Canadian Pacific Railways for the development of an entire complex of major structures to serve a wide range of purposes, utilizing air rights over the railways' rights-of-way between Bathurst and Yonge Streets, occupying nearly two hundred acres and estimated to cost somewhere in the neighbourhood of a billion dollars. Added to all of these were questions relating to the future of the Island Airport and, somewhat removed from the central sector, suggested expansion schemes at the Canadian National Exhibition which included plans being rapidly developed by the province for the creation of Ontario Place as a display and recreational facility projecting into the lake off the Exhibition's shoreline. It was little wonder that at this point the Board of Trade was calling urgently for the formation of a comprehensive design which would establish objectives and procedures and for an agency which could correlate all elements involved into a workable pattern in terms of space, time and the best interests of the city as a whole.

While all these projected developments, constituting a package of undertakings bigger than anything ever contemplated in Toronto or, very likely, any other Canadian city, focused attention on the relatively small central sector of the waterfront, the Board of Trade since 1961 had been calling for complete planning of the fifty miles of shoreline within the metropolitan planning area, stretching roughly from Ajax to Clarkson. The Metropolitan Planning Board undertook studies in 1965 which led to a report recommending in general terms the features that should be either encouraged or produced over a period of time over this long and valuable stretch of lakefront land, incorporating liberal park and recreational areas and providing for the effective co-ordination of private industrial, commercial and residential components. The Board of Trade had reservations about some elements of the plan but recognized that it was of necessity conceptual and therefore flexible. General approval was registered but, once again, the Board strongly urged the creation of an agency to which could be assigned the responsibility for working out the details and organizing a program of implementation. Assuming that some at least of the contemplated major projects would reach fruition in due time, it was beginning to look as though the city might one day achieve the full potential of its magnificent waterfront, an objective which the Board had struggled to realize for about a hundred years.

While these land developments associated with the lakefront were proceeding the activities of the port itself were increasing. In 1956 an all-time record of nearly 5.5 million tons moved through the port in 2,450 vessels of which 455 were on direct overseas service. The latter were still relatively small ships able to negotiate the restricted canal system, but, according to an agreement finally reached between Canada and the United States in 1954 to build the St Lawrence Seaway, work was progressing on this vast undertaking which, when completed, would make the port of Toronto accessible to some 80 per cent of the world's shipping and begin a completely new era. The construction of the Seaway involved the labour of 15,700 men over a period of more than four years and cost in excess of $470 million, of which Canada's share was about $329 million. Associated works to produce some 1,250,000 horsepower of electrical energy in the stretch from Iroquois to Cornwall cost an additional $600 million, shared equally between the United States and Canada. The Seaway was formally opened by Queen Elizabeth and President Eisenhower on 26 June 1959; the Queen then travelled its length and visited Toronto in the Royal Yacht *Britannia*. In September of that year the Toronto Board arranged its own tour of the Seaway: 250 members boarded the S.S. *Tadoussac* in Toronto, sailed down the St Lawrence through the new locks and channels as far as the Saguenay and travelled up that river to Chicoutimi.

With the opening of the Seaway the Welland Canal, the only shipping access to the Upper Lakes, assumed even greater importance. The Board had traditionally been opposed to tolls on the Welland and in 1957 it brought together representatives from Hamilton, St Catharines and Thorold, the places most directly concerned, to devise a strategy that would induce the federal government to keep it toll-free. In spite of vigorous representations made to government authorities, including the Prime Minister, tolls were imposed for a short time. The position taken by those who opposed tolls was that assistance to transportation was a historic necessity in the economic development of Canada, and that in Ontario such assistance should apply to the carriage of bulk commodities for export and for use in Canadian industries. It was felt, moreover, that charges applied to passage through the Welland discriminated against shipments in and out of Lake Ontario since waterborne traffic in the Upper Lakes was toll-free. There was also some reason to fear the imposition of retaliatory charges by the United States on locks and canals under its control.

A Great Lakes Waterways Development Association was formed in 1959, with the Toronto Board a member, to deal with this situation in an organized way and generally to encourage economic development in Canada by ensuring low-cost transportation through the St Lawrence Seaway and the Great Lakes. When a new order was issued in 1963 for the re-imposition of tolls successful action was taken to block it, although the argument started all over again a few years later with the imposition of lockage charges. The St Lawrence Seaway itself was tolled by international agreement; those working for maximum use of the total St Lawrence–Great Lakes Waterway continued to insist in a toll-free Welland and no increase in charges on the Seaway, and when the Canadian and United States Governments brought the conditions governing operations in the Seaway under review in 1965 they suggested that an attempt be made to negotiate a new deal which would completely free the system from passage charges. The effort did not succeed but the creation of a waterway free of artificial barriers remained a major objective of those concerned with the economy of the region.

In the matter of rail transportation, representations were made by the Board in 1959 to a Royal Commission on Transportation urging the incorporation of greater flexibility in the freight rate structure so as to provide more competitive freedom for the rail carriers, while still preserving the basic principles underlying the existing system of rates and services. It was suggested that when it became necessary to grant aid under statutory rates they should be in conformity with a national policy, such grants to be a charge against the consolidated revenue fund.

The most spectacular increase in passenger and freight traffic was occurring in the air. When the federal Department of Transport indicated in 1967 its intention of hugely increasing the capacity of Toronto's air terminal at Malton the Board expressed its concern over the virtually inevitable impact on a large segment of the community in the airport's vicinity as a result of increasing usage by aircraft becoming ever larger and noisier and making ever accelerating demands for supporting ground services. It urged the fullest consultation with local authorities before any decisions were made respecting the extension of facilities. The next year the Department of Transport put forward its proposal for the expansion of Malton Airport in terms of both land area and terminal buildings. It was presented to all interested local authorities and to citizens' groups and aroused immediate opposition. The Board of Trade found itself among the critics; there was no question of the need for facilities on the scale suggested, but it seemed obvious that their creation at the fringe of Metropolitan Toronto would produce major noise and pollution problems and havoc in the roads system. Another hazard foreseen was that resentment of the undesirable features of an airport on the scale contemplated might lead to a curtailment of its use and hence a result completely opposite to the one intended. In the Board's view a preferred procedure would be the provision of interim facilities to relieve the existing overload situation and new studies directed to finding preferable long-term solutions. In the face of widespread hostility the Department of Transport withdrew its plan and undertook to explore alternatives.

Malton's facilities were in fact undergoing expansion to meet existing traffic pressures, but although consideration of the larger needs of the future was proceeding at the federal-provincial level there was for a long time no evidence of a new proposal and by 1970 the Board and others were expressing impatience. When at length it was announced that a second airport to serve the Toronto area would be built near Pickering, to the north-east of the city and far from Malton, the Board, like most others, was caught somewhat off guard but upon consideration expressed mild approval in the interests of getting on with the job. There was also the question of the Island Airport: was it simply to disappear in the new planning, or be reconstituted in a new form and a new location? The Board favoured a waterfront airport for private and inter-city flying and in view of the probable introduction of aircraft with short landing and take-off characteristics believed that an airport near the central city for such restricted uses was both feasible and desirable.

Traffic within the metropolitan area was posing serious problems as the number of people and vehicles increased; the movement of traffic might have been brought to a virtual standstill had it not been for the creation of the subway system and the building of expressways, with substantial assistance from the province, to provide lines of grade-separated communication serving as main arteries through the centre of the community and connecting with the highways radiating from it. The Toronto Transit Commission (reconstituted from the Toronto Transportation Commission after the formation of the metropolitan administration) was providing an adequate service, although confidence in it was shaken in 1959 when deficiencies appeared in its internal structure. The Board of Trade recommended a number of changes in the Commission's function and personnel, some of which were acted upon, but the metropolitan council was reluctant to introduce any basic alteration in a system that over the years had worked well.

The question was whether to concentrate money and effort in building expressways for motor vehicles or in public transit facilities. General policy was to maintain a balance, but among Toronto citizens there was increasing polarization of opinion. Many warmly supported all of the road-building necessary to accommodate the city's vehicles; they saw no reason to be denied the free use of their automobiles for every purpose, to which they had been long accustomed. There was, however, an increasing number who saw destruction of the city's more desirable characteristics in the proliferation of multi-lane traffic arteries and who were therefore the proponents of public transit at the expense, to some extent, of the expressways. Their case was strengthened by a new awareness of the evils of atmospheric pollution, to which the motorcar was a major contributor. The differences between the two factions were brought into sharp focus when in 1961 it was proposed to build the Spadina Expressway, an artery designed to channel traffic flow from the populous northwestern area into the central city. The facility was designed and work on a segment of it was begun. The Board of Trade supported the project on the principle that it fulfilled a necessary function but with a rider that what was really needed was a full-scale transportation plan against which the value of this or any similar sizable undertaking could be measured.

The introduction subsequently of plans for the Spadina Expressway in its entirety created something of a *cause célèbre* in Toronto; those who objected to the undue incursion of motor roads into the city bitterly opposed the advocates of bigger traffic arteries. After interminable argument, in the course of which the Board of Trade again signified its concurrence in the construction of a combined expressway and rapid transit line, the Expressway was approved by the metropolitan council and, what was expected to be the last hurdle, by the Ontario Municipal Board. To the surprise of everyone and the delight of the 'anti-Spadina' forces the Ontario Cabinet then stepped in with a veto. It was an unprecedented situation, creating wholly new parameters for future city planning.

Studies of the metropolitan government structure were undertaken anew in 1961 on the initiative of the metropolitan council as a means of determining on the basis of past experience what if any revision appeared necessary. The province appointed a Royal Commission under Carl Goldenberg to make a full-dress enquiry. The principal recommendation in the Commission's 1965 report was to re-cast the federation into the city and five boroughs in place of the original thirteen municipalities. The Board of Trade found little exceptionable in the report and wholly favoured its recommended three-year term for elected civic, borough and metropolitan officials; once more, however, in the interests of better planning, it advocated an extension of the metropolitan boundaries and planning powers so as to apply to areas beyond even these new political boundaries. A new metropolitan format was adopted, comprising the city and five boroughs but with no boundary changes, and was brought into effect on 1 January 1967.

When the provincial government came under self-scrutiny in 1958 with the appointment of a committee of the Legislature to enquire into the organization of government in Ontario the Board took the opportunity to comment on some general characteristics of constitutional law and parliamentary government and to put forward a number of proposals, among them that greater use should be made of committees of the legislature to provide for the submission of views by concerned bodies on legislative proposals, that the power to make regulations under existing legislation be restricted to matters of procedure and administration, and that no greater powers be conferred on ministers, officials, boards and commissions than were required for the discharge of their prescribed functions. It was further recommended that there should be access to the courts on points of law and supervision of proceedings in all judicial functions, that greater security should be provided in tenure of office by officials whose primary responsibilities are of a judicial nature and that there should be better definition and co-ordination of the functions of provincial agencies involved in planning and development.

In a somewhat broader context but with similar intent a brief was submitted a few years later to a provincial Royal Commission of Inquiry into Civil Rights. In it the Board pointed out that under the system of constitutional law and parliamentary government in Ontario there were no internal checks on the powers of the legislature; it was hence necessary for the legislature voluntarily to find within itself the restraints and disciplines essential to good government and to avoid encroaching upon the commonly acknowledged civil rights and freedoms of citizens. The function of the courts was to restrain unlawful interference with the person or property, and hence the freedom, of the individual, and there could be no intrusion into the function of the courts without diminishing the protection afforded by established law. The objects of a Bill of Rights were supported, but it was contended that they would be better attained in the protection afforded by the common law as administered by the courts. The Board's brief recapitulated much of its earlier advocacy regarding the administrative functions of government, its main intent being the creation and maintenance of a system which would preserve the rights and dignity of the individual without eroding essential legislative powers.

The introduction of health insurance measures by the province was viewed by the Board with mixed feelings. It agreed with the policy announced in 1957 of providing an essential 'floor' of protection against hospital costs, but believed that it should be integrated to the greatest possible extent with existing private contracts, especially those negotiated under labour agreements. Satisfaction was expressed over the incorporation in the 1963 Medical Services Insurance Bill of many provisions advocated in the Board's earlier representations to a Royal Commission on Health Services, and when Medicare proposals were under discussion between the federal and provincial governments the Premier of Ontario was strongly urged to retain the right to determine how any federal grant would be applied in the operation of a medical plan in Ontario. The Board was basically of the opinion, however, that Canada at its stage of development in 1968 could not afford Medicare since it would add materially to an already heavy tax burden. Nor was it considered necessary, particularly in Ontario where 97.3 per cent of the total population were already protected by some form of medical insurance. Instead of universal Medicare adequate coverage was needed for those who, for valid reasons, were unable to protect themselves. The Ontario government itself for a time seemed reluctant to become involved in medical insurance, but at length accommodated itself to the system of federal grants and introduced its Ontario Health Services Insurance Plan in October 1969. The only contribution the Board could make at this point was to undertake a survey in order to produce data which would assist companies in determining their policies with regard to the premium costs levied against their employees enrolled as members of a mandatory company group.

In other areas of provincial affairs the viewpoint of the business community was conveyed to the appropriate authorities on proposals to enact a new uniform Companies' Act and action was co-ordinated to secure a revision of the Bulk Sales Act. Caution was urged in the devising of conditions to control the portability of pensions, and action was taken in response to the request of a number of interests to establish a Joint Conference on Mechanics' Liens to investigate problems of financing in the construction industry and formulate proposed remedies. Expropriation compensation was the subject of a brief to the Ontario Law Reform Commission in 1966; the main issues were the bases of valuation and the adequacy of existing scales of recompense. A year-long study of the Business Corporations Act of 1968 led to extensive representations designed to ensure that conditions governing corporate operations were fair, realistic and conformed with modern practices.

Commentaries on the statutory conditions applicable in the field of labour relations reflected current employer attitudes. In a 1957 brief to a Select Committee of the legislature appointed to enquire into the Labour Relations Act, reference was made to the great power in the hands of trade unions as a consequence of their extensive memberships and considerable financial resources, and their ability to bring about a cessation of production by strike action; it was therefore recommended that they be assigned the normal responsibilities under the law that apply to all other persons and groups of persons. A further proposal was that the judicial decisions rendered by such agencies as the Ontario Labour Relations Board and Arbitration Boards be subject to review as to both fact and law by a Justice of the Supreme Court of Ontario so that they, like other similar bodies, would not exercise final authority with respect to their own judicial decisions. Federal legislation introduced in 1966 which had the practical effect of eliminating the services of judges from arbitrations arising out of disputes under collective agreements was strongly opposed, as it had been years before, but in spite of objection by both management and labour organizations the legislation passed. The Board was quick to point out soon afterwards that failure to agree on persons other than judges deemed qualified to act as arbitrators was creating a backlog of unsettled arbitration cases.

To the Rand enquiry into labour disputes the Board in 1966 recommended that there be no compulsory arbitration except in the event of a strike or lockout involving essential services and argued that financial damage suffered by an employer as a result of an unlawful strike should be recoverable from the union concerned as a legal entity. It branded secondary picketing illegal, advocated application of the criminal law in cases of criminal offences in picketing situations and commented on the vexed question of injunctions in labour disputes. The eventual Rand Report was found generally acceptable, although its proposal to establish an Industrial Tribunal with virtually unlimited power was not well received.

While the general level of business activity remained relatively high, the cost of government and of increasing government services and the constant pressure for additional tax revenues in consequence were unfailing sources of concern. Taxes were an element of the inflationary pattern becoming clearly evident in the mid-1950s; in an address to the members in 1957 James S. Duncan, a former President of the Board, was warning of the insidious effects of inflation and the great danger it presented to the Canadian economy by undermining the whole structure of public and private social security. He urged comprehensive government studies of its causes, leading to remedial action. The Board's commentaries on tax matters were regularly directed to Ottawa when work was in progress on each year's Budget, their general tenor being the need to preserve both levels and methods of taxation that would stimulate rather than inhibit Canadian enterprise. In effect this usually resolved itself into a plea for an actual reduction in the rate of tax applicable at both the personal and corporate levels, although questions of tax applicability and administration leading to this desired end were often dealt with in considerable detail.

In the matter of federal-provincial fiscal problems, briefs were directed in 1960 to the heads of both the federal and the Ontario governments advocating that taxing authorities at all levels have responsibility for raising the moneys they expend, and that no two levels of government should occupy the tax fields of succession duties or estate taxes, individual income and corporate profits. If this were not avoidable, as a minimum there should be collection of tax at only one point with uniformity of conditions in all respects save possibly of the rates applied by the participating jurisdictions. With the appointment of a Federal Royal Commission on Taxation (the Carter Commission) the Board in 1963 submitted extensive new representations, being principally concerned at this stage with evidence that the introduction of a capital gains tax was being favoured. Such a tax was opposed on the grounds that it would not produce sufficient revenue to justify the costs of compliance and collection, and would have other undesirable consequences. 'A capital gains tax,' said the Board's brief, 'would create inequities, deter risk-taking investments and act as an impediment to the realization of investment and the free movement of capital.' Other recommendations included the adoption of a single rate of corporate tax somewhere between the existing rates, the establishment of more equitable provisions for the determination of taxable income and the assessment of the federal sales tax in terms of its effect as between imported goods and those manufactured in Canada.

At the same time the attention of an Ontario Committee on Taxation was being drawn to the fact that, in the preceding ten years, although the amount of personal taxable income had doubled, the expenditures of the provincial government had tripled, and that the effect of compensating tax increment was to weaken the competitive position of Ontario industry. Again the desirability of unitary tax incidence was emphasized, with a plea for the elimination of nuisance taxes, and it was further suggested that the whole question of the fiscal relationship between the province and its municipalities deserved a proper airing. A year earlier the Board had been impressed by the high yield obtained from the newly-introduced Ontario Retail Sales Tax and expressed the view that the government should act decisively to ensure that this additional revenue not be absorbed by increased expenditures inevitably invited by the availability of funds. A better use for apparent surpluses would be the removal of unfairness and discrimination in taxes and the provision of tax relief to promote capital formation and economic growth.

The issue of the Carter Report engendered considerable dismay in the business community and new representations objecting to a number of its proposals, particularly those advocating the introduction of a tax on capital gains. However, the biggest explosion of resentment was reserved for the federal government's White Paper on Tax Reform issued toward the end of 1969. Ostensibly an expression of attitude in tax matters offered to inform and invite opinion, the view was widely held by businessmen that it was in fact a blueprint of coming legislation; the document departed in so many ways from generally accepted tax principles and foreshadowed statutory innovations that were held to be so contrary to the country's best economic

interests that a wave of unusually strong protest was immediately generated. The Board of Trade took unprecedented steps to organize its own
response to the White Paper: a steering committee was set up to guide
overall procedures, the services of an economic adviser were retained, an
intensive study was undertaken of the actual document and a summary of
its main provisions, with an explanatory commentary, was incorporated in
the Board's *Journal* for circulation to all members. The members were
urged to convey their own views on the more significant features of the
White Paper to the appropriate government authorities, and many of them
did so. Three separate seminars were necessary to accommodate some
twelve hundred members who desired to confer with the Board's experts
on the salient features. A detailed brief was presented by a delegation led
by the Board's president, James W. Kerr, to committees of the Commons
and the Senate dealing with the matter in Ottawa early in 1970. The Board's
strong reaction was similar to that of many other concerned individuals and
organizations whose combined efforts were undoubtedly responsible for
the considerable amelioration evident in the tax legislation eventually
introduced. There were, of course, still areas of substantial disagreement,
and the Board was especially critical of the federal government's failure to
take adequately into account tax reform policies which had been developed
by the Ontario and other provincial governments.

The traditional dislike of government intrusion into the operations of
private enterprise was further evidenced in the representations made by
the Board to the Royal Commission on Energy in 1958. The need to market
Canada's energy reserves in such a way as to protect the long-term requirements of Canadian consumers was appreciated and it was acknowledged that this function could only be adequately performed by the government. The Board urged, nevertheless, that in any approach adopted due
recognition be given to the contribution made by private interests under the
free competitive enterprise system in the discovery, development and
distribution of energy resources, and that they be encouraged to continue
and expand their activities with the least possible interference. The implementation of a national policy on energy resources was considered to be
a function of appropriate existing departments of the government; the
establishment of a National Energy Board was opposed as yet another
medium of control – readily extendable – over business enterprise, deeply
disturbing to those in private industries working for the country's development.

A good deal of work was carried out by the Board in 1960 in connection
with an investigation of the various forms and returns required by the

federal government undertaken by a Royal Commission on Government Organization. The demands made upon business had become extremely onerous, and the proposals made by the Board, after a very careful survey, were expected to permit important savings of time, trouble and expense for both government and business. As important as the practical effect would be the feeling of at least a small measure of relief from ever-increasing government surveillance.

Akin to its innate dislike of the socialization of health services was the Board's reaction to the proposed introduction of a Canada Pension Plan. Again it was a question not so much of being against an adequate pension system as of fearing the effects of new and uncontrollable costs in an area where the private sector had been doing a pretty good job. If there was to be a national plan, the Board suggested that it be funded and the custody and investment of its funds placed in private hands. The argument made little headway.

The Board's preoccupation with matters of local, provincial and national concern throughout this period had to some extent diverted its attention from the field of international trade which in previous years had occupied much of its time. Floods of enquiry were still being received and dealt with as a regular departmental operation, and trade delegations from all parts of the world were being received in increasing numbers and assisted and entertained, but for a long time after the adoption of a Commonwealth preferential tariff system, for which it had fought so hard, the Board had not engaged in any major undertaking directed towards the development of overseas markets. By 1956 there was rueful recognition of Canada's $1,300 million adverse trade balance with the United States, while Britain was running a $334 million adverse balance with Canada. There was mixed reaction to a remark made by Neil H. McElroy, a prominent American businessman, in the course of his address at the Board's annual dinner in 1961. 'In my opinion,' he said, 'the next few years will see the evolution of a kind of common market or customs union thinking in the economic relationship of our two countries ... there would be no intent to consider political integration to be a desirable sequel to economic integration. This would be a fundamental difference as compared with the European Common Market.' Many were made uneasy by the prospect of such tightened economic bonds and saw a better future for Canada in a diversified trading pattern.

Japan, for instance, was becoming one of the world's great trading powers, and recognition of this fact led to the Board's undertaking a new venture – or rather the large-scale extension of a traditional activity. For more than half a century tours had been organized for members to let them see at first hand some of the important and interesting things going on outside their own community; these had been for the most part confined to the provinces of Ontario and Quebec and lasted no more than five or six days. The Board's President in 1960, W.E. Williams, and a former President, Courtland Elliott, had recently been in Japan; they had returned much impressed by what they had seen of that country's post-war economic recovery and suggested that a tour be organized for a group of interested Board members. The project was found to be quite feasible, details were worked out, one hundred members enrolled, each paying his own complete share of the costs, and on 21 October 1960 the expedition set off in a chartered Canadian Pacific aircraft. Ten days were spent in Japan, four more in Hong Kong and the long journey back across the Pacific was broken by a brief stop-over in Hawaii. It proved a memorable experience for the travellers, opening a door into a new world and demonstrating in a dramatic way the possibilities for the development of trade and social contacts on a global scale.

So successful was the venture that another was organized two years later, this time a three-week trip to six Latin American countries, with 142 participants occupying two aircraft. The enthusiasm generated led to a decision to undertake an overseas tour every other year with shorter domestic ones in the intervening years. In 1964 the destination was Scandinavia and several northern European countries, including the Soviet Union, and in 1966 it was the Middle East. Plans for a tour of Eastern European countries in 1968 were aborted at the last moment because of internal troubles that had flared up in those parts, but 1970 saw a return to the regular schedule with a visit to Expo 70 in Osaka and from there to Taiwan. In 1972 a smaller group visited Australia and New Zealand and continued around the world. The overseas trips were not billed as trade missions but were designed to provide an opportunity for Canadian businessmen to see some of the world beyond the main travel routes under specially arranged conditions which permitted them to assess the potentials for future trade and commercial liaison. There was ample evidence that excellent use was made of the opportunities and the visits had the added advantage of generating much good will, the ultimate value of which could hardly be estimated.

A reorganized International Trade Department was set up in 1961 and an expanded program of activities was undertaken, including the regular monthly publication of *Trade Winds*, a modest but effective summarization of market data, trading opportunities and general information of use to traders. In addition, an increasing number of seminars was conducted to assist Canadian producers who felt there was a future for them in exporting, but who lacked experience. When the government in 1969 showed some signs of reducing its foreign trade services and activities the Board, while commending the money-saving motivation, expressed its concern about any move that might weaken Canada's excellent Trade Commissioner Service abroad and urged that there be no serious diminution in the effective efforts being made through participation in trade fairs and similar overseas enterprises to make Canadian products better known in world markets. The Board had been enthusiastic about the federal government's establishment of the Canadian International Trade Fair in Toronto in 1951 as a medium for promoting Canada's greater involvement in world trade and had supported the activity in a number of ways in an effort to ensure its perpetuation. But by 1955 the government reluctantly concluded that the Fair was more successful in fostering sales of foreign goods in Canada than the other way around, the opposite effect to that intended, and it was discontinued.

A few years later the Board was again evincing unhappiness in the Canadian National Exhibition: for a long time no effort had been made to improve its image and it seemed to be slipping into a routine operation with little serious purpose. When this criticism was conveyed to the directors of the CNE they reacted promptly by requesting the Board to investigate the Exhibition's operating policy and submit recommendations for improvement. This the Board's Council firmly refused to do on the grounds that as a purely business organization it was not competent to function in such a highly specialized field; instead, it suggested the appointment of independent consultants and offered its own services in any supplementary way that might be useful. Some studies were undertaken, with the Board playing a part, but they led to no substantial change. The subject continued to receive attention, however, and in 1970, with the assistance of the Metropolitan Planning Department, a new conceptual plan for the Exhibition's long-term development was produced and it received the Board's endorsement in principle, although some weaknesses appeared to require renewed attention.

As plans developed for the enormous Metro Centre project in downtown Toronto, the Board undertook, with the aid of consultants, an examination of the city's needs for new and vastly increased facilities to accommodate convention activities and recommended that these be provided in a Convention Centre incorporated as a part of the Metro Centre plan. This was not intended as competition for the Canadian National Exhibition but rather to attract to Toronto the large and lucrative conventions which were going to other cities, mainly in the United States, because Toronto could not offer the needed amenities.

By the 1950s it had become clear that Toronto, even by world standards, was becoming a big city, and twenty years later the unrelenting pressures of growth were beginning to cause some alarm. In less than two centuries the tiny settlement on the shore of Lake Ontario had become a metropolis spread over 240 square miles containing more than two million inhabitants. Its population was increasing at a consistent rate of some fifty thousand each year and there was no sign that the growth was likely to abate. A steady demand for new housing and land for industrial, commercial, transportation and recreational purposes was challenged by the declining availability of new land that could be assigned to any of these needs; the inevitable consequences were skyrocketing land costs, the gradual elimination of uneconomic uses, and structures climbing upward ever higher and higher. The problems attending such growth were becoming more difficult and pronounced each year and solutions could be sought only by dogged attention to the pressures of immediate demands while keeping within what seemed to be a reasonable pattern for the future.

The process was difficult and complicated further by an increasing realization that urban concentrations on such a scale become ever more dependent on an effective integration with government processes applicable over a much broader jurisdiction. It was apparent, too, that urbanization inevitably affected the quality of life and that citizens were no longer prepared to accept a deterioration in that quality by changes justified solely on the grounds of pragmatic adaptation. People wanted to live in the city but clearly the maintenance of livable conditions would demand scrupulous attention to all conditions of urban growth and an enlightened and courageous attitude on the part of those responsible for political decisions. The effects of pollution in all its manifestations, a major issue demanding protective and remedial measures likely to conflict directly with the traditional belief in unrestricted development, led to a worried search for practical compromise. Smoking chimneys and waste-discharging industrial processes, long regarded as the insignia of a prosperous community, could no longer be tolerated yet they remained a part of the structure on which jobs and family incomes depended so that any modification demanded extreme caution to avoid disturbing a fragile economic balance. The Board of Trade, alert to changing attitudes as well as to the realities of an industrial society, decided in 1971, after a good deal of exploratory work, to set up a special committee which would concern itself with the whole question of environmental quality. There would be no ready answers or firm policies but, as in the field of urban planning, it was believed that such representative and objective proposals as the Board might produce could contribute to a conciliation of opposing views and the development of integrated approaches.

The Board's own growth, like that of the city, although gratifying, created problems. Its membership by 1959 exceeded nine thousand and was spread over the entire Metropolitan Toronto area and considerably beyond. Such a wide dispersion made it extremely difficult to maintain contact and furnish services conforming to the desired standard. The creation of a regional committee in the western suburbs had been a successful but limited answer to the problem but had not been found applicable in other areas. What members in the outlying districts needed was access to club services such as those available in the central region. The Board's experience left no doubt that membership affiliations were greatly strengthened by identification through use of and privilege in actual physical facilities.

The idea of setting up secondary premises with various social amenities was discussed at some length and an examination of membership densities indicated that to serve the greatest number the first such facility should be at some distance from the city centre in a northwesterly direction. Detailed studies of such an undertaking were begun in 1959 by a small committee headed by Vice-President Sydney Hermant; its conclusion was that the most satisfactory and economical form of suburban club would be one that incorporated recreational uses and thus permitted full use seven days a week. More specifically, this meant a full-scale golf and country club. No Board of Trade or Chamber of Commerce had ever before contemplated such a project and at first the very idea was intimidating, but feasibility studies placed it at least within the realm of possibility and by 1962 enthusiasm was mounting. A tract of land ideally suited to the purpose had been located in the Woodbridge area and on 15 March 1963 an option was obtained for the purchase of its 225 acres. In the meantime reaction from the membership had been sought and the interest evidenced was so strong that provision had to be made for *two* eighteen-hole courses. Arrangements were accordingly entered into for the acquisition of an additional seventy-five acres.

The major consideration involved was, of course, financial. Substantial reserves had been accumulated by the Board, and when financial institutions in Toronto agreed to fund the project on mortgage bonds to the value of $1,950,000, the last barrier to accomplishment fell. Messrs Shore & Moffat & Partners were selected as architects for the clubhouse on the basis of submissions made by all interested architectural firms in the membership. Howard Watson, a noted golf architect, was appointed to lay out a thirty-six-hole golf course, and by early 1964 the country club was fully planned and actual work on the site had begun. Construction was completed on schedule and the clubhouse was opened for the use of members on 1 June 1965. An official opening by William R. Allen, Chairman of the Metropolitan Toronto Council, took place on 29 June, play on the completed twenty-seven holes of the golf course having begun the previous day.

Since all members were automatically to have full country clubhouse privileges, to support the cost of the operation the unit amount of the Board's annual membership fee was increased from $50 to $60; those desiring golfing or curling privileges had to pay a separate additional fee. Well before the club's opening the golfing membership had reached its full complement of one thousand and there was a long waiting list. It was immediately decided, therefore, to proceed with the construction of the remaining nine holes, thus providing two eighteen-hole courses of championship calibre and permitting the golfing membership to be increased. The country club gave a decided fillip to membership and the total advanced to 12,700 by 1965, an increase of 100 per cent in ten years. It continued to grow steadily and passed the 14,000 mark in 1970. A tribute to the calibre of the golf course was its selection as the site of the Carling World Golf Championship in 1967, and the event was promptly adopted as the Board's Centennial Project. Held in early September, it attracted as contestants 150 golf professionals from sixteen countries, who competed for $200,000 in prize money. The tournament was conducted with great success and received world-wide press attention.

The country club was produced at a cost approaching $3 million to serve a well-defined purpose. It was a unique and successful experiment that combined with the downtown club to provide social amenities at a relatively low cost and materially enhanced the value of membership affiliation. This aspect of the Board's services appealed particularly to businessmen in middle management positions who wanted dignified quarters where they could lunch, meet their friends and business associates, engage in recreational activities if they wished and conduct business meetings, but who had no affiliation with existing private clubs. The popularity of the idea was made clearly evident by the large influx of new members that attended the announcement of the new facilities. Nevertheless, by entering this field the Board had not the slightest intention of changing its essential character or deviating from its traditional course as an organization representing the interests of the business community and acting whenever and however those interests might best be served.

From a small beginning and a slow start the Toronto Board of Trade had become in a century and a quarter one of the largest bodies of its kind anywhere in the world and in its capacity as representative of a vigorous and growing city it will undoubtedly continue to grow and adapt itself to the perpetually changing conditions that influence the conduct of social and commercial affairs. Recognizing a subtly changing outlook and responsibility, a special 'action committee' appointed in 1971 was assigned the task of assessing and defining the Board's current status and future role in order to make specific recommendations for a plan of action. The committee members, widely representative of the Board's interests, have made a critical analysis of structure and objectives and have developed procedures designed to strengthen and improve efficiency of operations. Of some significance was the departure, by resolution adopted at the 1973 Annual Meeting, from the informal but nevertheless rigid practice of limiting membership in the Board to males. It had always previously been quite simply and logically a 'businessman's' organization, but the increasing importance of the contributions made by women to business had long been recognized and the removal at last of the barrier to their admission to membership was the inevitable culmination of a natural process.

During its lifetime the Board, under the leadership of capable and dedicated citizens, has busied itself unceasingly to achieve what it considers to be the conditions which build a good community, one in which business enterprise can function effectively and thereby produce the widest possible benefits. It faces a challenging future and will meet the challenge with those qualities which have been the source of its strength for so many years.

# Presidents of the Toronto Board of Trade 1845–1974

| | | | |
|---|---|---|---|
| 1845–51 | George Ridout | 1895 | Stapleton Caldecott |
| 1852–58 | Thomas Clarkson | 1896 | E.B. Osler |
| 1859 | E.F. Whittemore | 1897 | Edward Gurney |
| 1859–62 | Wm P. Howland, M.P.P. | 1898 | Elias Rogers |
| 1862–64 | T.D. Harris | 1899–1900 | A.E. Kemp |
| 1865–69 | James G. Worts | 1901–2 | A.E. Ames |
| 1870–71 | William Elliot | 1903–4 | J.F. Ellis |
| 1872 | A.R. McMaster | 1905 | J.D. Allan |
| 1873 | William Thompson | 1906 | Peleg Howland |
| 1874–75 | W.H. Howland | 1907 | R.C. Steele |
| 1876 | W.F. McMaster | 1908 | Lionel H. Clarke |
| 1877 | A.M. Smith | 1909 | J.P. Watson |
| 1878 | A.B. Lee | 1910 | W.J. Gage |
| 1879 | R.W. Elliott | 1911 | R.S. Gourlay |
| 1880 | John Morison | 1912 | G.T. Somers |
| 1881 | W.B. Hamilton | 1913 | Henry Brock |
| 1882 | G.M. Rose | 1914 | W.P. Gundy |
| 1883–86 | H.W. Darling | 1915 | J.W. Woods |
| 1887 | W. Ince | 1916 | Arthur Hewitt |
| 1888–89 | W.D. Matthews | 1917 | John G. Kent |
| 1890–91 | J.I. Davidson | 1918 | Clarence A. Bogert |
| 1892 | H.N. Baird | 1919 | K.J. Dunstan |
| 1893 | D.R. Wilkie | 1920 | C. Marriott |
| 1894 | Hugh Blain | 1921 | W.H. Alderson |

| | | | |
|---|---|---|---|
| 1922 | D.A. Cameron | *1956–57 | A.J. Little |
| 1923 | A.O. Hogg | 1957–58 | J.F. Ellis |
| 1924 | R.A. Stapells | 1958–59 | G.H. Sheppard |
| 1925 | S.B. Gundy | 1959–60 | Sydney Hermant |
| 1926 | George Wilson | 1960–61 | W.E. Williams |
| 1927 | Brig. Gen. C.H. Mitchell, C.B., C.M.G. | 1961–62 | Clifton H. Lane, Q.C. |
| 1928 | C.L. Burton | 1962–63 | G. Allan Burton |
| 1929 | John A. Tory | 1963–64 | G.E. Phipps |
| 1930 | F.A. Rolph | 1964–65 | John H. Taylor |
| 1931 | C.H. Carlisle | 1965–66 | Alan Y. Eaton |
| 1932 | J.H. Black | 1966–67 | Donald K. Tow |
| 1933 | Brig. Gen. C.H. Mitchell, C.B., C.M.G. | 1967–68 | Gage H. Love |
| 1934 | J.M. Macdonnell | 1968–69 | Wilson E. McLean, Q.C. |
| 1935 | James Y. Murdock | 1969–70 | James W. Kerr |
| 1936 | T. Frank Matthews | 1970–71 | Donald S. Anderson |
| 1937 | J.J. Gibbons | 1971–72 | R.V. Hicks, Q.C. |
| 1938 | Col. K.R. Marshall, C.M.G., D.S.O. | 1972–73 | B.R.B. Magee |
| 1939 | D.H. Gibson | 1973–74 | L.R. Smith |
| 1940 | R.C. Berkinshaw | | |
| 1941 | James S. Duncan | | |
| 1942 | F.A. Gaby | | |
| 1943 | L.F. Winchell | | |
| 1944 | Robert Fennell, K.C. | | |
| 1945 | E.W. Bickle | | |
| 1946 | H.M. Turner | | |
| 1947 | W.L. Gordon | | |
| 1948 | H.H. Lawson | | |
| 1949 | E.G. Burton | | |
| 1950 | Beverley Matthews, C.B.E., K.C. | | |
| 1951 | J. Gerald Godsoe, C.B.E. | | |
| 1952 | W.P. Scott | | |
| 1953 | N.J. McKinnon | | |
| 1954 | Courtland Elliott, C.B.E. | | |
| 1955 | David M. Woods | | |

* As of 1957 the period of the presidency was changed from the calendar year to the period from the annual elections in June of each year to the corresponding date in the following year.

# Index

Nest Pass 75; Temiskaming and Northern Ontario 91, 167–8; and capital imports 115; monopoly of 119; Canadian National 132–3, 147, 188, 240; terminal facilities 215; commuter services 225–6

Rand enquiry into labour disputes 248

Rapid transit 224–5

Reciprocity Treaty with United States: proposal 17; introduction 18–9; abrogation 27–8; new proposal 33, 43–4; failure to negotiate 70; comments on 88–9

Redevelopment Advisory Council 238

Rehabilitation Committee 141

Research, industrial 134–5, 170–1

Retail Sales Tax, Ontario 249

Revell, Viljo 227

Ridout, George Percival 6–7, 12, 13, 17, 24, 259

Roads improvement program 111–12, 164–5

Robertson, Charles 36

Rogers, Elias 71, 97, 259

Rollo, J. 36

Rolph, Frank A. 140, 185, 260

Rosebery, Lord 69

Ross, Allan 140

Ross, George W. 86, 87–9, 99

Rouille, Fort 1

Royal Agricultural Winter Fair 143, 179

Royal York Hotel 149, 184, 207, 231

St Lawrence Waterway: deepening of 28, 76–7, 84, 149–50, 168; improved utilization of 15, 81; tolls on 81, 242; and power development 149, 241; Seaway project 215, 241–2

Saugeen territory 16

School of Practical Science 94

Secretaries of the Board 5, 7, 25, 36, 49, 62, 156, 233

Security Frauds Prevention Act 177

Sewage treatment 48, 59, 77, 113, 191, 226–7

Shaughnessy, Sir Thomas 103

Shopping centres 221–2

Siemens, Sir William 97

Signs, removal of 164

Simcoe, John Graves 2

Simpson, Robert 30, 56

Smith, R. Home 91, 107

Smoke Abatement Advisory Committee 226

Social welfare, co-ordination of 120, 142, 183–4, 194–5, 205, 228–9

Solicitations Advisory Service 229

Somers, G.T. 90, 108, 113, 122, 259

South Africa 84

Spadina Expressway 244–5

Stamp Act 39

Standard Stock and Mining Exchange 57

Stanford, G.H. 233

Stapells, R.A. 141, 153, 260

Stevens, H.H. 189

Stevenson, John 36

Stock Exchange: establishment 22; expanded operation 56–7

Street railway: early service 30–1; Toronto Railway Company 55; municipal ownership 100, 110–11, 145; underground 224–5, 244

Streseman, Dr Gustav 90

Subway 111, 221, 224–5, 244

Suez Canal 80

Surveys 231